D1570192

"Mark Bell's *I Think, Therefore I May Become* is not only a book; it is a journey through time and space and defines the human condition within a scope and sequence that is compelling, powerful, and above all thought-provoking. In terms of scope, we are led along a broad river that begins with the basic historical tenets of humanity and guides us through our world of today . . . the human personae. It delves into the mind/brain dynamic, shaped by the development of emotion and the good and the bad of human interaction. Regarding sequence, it is a rational map of where we came from, where we are, and of utmost importance, where we are going. THAT is what is most powerful: Bell's prediction of a future life that we may or may not embrace. In closing, in this reader's humble opinion, we MUST embrace!"

—**HOWARD KARLITZ,** EdD, Author of numerous articles
concerning educational administration and child
development

"The present study represents a significant reflection on the fundamental aspects of the human condition. Bell investigates almost all the main categories that both define human life and divide human beings: political competition and economic behavior; nationalism; and on a more personal level, the family, the role of women, the cause and nature of violence, the stresses of parenting, and finally, the demands of morality and the centrality of reason in directing the actions we choose to take. Bell has interesting things to say about these foundational issues. Accordingly, this book repays reading."

—**STEVEN T.** Katz, Alvin J. & Shirley Slater Professor of
Jewish Studies, Boston University

"*I Think, Therefore I May Become* is a one-stop master class surveying myriad thinkers on the most important facet of history—how humankind has evolved to our current precarious moment. Author Mark Bell dives deeply into a comprehensive portrait of our shared existential fork in the road, the choice facing us right now: will we choose to wither or to flourish? (If you're a fan of the blogged "listicle" or bulleted "5-steps-to-utopia" TikTok approach, put this book back on the shelf, and consider your choice already made.) While Bell is surely not the only writer today calling for a collective species-saving awakening, he is unique in including the extraordinary opportunity during pregnancy to prepare our newest citizens to be those who will help us all thrive into the future . . . or not."

—MARCY AXNESS, PhD, Author of *Parenting for Peace: Raising the Next Generation of Peacemakers*

"Mark Bell brings forth and explores our past, focusing on the evolution of the human psyche and the consequences of our actions with regard to our survival, in the hope that they'll help the reader make some sense of our bewildering modern era."

—KATHLEEN SAMPEY, Editor

"In *I Think, Therefore I May Become*, Mark Bell provides a rich set of ideas to contemplate and discuss. Readers who take this text to heart and deploy its suggestions may be critical for turning humanity away from its march to destruction and instead restoring our sense of unity with and responsibility for the rest of Nature."

—DARCIA NARVAEZ, Co-Author of *Restoring the Kinship Worldview: Indigenous Voices Introduce 28 Precepts for Rebalancing Life on Planet Earth*

I Think, Therefore I May Become
Devolution or Realization,
The Choice is Yours

By Mark M. Bell

© Copyright 2022 Mark M. Bell

ISBN   978-1-64663-754-6

Published by

◄ köehlerbooks ™

3705 Shore Drive
Virginia Beach, VA 23455
800–435–4811
www.koehlerbooks.com

Also, by Mark M. Bell

I Think, Therefore I May Become:
Personal Primary Psyche Need

I THINK,
THEREFORE I MAY BECOME

DEVOLUTION OR REALIZATION,
THE CHOICE IS YOURS

MARK M. BELL

VIRGINIA BEACH
CAPE CHARLES

In their honor, through eternity,
my parents Lillian, Samuel, and sister Ann,
upon their foundation I am.

TABLE OF CONTENTS

UNBEKNOWNST TO ME, prior to my thinking about much of anything other than growing up, the germination of this work began early in my life. I was inclined to extract whatever objective truths that I could from my being on Earth. As I further focused on that effort, I directed myself to both formal and informal study of the ancient and modern social sciences, physical and theoretical sciences, and biological sciences. I have written aphorisms, musical compositions, and a psychological essay describing *personal primary psyche need.* This book is an amalgam of those concepts combined with a lifetime of experience, introspection, and research.

This writing is, in part, a treatise on Homo sapiens life in the cosmos, within the framework of our limited knowledge of both Homo sapiens and the cosmos. It also deals with our relationship to nonhuman life and what it tells us about ourselves. My purpose is to inform and challenge each reader to conclude whether to contribute to their *devolution* while our species becomes vestigial (or, at worst, extinct) or endeavor to foster their individual *realization* and contribute to our future evolutionary potential. The only time—

think *spacetime*—the human mindbrain (the term *mindbrain* is defined in the glossary and explained in the text) gives up is when a person presumes a circumstance is a fait accompli, which is both shortsighted and deadly. I suggest that the work toward the goal of *realization* is the greatest ongoing and long-term challenge human beings and humankind have always faced. I have no illusions that this writing which covers consequential subjects may resonate with an unlimited readership, as I have written it to provoke serious thought. But it will have served its purpose if it percolates in your mindbrain and results in self-examination and critical thinking about our past, present, and future. I do not mean it to lead the reader to any conclusion other than that of their own. In doing so, one may understand and realize what is humanly possible rather than what they may believe to be inevitable.

The research for this work includes conversations with people from different countries with whom I discussed the themes of this writing. Many of them are pessimistic about our long-term survival or do not care to think about the future. Their concern is to survive the emotional and material challenges of everyday life—not to focus on the insurmountable challenges over which they feel they have no control. I have learned that some people do not wish to discuss such topics as the mindbrain, the future, history, the sciences, etc., yet many do. I ascribe the degree to which people enquire or have any interest in these subjects into three metaphorical categories: *water skiers* who skim the surface; *scuba divers* who penetrate the surface to view the incredible world just below the surface; and *deep-sea divers* who cannot go deep enough even though the view becomes murky. I find the reasons for these predilections to be as complex as the human mindbrain from which they originate. Most people agree that their children and their children's children are the most precious beings in their lives and that there is something wrong with the way things are. I am grateful to them all for their feedback, which mostly encouraged me to continue drafting this book through to its conclusion.

We have accomplished increasing growth in societies, freedom, knowledge, and productive enterprise, for at least the past 5,500 earth years (EY) of recorded history. Concurrent with that *progress*, it is profoundly glaring that we have an ongoing and serious disturbance in our thinking and behavior that sabotages us as I write these words.

In cosmic time (CT) 5,500 EY is the equivalent of 13.75 cosmic seconds. Along with our achievements are our setbacks, as we have chosen more paths to divisiveness than unity. The unintended divisive consequences of governments, religions, ethnicities, races, and economic ideologies threaten all the growth we have achieved. Now that we have nuclear fusion and fission as of the fourth decade of the twentieth century, we can hear a time bomb ticking in the unconscious mindbrain.

My first employment following my college graduation was with IBM, and their well-known slogan was *THINK*. This did not evoke any stirring in me, as I had been thinking ever since I could remember. It was not until years later that I learned the hard way that the slogan was a one-word conglomeration of the terms "think carefully," "think critically," "think efficiently," "think ahead," "think wisely," and "that of which you think," which is of the greatest import. Reflected throughout this work is the fact that any future of substance will require the best of our individual and collective *thinking* from now on. Noted will be the fourteen billion EY that took nature from *quarks* to the human mindbrain. Respiratory life requires that a heartbeat, digestion, metabolism, and millions of coordinated electrochemical processes do not depend upon our conscious effort. Nature has subtly relieved us of that impossible chore specifically to free us for the one function that is ours to control—and that is to *think*.

Our existential problem is that despite nature's long and arduous effort to afford us independent and free thought, and all that it has produced, we remain on the precipice to this very day. It is apparent that we have not yet removed ourselves from that precipice, nor may we ever, until we plunge from it. Explored throughout the text are the reasons we continue to teeter on the edge of oblivion. Mentioned in brief will be several of the known, selectively bright, and curious mindbrains that have advanced our societies, discoveries, and technologies; many more have done so in relative obscurity and must therefore forgo recognition in this text. Their collective contributions have given us a false sense that we are a "special" species with rampant enlightenment and one that possesses the superior stratagems to have successfully enabled our survival to date. Think more thoughtfully and you learn that we are merely one of the many millions of species with which we have coexisted and survived, many despite us. We will give attention to our understanding and lack thereof of nonhuman species being researched and found to have advanced human-like skills and abilities, and some are just being investigated. Discussed in some detail will be the history to date of our relationship with them.

And as knowledgeable as we may collectively believe we are, our entire body of accumulated knowledge is infinitesimal relative to what we do not know and what we may never know. We have been relatively clueless as to the function of our opaque mindbrains (fount of our thinking, emotions, and behavior). It is a problem that threatens not only us, the human progenitors of the problem, but every other species. The answers to why we continually, violently, and destructively flounder and flop about on the deck of the Earth lie therein.

I touch upon historic philosophies and ideologies and how they have shaped us to date. An examination is made of the changes possible concerning parenting, education, government/leadership, economics, and our treatment of nonhuman life, upon which our future success or failure depends.

We will discuss the female and male auras from a biological perspective, and not the familiar and well-trodden superficial male-female emotionally charged points of view. Genetics/heredity are briefly reviewed and how we may have mistakenly interpreted their effect on our nature, emotions, and behavior. I have written the book to be user-friendly and tried to avoid the technical details and minutiae. At various points in the text, I direct questions to the reader; I hope you will reflect and think your way through them.

Profound and eternal gratitude goes to my wife Sandee and a few of nature's miracles, our children, Lowell, Shoshana, and Jed. I also wish to offer thanks to our extended families and friends for their love and support.

I THINK, THEREFORE I MAY BECOME™

"This is not a place for romanticists, sentimentalists, or for emotion. This requires a good brain, which does not mean being an intellectual, but a brain that is objective, fundamentally honest to itself and has integrity in word and deed."
  —Krishnamurti

"The cosmos is within us. We are made of star-stuff. We are a way for the universe to know itself."
  —Carl Sagan

"Have a true understanding of Nature about, to allow your complete awareness of Nature within."
  —Symmetrias

"Humans are a part of nature, not apart from nature."
  —Marc Bekoff

"Nature, to be commanded, must be obeyed."
  —Francis Bacon

"The world as we have created it is a process of our thinking. It cannot be changed without changing our thinking."
  —Albert Einstein

PART I
MISCONCEPTION, PHILOSOPHY, IDEOLOGY

"The question of whether or not there is a God or truth or reality or whatever you like to call it, can never be answered by books, by priests, philosophers or saviours. Nobody and nothing can answer the question but you yourself and that is why you must know yourself. . . . When I understand myself, I understand you, and out of that understanding comes love."
    —J. Krishnamurti

"Once we take ownership of an idea—whether it's about politics or sports—what do we do? We love it perhaps more than we should. We prize it more than it is worth. And most frequently, we have trouble letting go of it because we can't stand the idea of its loss. What are we left with then? An ideology—rigid and unyielding."
    —Dan Ariely, author of *Predictably Irrational: The Hidden Forces That Shape Our Decisions*

All of nature's conceptions and creations are in accord with its wholeness and perfection. The birth of the human being, however, is into a world we ourselves have divided as we have *progressed*. Seven billion human beings are alive on Earth currently and estimates project there will be ten billion of us by 2050. We have lived within separate, structured, and organized groups since the beginning of civilization 10,000 EY ago. We are born into the divisions of 4,250 religions[1], 1,192 nations[2], 6,950 languages[3], not to mention the economic and racial differences. Many of these divisions have served an organizational purpose over the last 10,000 EY of civilization, or they would not have survived to date. There have been significant costs, however, because of such divisiveness, as nations, religions, ideologies, and self-interest have competed for power endlessly. Divisiveness from birth to death, conflicts of interest, strife, and war have followed. Is this our only path, our destiny?

1
CONCEPTION MISTAKEN

"If 'genius' is the ability to conceive the relationship between seemingly unrelated variables, what then should we call divisiveness?"
—Symmetrias

EVERYTHING WE KNOW that has occurred from "quark soup" to consciousness, has occurred within what we have measured as approximately 14 billion EY or only one year of CT *-cosmic time.* Within the framework of the meaning of the word "spacetime," nothing can exist in its absence. Evolution Is defined as "the process by which different living organisms have developed and diversified from earlier forms throughout the Earth's existence." Our common knowledge implies that the segment of spacetime that we have measured as having passed is our history, but what passes? Our egocentric and unenlightened misconception is that spacetime passes us by, but isn't it more factual to state that all the living and non-living entities upon Earth are passing through spacetime rather than vice versa? It is we who age and pass as we go through what we measure as spacetime. We have no proof that spacetime as we understand it will ever end, for like space it is expanding constantly and making new spacetime. Spacetime expands, and individual lives are finite, therefore it behooves us to use our limited lifetime wisely, within the perspective of reality.

In 150 AD, almost 1,900 EY ago, Ptolemy described our Earth

as being in the center of not only the solar system but the entire universe. That theory helped explain the known science of the day for observed planetary motion, influenced in part by the ruling religious doctrines of the day. It wasn't until some 1400 years of misconception later that Copernicus in 1543 posits his theory that a heliocentric solar system was the scientific reality, and even that concept took 100 EY of "holy" opposition to overcome. Wasn't the Earth flat until 1492, when Columbus failed to sail off it into oblivion during his trip West from Spain? Fast forward to two of the more dangerous and current misbeliefs and those are the beliefs that we use only 10 percent of our mental power[4] and the larger the physical mental capacity grows, the "smarter" we become. If it is not the amount of it we use, nor the increasing amount of it we have available to use, could it be that it just may be how we optimize its use, and for what it is that we use it, that is the key to its maximum health and productivity?

Humankind has survived and "progressed" for at least 2.5 million EY as the genus Homo, despite the thousands of misconceptions regarding the external and internal world. Most of those inhabiting this planet in that span of spacetime have had brief lives because of accidents, the environment, famine, disease, and violence; not their misconceptions. As our ignorance of the external and internal world continues to dissipate, the scientific method will expand our knowledge and enlighten us even more. Does this offer us hope for survival? Not likely, now that we have created enough nationalistic and religious fervor to divide us into many clashing cultures and beliefs, not to mention the thousands of languages and dialects that make it impossible to communicate directly with one another.

Despite the scientific unveiling of misconception into fact, our mistrust and fear germinate amongst the segmented populations of the world, as continual clashes between powerful leaders of governments and religions persist. Self-interests, business interests, national interests, and religious interests sway our leader's thoughts and actions between cooperation and conflict and continue ad nauseam to this day. Through the entirety of philosophical, political, and religious doctrines bequeathed to us since 3500 BC, the dawn of recorded history, the human species have destroyed nearly 555,000,000 of their own; not included in the figure is pre-recorded history. War is this massive, intentional, wanton, destruction of life.

We have lived with misconceptions just as we have lived with war, and both have been hallmarks of our several million EY existence. The difference now is that as our misconceptions dissipate, our increasing divisiveness in a nuclear-triggered world can destroy everything.

THE GREEK ROOTS of the word *philosophy* are "love of wisdom," as in sagacity, intelligence, sense, common sense, and shrewdness. There have been at least 234 "isms," beginning with the first known Greek philosophers, circa 625 BC, through today, each one representing a philosophical belief system.[5] The modern meaning of the word philosophy is the rational investigation of the *truths* and *principles* of existence, reason, and conduct. This collection of thought had wonderful potential, as it showed that we possessed a power capable of formulating meaningful questions concerning our very being. It showed us that there were people who would devote their lives to our enlightenment and education, in a search for the why, what, and how of our being. We are fertile receptors of the spoken and written word, as most of humanity searches to comprehend the meaning of their lives.

We are a curious lot and have always sought answers to our questions. What is a human mindbrain? Can we know the essence of the human mindbrain? Why are we here? What is consciousness? What is the meaning or purpose of matter, life, the universe? Is there a meaning or purpose at all? Is there a supreme being? Who is to judge, good or evil? Is free will possible? These questions result from our musings ever since our thought processes began, which scientists and philosophers have sought answers to.

Ancient Greek and modern-day philosophers, whirling dervishes, scientists, and psychiatrists have all contributed their energies to free Homo sapiens from a lack of awareness and understanding of both our external truths and internal ones. There have been many credible and fruitful efforts made to enlighten us from cradle to grave, and to improve our lives, and it has accrued to our collective benefit. *Yet we are still destroying one another.* The keys to our survival, our thoughts, and our *emotional* processes will receive greater focus in later parts of this book, as they are crucial to this text.

The scientific mindbrains in the physics world gave us fusion, fission, and the recipe for nuclear power. As a result, we now have the blueprints to manipulate matter and turn it into enough destructive energy to render all life as we know it extinct. There are several reasons we are still inhabiting the Earth, apart from the fact that we have not blown ourselves up. We have had an uninterrupted supply of oxygen at a perfect distance from a star, a functioning autonomic nervous system, and continual birthing, and we have not, as of yet, blown off the wheels of economic and societal progress.

Most modern philosophies came to fruition from the late nineteenth century through to the late twentieth century in Europe, and we should understand that philosophies are mostly the opinions of people driven by their emotions and beliefs in their particular milieu. It includes the cultural milieu in which they grew up in, with all the associated subtleties of the religious and political undertones. It is always wise, therefore, to place oneself in any philosopher's shoes to understand their mindset at a spacetime particular to their philosophy, when possible. It is sometimes the case whereby the work of their peers or those who preceded them infused and influenced great mindbrains—whether it be in philosophy, science, or the arts. As fate would have it, much of philosophy does not measure up to the aforementioned meanings of the word. The broader the originality and appeal of a given philosophy, the more interest, interpretation, and debate it accrues. Were we to examine each of the myriad "philosophies" known, we would find that they run the gamut from ridiculous to consequential and thought-provoking.

One might deem it impossible to believe that circumstance could ever allow *ignorantism*, or those who extol the advantage of ignorance over knowledge and the spread of knowledge, to have ever entered our lexicon; yet, it did. Likewise, *immoralism* is the rejection of morality, and *psychomorphism*, which states that inanimate objects have a human mentality, does as well. There are many others I cannot unabashedly mention. Some philosophies bear witness to the fact that, through the ages and into the present, some people will believe almost anything there is to believe, under the guise of *philosophy*.

There have been sagacious people who have expressed their believed truths and broadened our collective understanding of life positively. The more thoughtful and expansive philosophies stress the critically reasoned probe of highly gifted mindbrains expressing their interpretation of universal truths, individual worth, rationality, and the potential goodness of human beings, and emphasize common human values rather than the supernatural. Others may define the individual as a free and responsible agent who is the sole determinant of their development through acts of the will whilst concentrating on the study of consciousness and the results of direct experience. Finally, some only adhere to assertions that one can verify scientifically or are capable of logical or mathematical proof, such as humanism, existentialism, phenomenology, and positivism—all of which reject hidden reality theories and theism.

The work of those who have contributed their efforts through the written or spoken word in a public forum did so hoping it might bring about an *awakening* in our species' mindbrains. Their hopes for revelations had to do with their subjective heartfelt assessment of what they believed were universal truths dealing with the questions posed at the outset of this section. If any of the established philosophies still resonate today, we may consider it some validation of the truths their progenitors gleaned and conveyed.

We will continue to filter the philosophical knowledge, to date and to come, through the lens of our continually advancing scientific understanding of the human mindbrain and our surrounding universe. A combination of life-affirming values and scientific breakthroughs—along with the complete assimilation of the same by parents, educators, and leaders—is the only way to experience a unity of awareness and understanding on this planet. Regardless, the key is to encourage your mindbrain's expansive growth, both in awareness and understanding of all you can know. Your general well-being depends upon your navigation of life with your continually questioning, adjusting, and expanding self-directed mindbrain map. This will serve you far better than a fixation on or adherence to any philosophy or group of philosophies.

3

ECONOMIC IDEOLOGY:
WHO MAKES IT, WHO FAKES IT, WHO TAKES IT

"The curious mind embraces science; the gifted and sensitive, the arts; the practical, business; the leftover becomes an economist."
—Nassim Nicholas Taleb

"Money is not the root of all evil; fear, misguided thoughts, and thoughtless emotions are."
—Symmetrias

"Money is only a tool. It will take you wherever you wish, but it will not replace you as the driver."
—Ayn Rand

AT THE CORE of any organized social system, *especially* an economic one, is human nature and the need to survive and improve oneself or one's family's prospects for the future. Driven by the *angels* of our nature and expressed in our economic systems are the provision for sustenance, self-expression, self-endeavor, pride, productivity, and accomplishment. Greed, jealousy, envy, power, hate, prejudice, etc., are some of the underlying *devils* of our nature expressed in our economic systems.

Any system, be it economic or otherwise, which is controlled by the *self-interest* of an individual—of those born into power, of those who bought or earned their power, of those who fraudulently gained power, or even of those who were honestly elected to power—is one on the path to *devolution*. This is especially true when power and self-interest infiltrate government, education, and the media; it is the greatest betrayal of public trust. The more perfect economic systems await, the more perfect human beings.

Pillaging, plundering, marauding, and looting were ways of life for some people throughout our uncivilized and civilized history, especially during times of war. The Vikings, Huns, and Vandals were barbarian groups that engaged in this most heinous means of property acquisition. Fraud, theft, corruption, and subterfuge in any economy are present-day reminders of our ancestral past.

Throughout it all, since the origin of modern civilized societies 7,500 EY ago, it has been necessary for most of our species to compete for a legal livelihood to sustain themselves and their families. Initially, it was the male who took the helm in this pursuit, and it has only been thirty years prior to this writing that females joined in the competition, an undoubtedly excellent sign. Just as there have been political ideologies that have organized masses of human beings, economic ideologies have, by necessity, accompanied them. Both must function hand in hand for either to work effectively and for the long term. As various civilizations and nations developed, they chose different economic structures. Every path selected was at first founded upon their geographic location and resources. What followed were a variety of governmental institutions and agencies to decide upon and implement the decisions necessary to deal with the maximization of their resources and productivity. This was imperative to produce and distribute goods and services for consumption, yield income within a given geographic locale, and provide revenue for the government.

Economic systems have been, in effect, types of social systems.[6] A country's economic success has preceded its political liberation, and the countries that have achieved economic growth first have been the first to democratize. The increasing rate of economic growth in the poorer countries of the world, therefore, offers hope for the future democratization of the Earth. History displays that, when a society is managed by a self-interested few in power, it will fail; if managed by people with society in mind, it will succeed. Any true and lasting wealth created through commerce and economics will be used to increase the individual liberties of their global populations. Economics has survived dictators, autocrats, oligarchs, politicians, monarchs, war, famine, the rich, the poor, and everything in between. Any established economic system has recognized that control by the people for the enrichment of the people must be its inevitable hallmark.

Forged by the inventions of industrialization and automation, we have devised what we believe to be the best methods of extracting the most productivity out of our organized economic systems. The analysis of these systems shows the dominance of socialist/ communist economies and free-market/capitalist economies.[7] Modern communication across the globe, and trial and error, have fostered the expansion of economic systems to include other models that do not conform to the traditional.[8] In the early twenty-first century, the dominant form of economic organization at the world level is the *mixed economy*[9], because pure socialism or communism cannot succeed any more than pure capitalism can.

Given our differing psyches and complexities, the government-controlled classless, unmotivated societies of socialism or communism fail. Pure capitalism cannot work because of the growing disparity in wealth of those populations. Regardless of the labels, we will move toward offering a rising standard of living and greater *individual freedom,* as we *feel* our way along. We will inevitably eliminate the systems that cannot meet our need for freedom and independence through attrition, or we will devolve.

The market-oriented mixed economic model has been driven by the economic success of the wealthiest economies on the planet who have incorporated subsidies for health care, shelter, and education for their low-income population. The models which fail will disappear, as people do not wish for a life of ongoing hunger, poverty, and restricted individual freedoms. This will not be an overnight transition; it involves critical sea changes within each one of the 192 separately bounded nations on this planet.

It is the purpose of this section, with an eye toward the future, to address the possibilities of utilizing efficient technologically and scientifically driven tools to support economic methodologies to improve them—a future that will include robots, cyborgs, and artificial intelligence doing most of the physical work. It will also include the mapping sciences which will help yield personal mindbrain profiles to help predict the future success of any individual's position within any future economy. This ultimately will involve their knowledge of every facet of their mindbrain and intellect and lead them to an informed free choice as to the part of an economic system best suited to their nature.

Is a person more suitable for individual or group effort? Will their suitability for a trade drive them? Will it be a white-collar or a professional endeavor, a need for risk or security, a leadership position or not, etc.? That will be the individual's choice, and it may cause trial and error periods until a person feels comfortable in their position within an economy. An optimal allocation of human and material resources worldwide should enable not only profit but capital for health, education, and general welfare. I expect we will not waste economic resources or spend them on weaponry or defense forces by then. Through it all, we must never ignore the endowment of every individual having inherently different natures, talents, and drives, the freedom to take their choice of paths to fulfillment. We should also recognize our basic humanity and treat the legitimately physically and mentally challenged amongst us with compassion and help to support their well-being throughout their lives. Family size should not be a method of gaming the social support system. People should not proliferate the size of their families unless they can economically and independently support them.

Were a Continent 8 system of societal organization, or the like, in use by then, and economic balance created amongst each, the movement of populations en masse for economic reasons would be unnecessary, eliminating the economic and population drains on one continent to the benefit of another. Each continent on Earth would use the same economic methodologies and mix because they would have proven the most utilitarian. One would hope that is the universal case whether the global population is fifteen billion or thirty billion people. There will always be the need to trade with one another, as we all have different natural resources and production capabilities. Trade opens paths of communication and codependence, which bring people together, so whatever the form of production, it will be more beneficial to produce and trade surpluses than control production for any self-contained people.

What, then, is the best way to achieve well-being and prosperity for a species that aspires to a *self-realizing* world, supported by economic endeavors? By trial and error, we will forge economic systems that judiciously address growing populations. In the highly mechanized, robotized, quantum computerized, and artificial-intelligent world of the future, we will eliminate the drudgery of performing many, if not all, repetitive and menial tasks. As we genetically engineer our way out of disease and the aging process, our longevity will increase.

This will allow us to increase our understanding and awareness so that we may engage in new challenges. Out of necessity, untapped resources will come from earthbound discoveries, harnessing and creating fresh energies—and new planets to mine and inhabit.

4
POLITICAL IDEOLOGY

"...armed conflict...depends more on ideology and bad governance than on resource scarcity."
—Steven Pinker

"Now man must learn to live without ideologies religious, political or otherwise. When the mind is not tethered to any ideology, it is free to move to new understandings. And in that freedom flowers all that is good and all that is beautiful."
—Osho

AN *IDEOLOGUE* ADHERES to a system of ideas and ideals shaping *political* or *economic* theory and policy, a.k.a., an ideology. Imagine the combination of an *idea*, as inflexible as a *log*. An ideologue is completely *dogmatic*, insistent, adamant, dictatorial, and uncompromising. It should not be surprising that one who is an ideologue in a position of power is in the wrong position, with the wrong mindbrain state. Throughout our glorious slog through history, these are exactly the people who have led their populations into black holes. They have convinced themselves and the governed that the hardened-like "concrete" thoughts in their mindbrain are the only ones upon which to base their actions. It is exactly this mindset that needs a steady increase in growth and flexibility—so that it may critically inquire and improve its capacity to think.

It will be wise to teach everyone on this planet, to the best of our knowledge, the accurate and objective history of every political ideology ever ideated and instituted, and how they have served their people—or were a disservice to their people. In that way, an informed populace will be better able to cultivate future systems that are always becoming more adaptive to the greater freedom and well-being of its citizens and the growth of world accord, not discord. The cliché, "if one does not learn from history, history will repeat itself," applies. It is important to recognize that this term is used to describe history with only negative outcomes and ones that we can never seem to correct. This is easy to comprehend because we have not yet developed our political systems beyond the self-interest, power, manipulation, corruption, and mistrust of most political leadership to date. The government has grown to the point where it is serving itself, rather than the people. Politics or political ideology affects the raw nerve of every nation. The underpinning of every country is its political system and how it serves or disserves its people. It will also affect how that country will act and react to exogenous events. Most of the rational among us favor our freedom rather than our suppression, and the record shows there has been a shift toward the more democratic systems of government in the recent past. It would seem reasonable that, as the instant communication of our twenty-first-century digital world increases, this trend will continue; as they say, if a "picture is worth a thousand words," an instant picture that goes worldwide should be worth a million words. One irony of life is the fact that one has no control over the type of political system of governance one is born into, and that eliminates choice from day one. People have mobility in democratic systems, while in more authoritarian systems, they do not, which is another irony; those who can exercise their freedom to leave do not wish to, and those who would do so cannot. The chance circumstance of a person's birthplace will have one of the greatest effects on their freedoms (or lack thereof) throughout their lives.

Throughout history, because of the complex nature of government, no two have been the same, and there have always been nuanced differences between them. If one were to analyze and simplify the major governance amongst political and economic systems that have historically existed, two come to mind—the *authoritarian* and the *democratic*. No one nation falls entirely into either category; ideologues and their ideologies are not owned only by either their democratic or authoritarian heads. There are more checks and balances on the people's representatives in a democratic state vis-à-vis an authoritarian one. History, however, has shown us that the leadership roles held by low AUQ mindbrains can cause devastation, be they authoritarian or democratic. The people must continually examine and challenge their governments to be more just and flexible.

We ideally built democracy upon principles that value the independent thought and rights of its citizenry within fair, just, and equal laws, respectful of freedoms of speech, the press, and religion, with an absence of media and public censorship. The majority votes in free, fair, and competitive elections, and holds sway with the candidates chosen by the people taking office. The composition of the candidates competing for leadership roles should be of a diverse citizenry, not merely a few elite individuals or families. Regardless of the outcome of any election, minorities must have their voices heard, and a truly democratic government will always respond to its citizens when they make themselves heard. The laws of a nation must be a true democracy's only dictator—not the inclinations of any given entrenched politicians, oligarchs, governmental departments, or agencies. And the laws must apply to leaders and citizens equally. If a governmental body falls short of these things, it falls short of being a real democracy. We must also be very wary of the devolution of our democracies—slipping or morphing into more suppressive forms of governing bodies. Freedom is not a given and must be continually and vigilantly attended to with a determined, engaged, and educated populace.

Monarchs, emperors, military leaders, dictators, despots, aristocrats, presidents, and prime ministers have controlled authoritarian governments most often coming from small elite groups.[10] Whatever the leader's moniker, the authoritarian state is only concerned with political power, and if the people do not contest its authority, it may give its society a modicum of liberty. It rarely cares nor attempts to improve the world or human nature.[11] Citizens under the thumb of an authoritarian regime never take part in their government and are a voiceless mass who must obey the power structure. The latter are the ones who pay the army with the former's money. Majority rule and minority rights do not exist, even though they may hold elections. When one makes a real observation of the populations subject to such a governmental structure, one would find an economically and educationally challenged nation. Such people have never had a lasting experience with the freedoms that real democracies provide and constantly aspire to improve. Authoritarian states pursue the policies of social indoctrination under the guise of education through propaganda in schools, media, and the regulation and control of production. The design of education under such systems is always to glorify the state's nondemocratic movements and historical, political importance to the nation, as well as ablating ideas inconsistent with core state beliefs.[12] The indoctrination of children from grade school on promotes homage and allegiance to whomever heads whatever form their governing system has taken. This is always stultifying, as generation to generation is manipulated to blindly follow the leader. The human tragedy is that this "force-feeding" in one's formative years disallows questioning and criticism. It is devastatingly harmful because it does nothing to foster the expansion of insight, growth, and critical thinking, and destroys it. There can be no free expression of thought and feeling under such restrictive and controlled circumstances. In such instances, the mindbrain trying to free itself is like a firefly caught in a sealed jar, gasping for air as its lack of oxygen slowly snuffs out its light. Regimentation and the stunting of mindbrain growth results in ideologies that retard our basic freedoms, wherein the only ticket out is imprisonment, exile, if you are fortunate, or your life. It is not as if authoritarian regimes had a monopoly on indoctrination. Depending on which governmental history books one reads, we obfuscate the harm some have done with their desire for hegemony, throughout history. Remember that all human history reflects the evolution of the AUQ of the human population. There has been much harm caused by countries developing toward a higher sense of freedom and liberty, and no political ideology has had a monopoly on the pain it has caused world populations. The key is to remember that, as we develop, the goal must be the open and free-flowing exchange of ideas and the *realization* of the human being.

The statistics of the world population living under some form of democracy have shown growth from 250 million out of two billion or 12.5 percent in 1940, to 4.1 billion out of 7.35 billion or 56 percent in 2017.[13] This is an encouraging trend, but our vigilance must be *continual to a fault*, to support and defend that trend. Authoritarian regimes have ranged from dictatorships, oligarchies, fascists, Nazis, socialists, and communists. There are currently fifty-two authoritarian states in the world or about *one out of four.* Looking at the 192 countries in the world shows some progress, yet almost *four out of ten* human beings inhabiting the planet, or almost three billion of us, are living under the thumb of an authoritarian regime.

The increase of the AUQ amongst our global population should lead to the recognition that there are differences in the *capabilities* and *personalities* of human beings while allowing them the freedom to realize their inborn potential whatever the political system. The realization of any human being is *impossible* if it is at the expense of another's realization. Like cells within an organism, individuals within a society each have different purposes and capabilities—each one functioning purposefully to keep the organism alive and healthy.[14] This can only occur when we are at a level of AUQ en masse, which has yet to be achieved.

5

ORGANIZED RELIGIOUS IDEOLOGY

"I cannot pretend to throw the least light on such abstruse problems. The mystery of the beginning of all things is insoluble by us; and I for one must be content to remain an Agnostic."
—Charles Darwin

"Doubt as sin. — Christianity has done its utmost to close the circle and declared even doubt to be sin. One is supposed to be cast into belief without reason, by a miracle, and from then on to swim in it as in the brightest and least ambiguous of elements: even a glance towards land, even the thought that one perhaps exists for something else as well as swimming, even the slightest impulse of our amphibious nature — is sin! And notice that all this means that the foundation of belief and all reflection on its origin is likewise excluded as sinful. What is wanted are blindness and intoxication and an eternal song over the waves in which reason has drowned."
—Friedrich Nietzsche, *Daybreak: Thoughts on the Prejudices of Morality*

"Science is not only compatible with spirituality; it is a profound source of spirituality."
—Carl Sagan

"Organized flawed religious ideologies are the result of the beliefs of those who first imagined them, and those who now proliferate them."
—Symmetrias

"The constant assertion of belief is an indication of fear."
—J. Krishnamurti

"Religion is the opiate of the masses."
—Karl Marx

THROUGHOUT ANCIENT TIMES (until the Middle Ages), alchemists searched for substances that could provide wealth, health, extended life, and whatever else one could wish and pay for. That business lasted until the modern sciences developed. Because of the power of the scientific method of investigation, which involves experimentation and examination, the modern world is still developing. Science explains with *proof* why phenomena occur— the beliefs and possibilities portended by alchemists, given enough spacetime may yet reach fruition, based upon the capabilities of modern and future science. Alchemists may just have been too early. The seeds of religion are the *beliefs* that were sown and spread in fertile ancient mindbrains. What has developed since are the ritualistic aggregates solidifying those beliefs as "faith," resulting from the labors of organized religion. Most organized religions have their foundations on the bedrock of "faith," preventing and eliminating the need for requisite scientific proof. Most organized religions have survived for several millennia, because they have incorporated into their "belief as reality" doctrines a panoply of so-called "miraculous" events inexplicable by known laws. They include afterlife rewards or punishments, resurrection, reincarnation, etc. Organized religion is far less exacting and far more reaching because it appeals to a much wider audience popularly known as "the faithful," all members welcome, no proof required.

Once individuals take ownership of a particular faith-based concept, there is no force quite like the human mindbrain to fight for it or over it, as if it were their appendage. Faith, like politics, is very personal and very emotional. It is a fact that people project their life frustrations onto their religious and political ideologies, creating a tinderbox of emotion. The bottom line is that when people disagree on either, it defines the term divisiveness. Nascent religions unified us. How did that work out in the long run? With twelve major (and 4,200 minor) religions, organized religions have taken many more paths that divide us. Some are "carrot and stick" religions, the *carrot* being the promise of "eternal life," "paradise," "nirvana," etc., and the *stick* being punishment for our inevitable sins or transgressions. We have many inflexible religions that are frozen in the past, ignoring cultural differences that dictate "it's my way or the highway."

One cannot understand most organized religions without first understanding two of the most basic, dominant, and prevalent human emotions—*fear* and *guilt*. Some of the earliest memories of our childhood involve our fear of the bogeyman and the dark, having the light left on and the door open with a security blanket tucked into bed with us at bedtime. This results from one's fear and anxiety of an *unknown* that may lurk and cause us harm. Some of us may remain more fearful than others because of hormone and neurotransmitter imbalances or the result of experiences that can affect the release of said molecules and persist into adulthood and old age.[15] Engaging in an activity that goes against social mores, whether as a child or adult, will cause a feeling of guilt in a normal human being. And making a guiltless person feel guilty is usually an effective way to induce them to do something they otherwise would not think of—or would be reluctant to do. *Fear* and *guilt* may as well be basic emotional byproducts of human nature—and religions have fully capitalized on them.

In a religious context, sin is the act of violating God's will by transgressing his commandments.[16] We can also view sin as any thought or action that endangers the ideal relationship between an individual and their God; or as any diversion from the perceived ideal order for human living. The root of Christian religious guilt is the promulgation that every sin committed—past, present, or future—adds to Jesus' suffering on the cross. Since everyone is a sinner, this is a very heavy burden to bear. It is bad enough that you must pay for your sins, but making Jesus take the rap is extremely hard for our mindbrain to bear. One may sum up the two outstanding forms of guilt in one of two ways. The wayward Jew thinks, *What an awful thing to do to somebody*. The Catholic sinner thinks, *What an awful person I am*.[17]

When one becomes a member of a long-established group that has the same beliefs and deep-seated needs, it solidifies a strong bond amongst them. Religious camaraderie offers the individual an enhanced feeling of security and acceptance, in that one feels a sense of community and trust amongst like mindbrained beings. This is true regardless of the belief. The old saying "there is strength in numbers" rings true. When we couple the need to be rid of the fear of the unknown and the guilt of "wrong behavior" with the need for fellowship, few solutions fill the bill like religion. Besides, most religions serve a deep-rooted longing in our mindbrain for an explanation of what this brief span of consciousness on an insignificant grain of sand in the universe means, and how we can keep it from ending.

At their best, faith-based doctrines are mostly an *idealistic* behavioral guide on how to live a moral life, and there is nothing wrong with that. Problems arise because religious precepts infer that we never grow up and that, if we act according to a proscribed ideology, our rewards will be eternal in another and improved realm of "being," a belief that this life cannot be all there is. This is not a solid foundation for a reality-based life, as it minimizes and diminishes the miracle of life on Earth as being just one phase of an eternal one. Another problem presents itself when *believers* attempt to proselytize *nonbelievers*, as that has led to incalculable misery and bloodshed throughout history. Interpretations of religious writings that lead their adherents to violence or coercive indoctrination are too often fatal to nonbelievers. Combine this with followers whose veneration and devotion leave them open to manipulation by nefarious leaders, and the results are devastating.

Some secular critics believe *all* religions indoctrinate their adherents as children and subtly coerce people to act and think based on a certain ideology. Their opinions are especially valid with religious extremism. Considering the differences in our emotions, personalities, and general nature, to be explored in-depth in the following subsections, when given a choice as thinking adults, there is a broad spectrum of adherence to religious ideologies. Atheists do not believe, agnostics suspend their beliefs and are awaiting conviction, and the not so pious amongst us round out the spectrum of religious leanings. Faith-based religious ideologies persist because humanity has not yet gone through enough spacetime to understand, using purely rational critical thought, how to handle the emotions of fear and guilt without palliative help. Most of our species cannot yet or have not yet done the work necessary to *realize* life-enhancing moral goals, without requisite religious support. You will learn in part X that many of the nonhuman species on Earth need no ideologies to instinctively and rationally understand behavior that exhibits empathy, kindness, and caring for their own, and other species.

A non-proselytizing, *non-faith*-based way of life that is inherently moral in both theory and practice which engenders kinder, gentler, wiser beings is plausible and doable. For almost three millennia of Confucianism, the Chinese form of humanism has been more of a belief system than a religion. It has guided adherents to fulfill their role in society with propriety, honor, and loyalty, with no associated supreme beings, nor afterlife, promised. This way of life describes the good, teachable, improvable, and perfectible human being through personal and communal endeavors, especially self-cultivation and self-creation. Early and secular Buddhists have no deities, but they insist on reincarnation. Jainism believes the universe is eternal, has no need for a creator deity, and it venerates all life, and it has a belief similar to reincarnation. In Judaism, the Sadducees, the prominent priestly class and overseers of the Temple, did not believe in an afterlife nor the resurrection of the dead, and their one God was a spiritual entity only.

BROTHERLY LOVE-HATE

Thus began the recorded history of religious beliefs and the organization of people around them. In ancient times, religion may have initially quelled conflict amongst the populations in an area, which had until then been more violent hunter-gatherer groups. Depending upon the political climate of the day and the leaders, the tolerance for different religious beliefs varied.

Cyrus the Great (580-529 BC), the founder of Persia, declared the first Charter of Human Rights known to humankind. He took the title of King of Babylon and King of the Land. Cyrus had no plans of forcing conquered people into a single mold and had the wisdom to leave unchanged the institution of each kingdom he attached to the Persian Crown[18]. Cyrus was, of course, an ancient ruler and leader and an "exception to the ruler" mindbrain.

The vicious persecution of Christians in the Roman Empire lasted 250 EY, from 64 AD, under Nero (37-68 AD), until 313 AD, when it became the Roman Empire's official religion by Constantine (272-337 AD). [19] One might say that a Christian birth before 313 AD was rather ill-timed. Unfortunately, some adherents to certain beliefs have gone to great lengths to force others of differing opinions to the point of torture and auto-da-fé (burning "heretics" at the stake), to either convert or recant their genuine convictions. The "Tribunal of the Holy Office of the Inquisition," a.k.a., the Spanish Inquisition (1478-1834), is one such power that saw to it that Jews were persecuted and tortured. The European Witch Hunt (1450-1750) witnessed the Protestants' and the Catholics' persecution of heretics, i.e., Jews, Moslems, and possessed witches, mostly all of whom were innocent women, with almost the same zeal.

Hitler, a pagan, and his Nazified precision killing machine of henchmen murdered six million of the Jewish faith and 5 million gypsies, homosexuals, and the infirm during the period 1933-1945. That these atrocious acts transpired in *modern* times, in one of the most cultured places on Earth, is unfathomable. The lessons to be learned here are that "civilization" is merely a thin veneer in a nation of emotionally manipulated people managed by spoon-fed distortions and lies—rather than reason and critical thought.

Many murderous conflicts, child molestations, genocides, and cult suicides have had a religious basis.[20] The "blood libel" is the unfounded accusation[21] that Jews kidnapped and murdered the children of Christians to use their blood as part of their religious rituals during Jewish holidays.[22] Historically, these claims, alongside those of well poisoning and host desecration, have been a major theme of the persecution of Jews in Europe.[23] Persecutions of Christians, Coptic, Yazidi, Buddhists, and Hindus have gone on since their religious ideologies have been with us. Islam hated Judaism and Christianity from the start. The Koran urges Muslims not to befriend Jews or Christians (Koran 5:51) and speaks of "enmity and hatred" with Christians (Koran 5:15) and the Jews (Quran 5:65) who are also to be cursed. They accuse the Jews of "creating disorder" (Quran 5:65), and they accuse Christians of worshiping their priests (Quran 9:31).

The Jews and Christians believe in evil things (Quran 4:52) and Allah's curse will be upon them (Quran 9:30).[24] The estimate is that 195 million have died in the name of religion, the equivalent of 2,500 Super Bowl stadiums filled with 80,000 people each. And if a toxic combination of ignorance and intolerance remains cloistered within the mindbrains of our species, poisoning divisiveness must ensue.

Taking a more scientific view, ponder, if you will, the number of chemical reactions in *one* human eukaryotic cell per second, estimated to range from hundreds of millions to several billion. The most current estimate is 37.2 trillion cells per human body; the result would yield thirty-seven with twenty-one zeros after it, or *thirty-seven thousand billion billion chemical reactions per second* in the human body. [25] Many of these chemical reactions are the basis of what we would consider life. They copy our DNA, manufacture new organelles and cell walls so the cells can multiply, and transcribe DNA into RNA into proteins, the building blocks of organic life structures.

Consider the fact that nature has taken almost 13.8 billion EY to sculpt this elegant cosmos, with all of its harmonious features and living entities, both known and unknown. More essentially, it took that long to produce the first model of a hominid with electrochemical energy that *thinks*. Nature can now gestate Homo sapiens in 39.5 Earth weeks, not to mention the gestation of the other 8.7 million *known* eukaryotic species on Earth. Is this not miraculous enough for our sense of majesty, sans the torturous divisiveness, hate, and a "my faith is better than yours" belief system? Is this something to argue about, or to become aware of and understand? It might bring us together.

PART II
HEREDITY AND COMPLEXITY

"Although Nature needs thousands or millions of years to create a new species, man needs only a few dozen years to destroy one."
—Victor Scheffer

CREATOR OF THE GRAND DESIGN of all that we know, think we know, do not yet know, and may never know is what we name God, the Eternal, Yawah, the Creator, the Supreme Being, Mother Nature, the All Knowing, the Ground of All, the Holy Father, etc. To be inclusive and diplomatic, I will refer to this awe-inspiring entity as *Nature*, a more universally recognized term that everyone should be familiar with.

We have muddled through civilization, by replacing our fear, superstition, and lack of scientific knowledge with the reverence, faith, and fragmented thinking that created myths, idols, pantheons, and deities filled with many Gods. The questions of being itself—such as the, however, whatever, whoever, whenever, or whyever—have been queries of the human mindbrain ever since we first acquired mindbrains. For Homo sapiens, 250,000 EY existence equates to only eight cosmic minutes, and our 7,500 EY of actual civilization is only twenty-three cosmic seconds. One might reason that this has been to brief a cosmic spacetime, with all due respect to our intellectual capabilities, to have answered these cosmic questions. Combined with the routines, pressures, and pace of modern-day life, one can understand why most mortals are not currently thinking about these questions, let alone finding answers to them. However, as the people who ponder such questions grasp together more and more of the threads of the grand design of Nature, we have begun to answer some of those questions.

Francis Crick and Thomas Watson revealed in 1953 that the DNA molecule had the structure of a double helix and, subsequently, our knowledge of its composition and how to manipulate it has grown exponentially. Having mapped the human genome and those of 3,569 other species, we are presently studying Nature's design for the recipes for the physical characteristics, personalities, and the behavior of human beings, as well as many other species.[1] We now know that all life on Earth shares a common ancestor known as the last universal common ancestor (LUCA)[2, 3, 4] which lived approximately 3.9 *billion* EY ago,[5] although a study in 2015 found "remains of biotic life" from four billion EY ago in ancient rocks in Western Australia.[6, 7] In July 2016, scientists reported identifying a set of 355 genes from the LUCA of *all* organisms *living* on Earth.[8]

We estimate that over *99 percent* of all species[9] that ever lived on Earth are now extinct.[10] Estimates on the number of Earth's current living species approximate nine million, and it will serve us well to think about these figures. We are not alone on this planet, nor should we dare to think our species is exemptional. We are merely the "New Kids on the Block" and most living or growing species on this planet have preceded our evolution. Science has proven that simple cells first appeared on Earth almost 4 billion EY ago, insects 400 million EY ago, dinosaurs 300 million EY ago, and flowering plants 130 million EY ago. Anatomically modern humans developed only 225,000 EY (or eight cosmic minutes ago), and we too are replaceable, barring a premature natural or a human-engineered obliteration, not only by evolution but by our technologies. Biological, genetic, cyborg, android, and AI engineering might replace human beings as we know them, all hoping to develop a "new and improving model."

Another matter to consider is that we are limited in spacetime. In 3 billion EY from now, Earth will travel out of the solar system's habitable zone and into the *hot zone*. The availability of water defines these zones. In the habitable zone, a planet, whether it be in this solar system or another, is just the right distance from its star to have liquid water. Closer to the sun in the *hot zone*, the Earth's oceans would evaporate, and conditions for any complex life would have become untenable before the planet entered the hot zone.

"It takes a very long spacetime for intelligent life to develop," lead researcher Andrew Rushby of the University of East Anglia in the United Kingdom said in a statement. Rushby and his colleagues developed a new model to project the spacetime a planet will spend in its habitable zone, to help evaluate the amount of spacetime available for the evolution of life on other planets. In the research, published in the journal *Astrobiology* on September 13, 2013, they applied the model to Earth and eight other planets currently in a habitable zone, including Mars. Mars' remaining lifetime in the habitable zone is 6 billion EY, with the Earth estimated to be 3 billion EY. "If we ever needed to move to another planet, Mars is probably our best bet," Rushby said in a statement. "It's very close and will remain in the habitable zone until the end of the sun's lifetime 6 billion EY from now."[11]

We will investigate human "nature" in the next section, to better understand our origins and how much spacetime our species has gone through to get to the moment you read this, and the degree to which it influences our present behavior.

6

HUMAN NATURE:
THE DIFFERENCE OF SIMILARITIES IN EVOLUTION

THE RANGE OF OUR SPECIES' THINKING, emoting, and behavior is known collectively as "human nature." Nature created us as social beings, and we have cooperated enough with one another to build cities, governments, economies, technologies, and institutions. Our social and psychological interactions are thereafter tempered in the cauldron of life. Throughout it all, we have *naturally* needed to maintain our identities with our associated self-interests, motivations, and personalities. It is *essential* that we always strive for the type of society that always respect our individuality and our inborn ability to realize our full potential.

A taxonomic description of the families of Nature indicates that 6 million EY ago, the evolution of the nasty, aggressive male-dominant chimp and the peaceful, playful, sexual, female dominant bonobo, our closest living relatives, began. We have passed through 6 million EY since then and on through that of the genus Ardipithecus—a key ancient link in our evolution discovered by a team led by the American paleoanthropologist Tim D. White which precedes Australopithecus—discovered by a team led by American anthropologist Donald Johanson, the latter of which is represented in part by the 3.2-million-year-old "Lucy." And then our genus *Homo* evolved with the appearance of Homo habilis ("handyman") 2.25 million EY ago. [12] *Homo* sapiens ("modern man"), the last extant species of the seven of our genus, emerged only 225,000 EY ago in East Africa, and then spread throughout Africa, Eurasia, Oceania, and the Americas only a mere 60,000 EY ago. [13, 14]

Our 6-million-year evolution through spacetime— and a shared common ancestry[15] with the ape—has taught us that we have a 98.7 percent DNA match with the bonobo and chimpanzee. [16] Though we share all but approximately 1.3 percent of our DNA with each, we should not incriminate our ancestors for our present behavior.

It is as essential to continue the empirical study of our genetics and our mindbrains as it is to hold ourselves responsible for what we collectively do with and to one another at this *very moment*. After all, 6 million EY is enough spacetime for our species to have stopped the "swinging from the trees ape association," and scapegoating our ancestral families for *our* behavior. If we choose to go down this *rabbit hole* of ancestral history to explain today's irreverent behavior and violence, it will fail to help us glean the factual reasons for our inability to succeed at peaceful coexistence today.

It is bogus and disingenuous that we selectively credit our mindbrain with the reasoning, imagination, creativity, and invention that has produced the entire body of human knowledge and organizational and physical structures of the modern world; yet, at the same spacetime, we selectively blame our ancestral mindbrain for war, genocide, terrorism, murder, rape, torture, and other violence. We cannot have it both ways and we must take credit for it all.

———————

An informative, beautiful, and graphic means of enlightenment— describing the "birth of spacetime" of the *known* universe from its beginning to the present—is the "cosmic calendar." It is a pictograph used to visualize the chronology of the universe by scaling its currently known age of 13.8 billion EY into a single year of Earth spacetime. In this visualization, the big bang occurs at the beginning of January 1 at midnight, and the "current moment" you read this occurs at the end of December 31 just before midnight. [17] At this scale, there are 437.5 EY per cosmic second, 1.575 million EY per cosmic hour, and 37.8 million EY per cosmic day.

The concept was created by a colleague of Carl Sagan's at Cornell University. Sagan, a gifted scientist and a brilliant communicator of science, popularized it in his book *The Dragons of Eden* (1977) and in his television series *Cosmos: Episode 1* (1980). Sagan goes on to extend the comparison in terms of distance, explaining that if the cosmic calendar is scaled to the size of a football field, then "all of human history would occupy an area the size of my hand." [18] The proliferate force of Nature has led to mindbrained species, and the electrochemical energy in the form of thought, consciousness, and feeling, following some 13.3 billion EY of evolution. Our species is brand new in *cosmic* spacetime, in that the cosmic calendar indicates we have experienced the following Earth events in mere seconds/minutes of cosmic spacetime:

24 hours—primates evolve
16 minutes—fire is domesticated
8 minutes—modern humans, Homo sapiens, evolve
14 seconds—the wheel invented
0.16 seconds—the first knowledge of genes

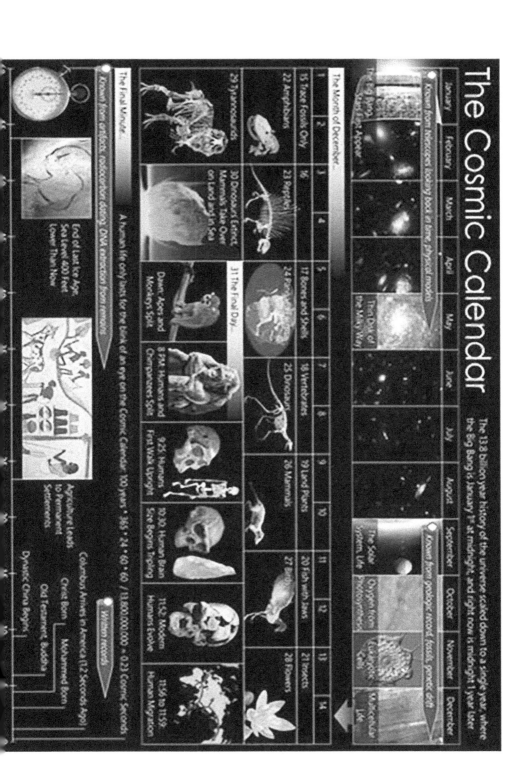

The Cosmic Calendar

The 13.8 billion-year history of the universe scaled down to a single year, where the Big Bang is January 1st at midnight, and right now is midnight 1 year later.

The Big Bang, Stars & Galaxies Appear

Then Disk of the Milky Way

Known from telescopes looking back in time; physical models

Known from geologic record: fossils, genetic drift

Oxygen from Photosynthesis

The Solar System: Life

Ecaryotic Cells

Multicellular Life

| January | February | March | April | May | June | July | August | September | October | November | December |

The Month of December

	1	2	3	4	5	6	7	8	9	10	11	12	13	14
15 Trace Fossils Only	16		17 Bones and Shells	18 Vertebrates	19 Land Plants	20 Fish with Jaws	21 Insects
22 Amphibians	23 Reptiles	24 Pterosaurs	25 Dinosaurs	26 Mammals	27	28 Flowers
29 Tyrannosaurus	30 Dinosaurs Extinct, Mammals Take Over on Land and in Sea													

31 The Final Day...

Darwin: Apes and Monkeys Split — 8 P.M. Humans and Chimpanzees Split — 9:25 Humans First Walk Upright — 10:30 Human Brain Size Begins Tripling — 11:52 Modern Humans Evolve — 11:56 to 11:59 Human Migration

The Final Minute...

Known from artifacts, radiocarbon dating, DNA extraction from remains

End of Last Ice Age, Sea Level 400 Feet Lower Than Now

A Human life only lasts for the blink of an eye on the Cosmic Calendar. 100 years ÷ 365 ÷ 24 ÷ 60 ÷ 60 / 13,800,000,000 = 0.23 Cosmic Seconds

Written records

Agriculture Leads to Permanent Settlements — Columbus Arrives in America (12 Seconds Ago) — Christ Born — Mohammed Born — Old Testament Buddha — Dynastic China Begins

In the eight minutes of CT that we have spent on Earth as modern humans, depending on when this sentence is read, we have created every human-made object and art form on Earth and some above Earth such as satellites, space stations, planes, drones, and rockets. We will inevitably conquer ever more diseases, extend our lives, and free ourselves from menial drudgery by using robots. We are now splicing genes in ever more efficient ways after only 0.16 seconds of the cosmic year, which is sixty-five EY. It is as if *thinking* has worked out well and shows great promise.

Ten EY prior to the gene's discovery, nuclear energy emerged as the sobering fundamental change. Ironically, Albert Einstein, the consummate mindbrain and pacifist, conceived that all matter contained locked-in energy. Fearing Nazi Germany would develop a nuclear weapon first, elite physicists from around the world gathered in the US and devised a means to harness and release the energy in matter. The genie is now out of the proverbial "bottle," and either we decide *collectively* as a species to productively use this energy, or we use it to incinerate all life. Nature has masterfully and impeccably assembled the individual hereditary components of *all* living things but has left no "How Best to Use Your Life, Before You Use It Up" instruction manual for human consumption.

Every nonhuman and human being has Nature's perfectly developing operating system installed from conception, except in the rare instances of inherited genetic disorders. You will learn as you proceed throughout the other sections of this work that the long evolution of the extraordinarily complex human mindbrain in which our operating system is located has, throughout civilized time, been subject to hacking and mental bugs. Enter all the divisive ideologies discussed in part I. They all have followers as did the Pied Piper of Hamelin, as he led the town's 130 children away, never to be seen again. Human beings have it in their nature to follow those deemed more knowledgeable than they are—to learn what they do not yet know. Parents, educators, and leaders are essential as our guides in the nascent and formative EY of our lives. This is where generation after generation helps mold and cast the future of a child and its success or failure in life. After we mature, we are left to our own devices on how to use our lives. Some have chosen well, some have chosen poorly, and some have had a limited choice or none. It continues to be hit and miss.

Nature is a prolific creative force, even when it is completely destructive by its natural upheavals, always reshaping its creation. Whether it is on the tiniest of scales where Nature creates and destroys particles and antiparticles in its exquisite dance, or where massive black holes vacuum away objects caught in its web of gravity, she is always in motion.

As Aristotle's saying goes, "Nature abhors vacuums," and we may be certain whether or not we as species progress positively, it will continue to do what it does best, having done so for billions and billions of EYS all over the universe, with *or* without us.

7

THE MINDBRAIN CONTINUUM

"Physics is really just about external relationships—between a proton and electron, between planets and stars. But consciousness is really physics from the inside. Seen from the inside, it's experience. Seen from the outside, it's what we know as physics, chemistry, and biology. So there aren't two substances."
—Bertrand Russell

"INNER SPACE," with regard to this work, references the area long thought to contain two separate and vital entities, one is our *mind* and our *brain*. This hyphenated *mind-brain* separation, however, has in every sense developed with us into one of our longest-held misconceptions. And though it has been a long-held belief, known as *dualism*, that the mind and the brain are dichotomous, as with every other lingering misconception, science will prove otherwise in time.

The two major reasons for this ongoing misconception, from this writer's point of view, are first the nostalgic and soothing concept of an eternal *soul-spirit* associated with the mind, and second, the functional complexities of the mind-brain, *mindbrain*.

Philosophers, mystics, religionists, spiritualists, laypeople, and even some scientists have bifurcated the mindbrain into the mind and brain. They have believed the *brain* to be a part of the material world controlling the body, while the *mind* is the invisible, esoteric, transcendent faculty expressing consciousness, higher thinking, and emotion. The mind is in one group concept called *soul, spirit, psyche, being,* or *essence*. Some believe that the body cannot confine it, as in possession, exorcism, and reincarnation, and it is eternal.

Any descriptions of the mindbrain being nonmaterial or ethereal are vestiges of spacetime when neuro-molecular biology and nanotechnology were not yet available and scientific bodies of knowledge and the technological tools enabling groundbreaking research were nonexistent. The misconception will fade as the mindbrain is more scientifically understood. In the words of the mathematician H. Minkowski, Albert Einstein's college math professor, "The views of space and time which I wish to lay before you have sprung from the soil of [Einstein's] experimental physics . . . Henceforth space by itself, and time by itself, are doomed to fade away into mere shadows, and only a kind of union of the two will preserve an independent reality."[19] His words are as true today—if one were to change *experimental physics* to *neuro-molecular biology*, and *space* and *time* to *mind* and *brain*.

Many of the experts who study the mindbrain believe it to be a materially complete system that operates as an extraordinarily complex interconnecting labyrinthian structure, the function and output of which is not yet fully understood. One such adherent is Dr. Christof Koch, chief scientist and president of the Allen Institute for Brain science, who, when asked how close we were to an understanding of the human brain, said as recently as 2018, "We don't even understand the brain of a worm." This statement is from the man who collaborated with Sir Francis Crick, co-discoverer of the DNA molecule with T. Watson, in an investigation of consciousness from 1990 until Crick died in 2004. Dr. Koch was only thirty-four EY old, and Sir Francis was seventy-four EY old when they began. They were at the time investigating human consciousness by looking at the minimal sets of neurons and mechanisms necessary for percepts to register subjectively and to be interpreted.

Dr. Koch and others feel that there are missing material processes regarding their ongoing studies which will help define the exact physical systems that make up the mindbrain and its output. They ground the mindbrain system in the material world. In the broader sense, one may say *scientific naturalism* defines all objects and events as a part of Nature, including the mental realm of human beings, and all are subject to scientific inquiry.

Imagine living on Earth in 140 AD, less than five cosmic seconds ago, at the time of the misconceptions discussed in the opening of this book. You would have believed you were looking up at the entire universe orbiting around you, at its center, while you were intermittently looking down so as not to fall off the edge of the planet. Those misconceptions of planet Earth are the same relative degree to which we understand the mindbrain as late as the beginning of the twenty-first century!

The investigation of the mindbrain began in the 1880s through the science of psychology, followed by neuropsychology and neurobiology in the 1960s. These were the only means available to analyze human thought and behavior. Now, as I write this sentence, the modern sciences used to investigate this subject—such as advanced genetics, advanced neurosciences, molecular biology, nanoscience, and bioengineering—find us still at the germinal stage of research and collaboration. To be effective, these undertakings will need to harness technologies that will investigate the biological, chemical, and electrical makeup of the mindbrain down to the size of several nanometers (nm) or one billionth of a meter (thirty-nine inches). To imagine this dimension, think of the Earth as the meter and a marble as the nanometer, or the width of an average human hair that can cover 60,000 nm.

As we analyze the mindbrain in the rest of this section, the research, taking decades, will be more challenging and complex than the investigation of outer space. When one thinks of it, this makes perfect sense. Were we to use 13.8 billion EY as the age of the universe; the stars and then planets began formation shortly thereafter. The mindbrain took another 13.3 billion EY of evolution—or half a billion EY ago—to develop in living beings such as fish, reptiles, birds, and then mammals. The mindbrain took 13.3 billion EY longer to evolve than planets and stars; all the components necessary for the mindbrain were not even available until then!

There is little doubt that the ongoing efforts to explore the mechanisms of Nature that explain our inner space will be monumentally more challenging, of longer duration and expense, than even the vast but less complex investigation of outer space.

The Obama administration's NIH BRAIN initiative was established to study the devastation of many currently incurable diseases originating in the mindbrain. Of equal or greater import—accruing from this and myriad extensive worldwide research—will be the heretofore unknowable complete and detailed compilation of information that will explain why we think, feel, and behave as we do. Many of the most respected institutes in the world are collaborating in this effort, including The McConnell Brain Imaging Center at McGill University, Montreal; Allen Institute for Brain Science, Seattle; Max Planck Institute for Human Cognitive and Brain Science, Leipzig; and the McGovern Institute for Brain Research at MIT, Cambridge, Mass. And this is an extremely short list, as remaining and growing research must go unnamed here, for the sake of brevity.

Our mindbrain comprises a billion neurons and a trillion interconnections, each multiplied by one hundred, not to mention its many structural components. When researchers increase the resolution of the instrumentation and enhance the revolutionary research tools with which they look at the mindbrain, additional levels of complexity reveal themselves and make it an endless search for an end to the search. At the beginning of the twenty-first century—by utilizing the human genome, enhanced mapping and imaging technologies, nanoscience, and supercomputers—things changed. Engineers and scientists made key discoveries that created the opportunity to not only follow and activate the paths of neurons but to ascertain the specific functionality of those mindbrain areas they interconnected with. We now determine in exacting detail, down to the cellular, atomic, and nano level, how and where the mindbrain is chemically and electrically energized to perceive, record, interact, process, store, and retrieve—*live and in living color*.

In the remainder of this section, the reader should judge for themselves whether the esoteric, transcendental concepts that have historically surrounded the mindbrain will have any relevance going forward. Or will we layer by layer replace the invisible unknown with the visible known.

8

MINDBRAIN DULLING

"The important thing is not to stop questioning. Curiosity has its own reason for existence. One cannot help but be in awe when one contemplates the mysteries of eternity, of life, of the marvelous structure of reality. It is enough if one tries merely to comprehend a little of this mystery every day."
    —Albert Einstein

"One has to be dull to feel happy amongst the dull."
    —Mehmet Murat Ida

"Getting used to something is to grow insensitive to it. This is destructive, as such a mind is a dull mind, a stupid mind."
    —J. Krishnamurti

"Imagination is more important than knowledge. For knowledge is limited to all we now know and understand, while imagination embraces the entire world, and all there ever will be to know and understand."
    —Albert Einstein (Smithsonian, February 1979)

REMEMBER WHEN YOU WERE A GROWING CHILD when everything was new and a learning opportunity, and you asked more questions about the "wonder of it all" than you do now? Everything was new, and you were not aware that you were endowed by Nature and nurture to grow physically, walk, learn, and yes, to be very curious. Your thirst for information led to questions, answers, and more questions than answers, in a glorious cycle of an awakening mindbrain. And then *life* sets in with its pressures as we grow through childhood to adulthood, such as peer pressure, responsibilities for raising children, earning a living, and battling the sometimes-overwhelming pace of life and its "slings and arrows."
    The stultifying way that a formal general education favors more

rote thought than insightful, critical, creative, and imaginative thinking carries over into the workplace, and we can become incurious as we age. It is a fact that most people do not have the time, energy, or inclination to inquire or learn about the vast unknown within us and about us. People are thus more preoccupied with *getting through the day* than being in a state of wonderment about it. For *most*, the everyday routine of life, regardless of what one produces, is always just that, routine and limiting to some extent. It is said that "familiarity breeds contempt." It also *impedes* creativity, spontaneity, imagination, and curiosity.

Conditioned by the structured rules of our schools, workplaces, society, etc., our mindbrains follow an agenda and we learn that straying from it can create problems, error, and failure. The structure is something that is constantly being ingrained in our heads, and we develop *routines* to handle it. Another factor is certainly the desire not to "ruffle feathers" and be "good soldiers" in the march through our educational and workplace activities. A routine, as Meg Selig of *Psychology Today* writes, is nothing more than a "series of habits." We follow them with the intention of making our lives easier and more convenient, but rarely ever stop to think about how limiting they might be as they allow us to do things without thinking, simply out of habit. According to Selig, routines allow you to "go on autopilot and still accomplish your goals. You wake up, hop in the shower, get dressed, grab a granola bar, double-check you have locked your door, and then get on the train. Your mornings require little thinking because you've been so programmed to do the same thing at every start of your day."

In an article for *Time* magazine, Annie Paul suggests your morning routine might also be a creativity killer. She writes, "The way most of us spend our mornings is exactly counter to the conditions that neuroscientists and cognitive psychologists tell us to promote flexible, open-minded thinking." Paul continues, "Adhering to a strict routine will cause the buildup of stress as you feel pressure to meet the demands of these routines, and when you don't, you'll feel as though you're falling short of your own standards." The stress hormone cortisol can harm myelin, the fatty substance that coats our mindbrain cells, and damage to our myelin sheaths decreases the frequency of what Paul refers to as "Eureka!" moments or the formation of those quick "light bulb" ideas. According to her, we are the most creative when we are slightly groggy because "the mental processes that inhibit distracting or irrelevant thoughts are at their weakest and allow unexpected and sometimes inspired connections to be made." By not following a strict morning routine, allowing your mind to unwind itself naturally, you will also be allowing yourself to carry out your most creative thinking. She adds, "This is why it is important to make constant revisions to your habits as the mind, like a knife, cannot be of optimal use, when dull.[20] The mental processes inhibiting new and creative thinking that Paul refers to are well-worn and, for lack of a better word, *furrowed* connections of neuronal pathways in our stored memory.

John Tierney of *The New York Times* has a slightly different view on maintaining routines and writes that humans are best served by following a routine of complete and utter "spontaneity"—no routine at all. In the Taoist school of thought, they believe, "Instead of following the rigid training and rituals required by Confucius," Tierney states, "they sought to liberate the natural virtue within and went with the flow." Taoists stressed the ideals of personal meditation as opposed to formally structured education.

Dr. Edward Slingerland, an Asian studies professor at the University of British Columbia, explains how our culture excels at pushing an agenda that requires attaining a certain set of skills, such as high grades, for getting into competitive colleges or a bulky résumé for a better job offer.

We should be cognizant that the mindbrain is the precious organ we use out of necessity for the routine and mundane, most of the time, but it is also the instrument of our freedom from them. A mindbrain that is alert and watchful will make certain it does not function habitually, and that it does not become insensitive, dull, weary, and ready to die. [21]

Thoughts that provoke questions, insight, spontaneity, and creativity—rather than programmed dogmatic, ideological, and ingrained thoughts that stultify and divide us—are the preferable path forward for human beings wishing to avoid mindbrain rust and, inevitably, mindbrain dust.

PART III
INTRODUCTION TO:
INTER, INTRA, AND THE AUQ

"The individual has always had to struggle to keep from being overwhelmed by the tribe. If you try it, you will be lonely often, and sometimes frightened. But no price is too high to pay for the privilege of owning yourself."
—Friedrich Nietzsche

"Trust is the sacred stride you make when your mindset to trust is more powerfully felt, than your mindset to mistrust."
—Symmetrias

"Madness is rare in individuals—but in groups, parties, nations, and ages it is the rule."
—Friedrich Nietzsche

"The most common lie is that which one lies to himself; lying to others is relatively an exception."
—Friedrich Nietzsche

INTER, AS IN INTERACTION, is the word used to describe your in-depth awareness/understanding of all of Nature's animate creations. *Intra, within,* is the word used to describe your in-depth awareness/understanding of yourself. The level of your *inter* and *intra* will decide whether we will survive long enough as a species to forge the awareness and understanding amongst us to foster peaceful accommodation for being, rather than nonbeing, on Earth. The problems caused by a lack of *intra* are not restricted to oneself and the damage it may cause to immediate family members, but also the extent to which the lack of *intra* negatively affects your *inter.* The challenges of *inter, intra,* and the AUQ suggest efforts that may very well exhaust future generations, and we still may not achieve our goal in sufficient spacetime.

Reference made to an *awareness understanding quotient* (AUQ) is the combination of *inter* + *intra* = AUQ. The more any being exhibits, both in *thought and deed*, an increase in the quotient's two components, the more elevated the AUQ and *realized* the being.

The table below illustrates the importance of these two factors as a basis for our prospects of survival. A perfect storm arises when a powerful faction or government finds itself headed by a leader who is in group 4. This has happened throughout history, to grave consequences for the lives of their unfortunate subjects, and the populations of the world, at times.

CHANCE OF SPECIES SURVIVAL
BASED UPON INTER AND INTRA LEVELS OF
AWARENESS AND UNDERSTANDING

Group	Level of INTER	Level of INTRA	Chance of Specie Survival
1	HIGH	HIGH	BEST
2	HIGH	LOW	BETTER
3	LOW	HIGH	WORSE
4	LOW	LOW	WORST

We have survived for some 250,0000 EY as modern humans without having much time or need for introspection, while the human population has been surviving, constructing, and destroying. As our communication with the world has become both ubiquitous and instantaneous, it is imperative to match the efficiency of our technologies and the effort it took to create them with the equally or more important efforts to speed up the maximization of our *inter* and *intra*. The imperative of all sentient individuals, parents, educators, and leaders should be the conclusion that our *inner space* is now the most important frontier of all to understand and master.

We are a social species, we are in control and accomplished when tasked to deliver mundane or great feats of the mindbrain, and we solve material problems, singularly and in groups. There is nothing, be it formulaic or material, that we cannot eventually bring to form from an idea. Our species takes on these challenges to provide financial sustenance, and for the satisfaction which accompanies the accomplishment of a goal. We discover, design, build, produce, and explore with relative ease. Given a task, we just do the work or someone else will. This is apparent when we look at how the world's populations have survived, grown, and developed their societies, regardless of our level of either *inter* or *intra*.

Call it "growing without knowing," if you will, as human beings have flourished and grown in wealth and size with no one to understand their very own mindbrain, and thus the ability to understand the mindbrains of other life. Accompanied by this growth, our species has also destroyed millions of its own through unimaginable thoughts and deeds, because of the lack of that understanding. Now, however, the nuclear clock is ticking away, and we must concentrate on inner space more than external space.

Our ultimate level of *inter* or *intra* has to do with the recognition that the divisions between us are because of a lack of clarity of not only *who* we are but of equal importance, *why* we are. When we answer those questions, we will better understand who *others* are. Inevitably, the answers must come from a complete knowledge of Nature, through the experience of life. To affect any long-term and continuing success in the future, our species must consider the awareness, understanding, and proficiency in the two major independent but importantly interrelated *inter* and *intra*.

9

INTER DETAILED

"To feel much for others and little for ourselves; to restrain our selfishness and exercise our benevolent affections, constitute the perfection of human nature."
—Adam Smith

WE MUST ADDRESS both *inter* and *intra* with an important caveat, and that is a firm understanding of why *inter* needs to be awakened in our children *before intra*, and as early as possible by eventual generations of high AUQ parents, educators, and leaders alike.

Inter—whether between individuals, powerful factions, or organizations such as governments—has to do with the development within our mindbrains of mutual respect, humility, honesty, empathy, compassion, and trust. We are subject to many challenges of an *inter* nature throughout our maturation, from childhood to adulthood, as highly social beings, and one must deal with any combination of insults to the mindbrain. This work touches upon the negative *mindbrain feed* that has accrued from parents, friends, schoolmates, teachers, religions, national agendas, etc., as we mature. There is not one human being that the above groups have not influenced. It is the balance of how positive or negative your experiences have been and how you react because of them that differentiates us.

Whether real, manipulated to appear real, or imagined, the perception of an *inter* threat to ourselves, family, or friends, by individuals, groups, or any outside force or power, has definite consequences. At that moment, our limbic-based old mammalian mindbrain survival system floods us with emotions that will be more controlling than rational thinking. When we are in the grip of an outer threat, fear, or terror, we may feel compelled to form groups and fortify ourselves in numbers. In a state where our emotions overtake us in this way, someone may easily prevent us from rational, insightful, and careful thinking, often inviting the possibility of *groupthink*. Social psychologist Irving Janis coined the term to describe a psychological phenomenon occurring when any group makes faulty decisions because group pressures for harmony or conformity discourage creativity or individual responsibility. They will lead to a deterioration of mental efficiency, reality testing, and moral judgment.[1]

Any experiences that have conditioned you to divide and enforce your *fear, ego, arrogance, exclusion, prejudice, scapegoating, superiority, mistrust*, etc. are mental *cancers*. Unless you become aware enough and continually *direct* yourself to function as your own *mental immune system* and free your thinking from the infective results of divisive rhetoric or action, you will devolve.

Informing your children through *inter* to value all life, be non-divisive, respect individual liberty and potential, and understand the interrelationship of all matter will be the most important education for your long-term survival.

EMPATHY

Empathy/compassion is the ability to understand, feel, and share the emotions of another living entity,[2] by caring for and having a desire to help them,[3] making less distinct the differences between oneself and another.[4]

Hoping to expedite the understanding of empathy, an international team led by researchers at Mount Sinai School of Medicine in New York studied the "anterior insular cortex." They have for the first time shown that it is the only area of the mindbrain which is the activity center of human empathy, whereas the other areas of the mindbrain are not. They published the study in the September 2012 issue of the journal *Brain*.[5] It shows that empathy deficits in patients with mindbrain damage to the anterior insular cortex are like the empathy deficits found in several psychiatric diseases, including autism spectrum disorders, borderline personality disorder, schizophrenia, and conduct disorders, suggesting potentially common neural deficits in those psychiatric populations. [6] This most recent study firmly establishes that the anterior insular cortex is where the feeling of empathy originates.

Patrick R. Hof, MD, Regenstrief professor and vice chair of the department of neuroscience at Mount Sinai, a coauthor of the study, stated, "Now that we know the specific brain mechanisms associated with empathy, we can translate these findings into disease categories and learn why these empathic responses are deficient in neuropsychiatric illnesses, such as autism. . . . This will help direct neuropathologic investigations aiming to define the specific abnormalities in identifiable neuronal circuits in these conditions, bringing us one step closer to developing better models and eventually preventive or protective strategies."

Xiaosi Gu, PhD of the department of psychiatry at Mount Sinai, working with researchers from the United States and China, evaluated Chinese patients at Beijing Tiantan Hospital. They showed the subjects color photographs of people in pain. Three patients had lesions caused by removing mindbrain tumors in the anterior insular cortex; patients had lesions in other parts of the mindbrain and fourteen "control" patients had neurologically intact mindbrains. The research team found that patients with damage restricted to the anterior insular cortex had deficits in explicit and implicit empathetic pain processing. "Patients with anterior insular lesions had a hard time evaluating the emotional state of people in pain and feeling empathy for them, compared to all the others," said Dr. Jin Fan, corresponding author of this study and an assistant professor at the department of psychiatry at Mount Sinai. This study suggests that we may develop behavioral and cognitive therapies to compensate for deficits in the anterior insular cortex and its related functions, such as empathy. These findings can also inform future research evaluating the cellular and molecular mechanisms underlying complex social functions in the anterior insular cortex and develop possible pharmacological treatments for patients. [7]

Might we be able to take an "empathy pill" someday and enhance our chances to spread compassion around? The notion that any complex human cognitive-emotional expression may be chemically or electrically enhanced by mapping anyone's targeted locus or loci is highly problematic. We need to focus on early parental and formal education and whatever other resources we can integrate to become more empathetic. Empathy is not as manipulative as depression, for example, with the use of mood elevators like serotonin and norepinephrine uptake inhibitors. Each individual will either thrive or dive depending upon a more acute understanding of their cognitive-emotional interplay, and the recognition of its essential role in our destiny.

"Without understanding the process of self, there is no bias for thought, there is no basis for right thinking."
—J. Krishnamurti

THERE HAS BEEN MUCH SELF-OBFUSCATION about *intra* when contemplating who we are as individuals throughout the ages. By ignoring or rationalizing the worst of our thoughts and actions and allowing the most favorable to enter and reflect in our consciousness, we disallow ourselves a clear and truthful understanding of our psyche. This is our way of avoiding *self-inflicted* mental anguish, having all that we can handle from external sources, preferring to live in a state of mild to strong self-deception, extending throughout our lives. It would be beneficial were we able to gain self-insight from the judgments of a consensus of people who are close to us or with whom we have had long-time associations; this must also fail because of the mask we present to ourselves, let alone others.

Had we the insight and acuity to investigate our psyches with the keenest of critical objectivity, no one could know us better, nor should they. This is understandable, as it is we who have incorporated every experience we have ever had into our psyches and reacted in kind to all of them, regardless of how meaningful or insignificant they have seemed. That would require a Buddhist-like insight which most mortals have failed to accomplish within our short evolution and lifespan. We view ourselves in the most favorable, benevolent light. Our selective self-views or self-support systems are a survival tool we use to help us navigate through life, bolster our spirits, and get us through to the next day intact.

We still lack an accurate understanding of who we are, even at the end of our lives, when we subjectively assess our words and deeds. With all the external circumstances in life that we encountered, we may have ignored, repressed, and minimized any memories of negative consequences that weakened our image of ourselves and enhanced the more favorable. Further impeding *intra* is what we refer to, for lack of an updated term, as the *unconscious*, which is the *mental repository* (memory) of all of life's past cognitive-emotional and sensory experiences. The neural highway of our mindbrain is busy processing current events, which instantaneously become the past, and assigning them to our mental repository as a matter of its normal function. We could not very well process life's continual stream of current input, with memories flowing at the same time. After consolidation, we store long-term memories throughout the mindbrain as groups of neurons that are primed to fire together in the same pattern that created the original experience, and each component resides in the mindbrain area that initiated it.[8] MIT research on mice has shown, for the first time, that there is a store of memories in specific mindbrain cells, and it's likely that the human mindbrain functions in the same way. By triggering a small cluster of neurons, the researchers could force the subject to recall a specific memory, and by removing said neurons, the subject would lose that memory.

Stored memories which are our *data banks*, barring organic deficits, are always accessible. Were they not, it would compel us to learn the same things over and over. These data are available and retrievable because that is how our mindbrains function and what makes us sentient human beings. The only reason to believe we cannot *recognize* these data (memories) anytime we wish is because we believe them to be too insignificant, or too painful. Were we both motivated and insightful enough to manage the psychic pain, the 350 psychotherapies that exist today would disappear as does the dark when infused with light.

Can we realize the unconscious level of the mindbrain? One

may enable this only when having the will and self-determination to control their psyche, rather than being controlled by it. By concentrating our mindbrain on hurtful memories we have chosen to not revisit, if determined enough through focused will, we will become aware of them. Once aware, we can feel and react from a more experienced perspective, creating new understanding, though our original memory will remain. Technology will eventually enhance this ability by retrieving the actual memory as initially recorded by our mindbrain, but you will still have to deal with it. To merely ablate the memory technologically, without destroying the neurons harboring it, would destroy our ability to become aware of it, understand it, and grow our *intra*.

PSYCHE

"We ourselves are the great danger. Psyche is the great danger. How important it is to know something about it, but we know nothing about it."
—C.K. Jung

The term *psyche*, is a seventeenth-century Latin word, originating from the second-century Greek word *psykhe*. It came to mean *"the soul, mind, spirit, or invisible animating entity"* which occupies the physical body. We have passed through spacetime for two thousand EY since then, and a more scientific update of the term is both long overdue and edifying. Even with the revelations of science, due to the intricacies and complexities of the psyche, traditional secular and religious interpretations will continue to oppose and question the more modern ones.

Throughout this work, the term *psyche*, the fount of which is the mindbrain, is used interchangeably with *personality*. It is the real-time combination of neurological processes that enable the conscious and unconscious interchange of internal and external percepts attributed to all sentient species—in turn resulting in memory, feeling, thought, and the resultant characteristic ways of a species' nature.

It is no surprise that we are a mystery unto ourselves. "Modern" human beings have been thinking for only eight cosmic minutes out of the *one cosmic year* that Nature has taken to develop the complex mechanics of the current modern human mindbrain. The modern human lifespan is less than 0.23 cosmic seconds as of this writing. This is a short spacetime for the layman to know what makes them function mentally and physically—with the scientific knowledge available now. With earnest effort, we will study, unravel, and understand the complex regions that chemically and electrically interact within us, such as electrochemical thought and consciousness, and the intricacies of our psyche. As if this were not challenging enough, we are using our mindbrain to analyze a key function of our mindbrain!

We have understood the model of our genes for only 0.16 cosmic seconds, and within that fleeting time, we have learned many of their functions, mapped entire genomes, and manipulated them with ever-increasing precision. Our physical traits have an obvious genetic basis, but what is more subtle is the influence of our genes on our psyche, which has been proven beyond question. In healthy individuals, both the neurotransmitters (dopamine, acetylcholine, norepinephrine, and serotonin [9]) produced by genes in the cell body of our neurons and our environmental milieu dictate how our psyches react to the chemistry influencing us. In a sort of tête-à-tête, the study of epigenetics is proving that not only our environment, but our thoughts, attitudes, and perceptions contribute to gene function. Science is confirming the possibility that we will eventually learn how to fulfill our potential for becoming finely perceptive and sensitive beings, by helping us to reframe our feelings, thoughts, and emotions to create positive cellular communications and gene responses.

As it relates to the field of psychology, we consider the psyche an amalgam of thought, emotion, and motivation, consciously and unconsciously directing the interaction of an entity with its social and physical environment. The *autonomic* nervous system physically enables all our *willful* functions by controlling our breathing, reproduction, body temperature, elimination, etc. Analogous to the central control board in an electrochemical generating station, it directs the interconnection of the billions of self-regulating bodily processes, nerves, and organs that maintain our lives unconsciously. *Nature has in effect freed all its sentient organisms, by placing them on automatic pilot, for the greater glory of thought.*

Psyche is synonymous with the more recognizable word *personality*. The word personality derives from *persona*, the Greek word for "mask," and it does much to delineate the understanding of our complex mental milieu. Because of the mores of any society, we learn which thoughts and behavioral characteristics are acceptable and which we should discard. Every sentient, noncriminal person will attempt to adhere to the accepted mores of society to avoid being ostracized, persecuted, defamed, jailed, or all of the preceding. The evidence of this "social mask" is most noticeable when well-known people fall from grace because of the unraveling of their real versus social persona and become newsworthy. The only reason the list does not include millions more is that we know only those who have reached fame, end up being publicly disgraced, do not resume their vocations, and are even jailed. Our social masking serves as a barrier, obfuscating self-knowledge by undermining our ability to understand our real psyche and personality. The major problem is that most of us are disinclined, do not have the need nor the will, to examine deeply our unmasked *psyche-personality*. We need not go through the insight, pain, and discomfort of true self-examination because we can slide through society unnoticed with our masks our entire lives. When problems arise because of our lack of a real understanding of our thoughts and actions, we ignore, medicate, or seek professional amelioration of our present state of mindbrain. This modus operandi has endured for centuries, and it always ends badly. Until we learn who we are, based upon our insight into our experiential lives and genetically based chemistry, we will suffer the consequence of unawareness and a lack of understanding.

Our dearth of knowledge of the psyche also adds to the difficulty of understanding that which exists outside of ourselves (*inter*), and so we live and behave unaware of the underlying whys of human motivations, defenses, and behaviors. One must spend a great deal of time, energy, and discomfort to understand their psyche; it is a frontier that few have explored, for all the above reasons.

EMOTION: COGNITION

"Thoughts are the shadows of our feelings—always darker, emptier and simple."
—Friedrich Nietzsche

"The solution for mankind is of a spiritual nature. It is not a political or religious solution. It's the ability to love each other. That's the only solution."
—Ziggy Marley

"I use emotion for the many and reserve reason for the few."
—Adolf Hitler

"Hate is natural and love is supernatural. Gender, ethnic, religious, and socioeconomic discrimination, are fueled by self-doubt and the feeling we cannot obtain the things we need to survive because of certain people. To make ourselves feel more secure we degrade those whom we fear. Sometimes hate is taught to young people and they believe this hate-talk because it comes from those whom they trust. Hate is sometimes passed down from generation to generation even though the hate-talk is illogical and lacks evidence. Hate requires nothing from us so it is easy to indulge in. All we need to do is dismiss reality and any facts that might differ with our hate-filled beliefs."
—James W. Cone, *Taos News* "OPINION" Posted Monday, February 3, 2014.

Emotions, like cognition, are with us from birth. They serve to preserve not only our sense of self but our survival and interpersonal relationships as well.

Understanding human emotion is an essential element for our success or failure as individuals and as a species. We may describe emotions as part instinctive and part personal, deriving from one's genetics, circumstances, mood, and experiences. The following metaphors describe basic emotions: let us say *life* is analogous to the *vessel*, our *thoughts* to the water flowing through that vessel, and our *emotions* are the spectrum of colors that the water may present at any spacetime. We have all heard the expression that one uses when overcome with rage: "I saw red"; *black* represents a dark mood or art (i.e., "black comedy"); feeling *blue* may describe a sad feeling.

In humans, we distinguish between *basic* and *complex* emotions. Anger, disgust, fear, happiness, sadness, and surprise are basic and almost instinctive, whereas emotions such as gratitude, pride, shame, guilt, embarrassment, contempt, and jealousy[10] may be considered complex, and require more cognition as in self-reflection and evaluation.

When we analyze the emotional life of Homo sapiens, from the basic to the complex, there is always an interplay of emotion and cognition, and they are *never* mutually exclusive. We conjoin even basic reflexive emotions with cognition, however automatic it may seem. The correlation between emotion and cognition is at a scientific point where we can no longer separate the two as distinct functions. Without our thoughts connecting to our emotions as a bridge, our emotions cannot stand on their own.[11] Try feeling rage or fear without a thought, be it ever so instantaneous. Likewise, decision-making is not necessarily only logical—it's in part emotional, according to the latest findings in neuroscience. If you help someone discover for themselves what feels right and is best and most helpful to them, they will base their ultimate decision on their emotional self-interest. If you get someone to reveal their problems, pain, and unmet objectives, then you can build a vision for them. They will not make their decision because it is logical, but because you have helped them *feel* it is to their advantage to do so. At the point of decision, emotions are particularly important for choosing. Even with what we believe are quite "logical" decisions, at the very point of choice, they all have an emotional basis.[12]

Another view from a neurological viewpoint illustrates this linking of cognition and emotion very well. People with lesions in the ventromedial sector of the prefrontal cortex have normal cognitive functions, they can reason, but it impairs their normal processing of emotional signals. As a result, it restricts their decision-making processes, even in everyday life decisions as simple as choosing between whether to hop on the bus or take the subway. In its broadest sense, cognition refers to all mental processes. However, the study of cognition has historically excluded emotion and focused on nonemotional processes such as memory, attention, perception, action, problem-solving, and mental imagery.[13] As a result, the study of the neural basis of nonemotional and emotional processes emerged as two separate fields—*cognitive neuroscience* and *affective neuroscience*. As science continues to peel the onion back, the distinction between nonemotional and emotional processes prove to be artificial, as the two types of processing often involve overlapping neural and mental mechanisms. [14] Thus, when one interprets cognition at its broadest neuroscientific definition, we may call affective neuroscience the *cognitive neuroscience of emotion.*

In the jargon of *quantum mechanics*, slanted less toward the probabilistic theory of Bohr and more toward the causality-based theory of Bohm-De Broglie, a *pilot* wave interacts with and propels a particle rather than defining it. [15] In the jargon of *being*, an emotion interacts with and is propelled by its thought component rather than being defined by it. Apart from the *basic* emotions, the less the thought component, and the greater the emotional component, the less the probability of securing a well-reasoned, favorable, sustainable, and productive outcome. This is true whether it involves business, national and international politics, affairs of the heart, or interpersonal relations.

For example, impatience or blind conviction are both driven by powerful emotions, and weak thinking is the poster child for failure. Ever hear the expression "headstrong, headlong, dead wrong?" To be clear, unless there is an organic deficiency or a neurochemical imbalance in your system, you always have the capability of thinking a great deal more about what you feel.

I have purposely avoided details informing readers of the specific areas of brain formation beginning 500 million EY ago from the evolution of the brains of lizards and mammals through to the modern human. Those developments chartered the brain's evolutionary course from that of a purely instinctive and emotional function to the higher cognitive functions of the more developed nonhuman and human mindbrain.

The main takeaway is to understand that we absolutely can use our highly evolved mindbrain to control all instinctive and emotional processes through reason and rational thought.

PERSONAL PRIMARY PSYCHE NEED

Intra, without the mention of *personal primary psyche need*, which creates a reflex-like systemic pattern of thought, would be remiss. Inborn in our genome, these needs cause mental *predispositions* from *birth* and are a predominant influence on our behavior throughout our entire lives. Any of the psyche *universal needs* germane to the average human being, such as the need for love, self-respect, and the respect of others, are of no relevance to this discussion.

Several personal, primary psyche needs include knowledge, independence, security, beauty/symmetry, adventure (exploration, travel, romance), solitude, community, power, control, acceptance, and accomplishment. These needs are as random as eye color and differ in degree and number from none to several in any individual. One may go through life without an awareness and understanding of their personal primary psyche needs—and therefore might never relate them to their motivations, actions, and emotions. Our awareness of any of these needs does not facilitate their satisfaction; yet, an enhanced *intra* is always more beneficial for our well-being than for us to be unaware of these drivers.

How, then, do these needs dictate much of our mood and behavior? When any personal need goes unfulfilled, it triggers frustration, anger, hostility, rage, fear, or sorrow. This inevitably results in habitual reflexive thought patterns that have furrowed out the same neural pathways time after time and are the fertile neurochemical bed where withdrawal, phobia, compulsion, obsession, depression, and anxiety originate. The takeaway is to understand which, if any, of these needs belong to you and the degree to which they are present; knowing your particular needs will give you more insight into your psyche and fulfillment. [16]

The NIH's BRAIN (Brain Research through Advancing Innovative Neurotechnologies) initiative of the Obama administration was designed in 2014. Its goal is to map the activity of the entire life operating mindbrain in 3D graphics, identify and record all neuronal cellular and circuit activity, and develop innovative scanning and microscopy techniques. Its hope is to further our understanding of the underlying biology of all mental processes and behavior and will advance treatment and prevention of Alzheimer's, schizophrenia, autism, and epilepsy, amongst other diseases. [17] Part XI details these and other dynamics of the in-depth research and progress that must continue as an aid to speed up our ability to increase our AUQ.

PART IV
Vive la Différence

"Basically, women are nurturers and healers, and men are mental patients to varying degree."
—Nelson DeMille, author

"The world of humanity is possessed of two wings: the male and the female. So long as these wings are not equivalent in strength, the bird will not fly."
—Abdu'l-Bahá

"There are millennia of genetic material in the female of the species to resolve problems without violence."
—Ian A Herron, Quora, June 15, 2017

"In time, and very soon, the idea of male dominance will be ancient history."
—Valerie Lynn Ryan, August 24, 2016

THE FEMALE AND MALE of all species are each one side of Nature's "coin of the realm." They are the two living "halves" that join in Nature—for Nature to perpetuate most of its species. The attractive force for males and females of Homo sapiens is "mentical" (rhymes with physical),[1] which describes the combination of a mutual *mental* and *physical* desirability, which is the aspired to ideal for long-term bonding. The result is the propagation of the species, the antidote to its extinction, and the best outcome for the nurturing, rearing, and growth of their offspring. And as the most altricial species known to exist on Earth, we need the longest traditional parental care. This work will not focus on the physical differentiation between the two sexes, amongst them the significant hormonal differences. It is worth noting, however, that Stanford University's findings wherein an *emotional* image shown to females and males caused nine different areas of females' mindbrains to light up—only two lit up in the males.

Research has established there is a marked difference in the circuitry of women's and men's mindbrains.[2] For our purpose, it will be more prudent to address how secular, religious, and behavioral differences have determined women's and men's positions in society.

When we view male domination throughout civilized history, *muscle* very much mattered. Whether it was hunting, farming, manufacturing, construction, defending, or warfare, it was a male designated enterprise for which their strength was the key element and resulted in their controlling position. Relegation to the safety of the hearth was a female's destiny, having been subject to gestation, childbirth, and the nurturing of her newborn. Those clearly defined roles—during that time and within that culture—might have been understandable then, but as we have gone through spacetime, circumstances have changed.

Technology has automated every *muscle* enterprise to accommodate our needs, and law enforcement has defended the innocent and enforced our laws. Whatever the historic reasons for the patriarchal mentality of supremacy, we should no longer tolerate remnants of it that exist today, under any circumstance, in any society, for any reason. Unfortunately, old roles die hard, and the male ego persists in fueling the entrenched patriarchal mentality. This is *especially true* regarding the female-male relationship, as there is nothing like the male need to exert control when he feels the lack of it. The underlying male fear of the female becoming liberated and independent enough to be less in "need" of him is the bedrock underlying the inequality, and it will persist until people understand it. This undertow is a major factor in keeping the male and female at odds with one another throughout the ages, and within our psyches, which include our unconscious and will have to be laid bare for us to realize that fact.

Religion is a male-dominated creation and enterprise, and it must shoulder some of the blame. "Women are prevented from playing a full and equal role in many faiths, creating an environment in which violations against women are justified," former President Jimmy Carter noted in a December 2009 speech to the Parliament of the World's Religions in Australia. "The belief that women are inferior human beings in the eyes of God," Mr. Carter continued, "gives excuses to the brutal husband who beats his wife, the soldier who rapes a woman, or the employer who has a lower pay scale for women employees."[3]

A part of human realization will be the awareness and understanding that the female of our species must be elevated to a place of equal economic and gender stature with the male.

Ancient Ideas Die Hard

The ancient scriptures of Islam, Christianity, and Judaism highlight the religious influence that supports male favoritism and dominance. If you wish to understand where the mindset of male ownership over females came from, take these words to heart. Islam gives the husband the leadership of his family.

Quran (4:11)—(Inheritance), "The male shall have the equal of the portion of two females" (also verse 4:176). In Islam, sexism is financially established.

Quran (2:282)—(Court testimony), "And call to witness, from among your men, two witnesses. And if two men be not found then a man and two women."

Muslim apologists offer creative explanations to explain why Allah felt that a man's testimony in court has twice the value of a woman's, but studies consistently show that women are less likely to tell lies than men, meaning they make more reliable witnesses.

Quran (2:228)—"and the men are a degree above them [women]."

Quran (4:3)—(Wife-to-husband ratio), "Marry women of your choice, Two or three or four." Inequality by number.

Quran (4:24) and Quran (33:50)—"A man is permitted to take women as sex slaves outside of marriage."

Christianity—Ephesians: 5:22-25 (New Testament), "Wives, submit to your husbands, as to the Lord. For the husband is the head of the wife even as Christ is the head of the church, his body, and is himself its Savior. Now as the church submits to Christ, so also wives should submit in everything to their husbands."[4]

Judaism—Exodus, "Thou shalt not covet thy neighbour's house, thou shalt not covet thy neighbour's wife, nor his manservant, nor his maidservant, nor his ox, nor his ass, nor anything that is thy neighbour's."

The tenth commandment forbids coveting anything the neighbor owns, and the wife is clearly regarded as equivalent to a piece of property.[5]

It has been thousands of EYS since the writing of these verses, yet they are indoctrinated into the mindbrains of generation after generation of worshipers. The most unfortunate result of this has not only been the subjugation of the female psyche with its concomitant damage—but the obfuscation of their sorely needed positive energy and nurturing qualities throughout history.

The International Crisis Behavior (ICB) project data set and multinomial logistic regression are used to test the level of violence exhibited during international crises by states with varying levels of domestic gender equality. Results show that the severity of violence in crisis decreases as domestic gender equality increases. [6] Prof. J. S. Nye Jr. indicates that Harvard professor Steven Pinker, an experimental cognitive psychologist and a popular writer, has presented research showing that the nations of the world that lag in the decline of violence are the same nations that lag in mainstreaming the participation of women.[7]

World Ranks on Gender Equality, by Colby Jones on January 09, 2018, and The WorldEconomic Forum's published findings called The Global Gender Gap Report looked at all countries globally and ranked them on a scale from zero to one in terms of women's economic participation, educational attainment, health, and political empowerment. *The closer to "1" a country gets, theoretically, the smaller the gender gap.* Iceland, Norway, Finland, Rwanda, and Sweden round out the top five, while the Islamic Republic of Iran, Chad, Syria, Pakistan, and Yemen make up the bottom.

Table 5: Rankings by region, 2017

EAST ASIA AND THE PACIFIC		
New Zealand	9	0.791
Philippines	10	0.790
Australia	35	0.731
Mongolia	53	0.713
Lao PDR	64	0.703
Singapore	65	0.702
Vietnam	69	0.698
Thailand	75	0.694
Myanmar*	83	0.691
Indonesia	84	0.691
Cambodia	99	0.676
China	100	0.674
Brunei Darussalam	102	0.671
Malaysia	104	0.670
Japan	114	0.657
Korea, Rep.	118	0.650
Fiji*	125	0.638
Timor-Leste	128	0.628

EASTERN EUROPE AND CENTRAL ASIA		
Slovenia	7	0.805
Bulgaria	18	0.756
Latvia	20	0.756
Belarus	26	0.744
Lithuania	28	0.742
Moldova	30	0.740
Estonia	37	0.731
Albania	38	0.728
Poland	39	0.728
Serbia	40	0.727
Kazakhstan	52	0.713
Croatia	54	0.711
Romania	58	0.708
Ukraine	61	0.705
Bosnia and Herzegovina	66	0.702
Macedonia, FYR	67	0.702
Russian Federation	71	0.696
Slovak Republic	74	0.694
Montenegro	77	0.693
Kyrgyz Republic	85	0.691
Czech Republic	88	0.688
Georgia	94	0.679
Tajikistan	95	0.678
Armenia	97	0.677
Azerbaijan	98	0.676
Hungary	103	0.670

LATIN AMERICA AND THE CARIBBEAN		
Nicaragua	6	0.814
Bolivia	17	0.758
Barbados	23	0.750
Cuba	25	0.745
Bahamas	27	0.743
Argentina	34	0.732
Colombia	36	0.731
Costa Rica	41	0.727
Ecuador	42	0.724
Panama	43	0.722
Peru	48	0.719
Jamaica	51	0.717
Honduras	55	0.711
Uruguay	56	0.710
Venezuela	60	0.706
El Salvador	62	0.705
Chile	63	0.704
Dominican Republic	70	0.697
Belize	79	0.692
Mexico	81	0.692
Suriname	86	0.689
Brazil	90	0.684
Paraguay	96	0.678
Guatemala	110	0.667

MIDDLE EAST AND NORTH AFRICA		
Israel	44	0.721
Tunisia	117	0.651
United Arab Emirates	120	0.649
Bahrain	126	0.632
Algeria	127	0.629
Kuwait	129	0.628
Qatar	130	0.626
Turkey	131	0.625
Mauritania	132	0.614
Egypt	134	0.608
Jordan	135	0.604
Morocco	136	0.598
Lebanon	137	0.596
Saudi Arabia	138	0.584
Iran, Islamic Rep.	140	0.583
Syria	142	0.568
Yemen	144	0.516

SOUTH ASIA		
Bangladesh	47	0.719
Maldives	106	0.669
India	108	0.669
Sri Lanka	109	0.669
Nepal	111	0.664
Bhutan	124	0.638
Pakistan	143	0.546

SUB-SAHARAN AFRICA		
Rwanda	4	0.822
Namibia	13	0.777
South Africa	19	0.756
Burundi	22	0.755
Mozambique	29	0.741
Uganda	45	0.721
Botswana	46	0.720
Zimbabwe	50	0.717
Tanzania	68	0.700
Ghana	72	0.695
Lesotho	73	0.695
Kenya	76	0.694
Madagascar	80	0.692
Cameroon	87	0.689
Cape Verde	89	0.686
Senegal	91	0.684
Malawi	101	0.672
Swaziland	105	0.670
Liberia	107	0.669
Mauritius	112	0.664
Guinea	113	0.659
Ethiopia	115	0.656
Benin	116	0.652
Gambia, The	119	0.649
Burkina Faso	121	0.646
Nigeria	122	0.641
Angola	123	0.6402
Côte d'Ivoire	133	0.6114
Mali	139	0.5831
Chad	141	0.5750

WESTERN EUROPE		
Iceland	1	0.878
Norway	2	0.830
Finland	3	0.823
Sweden	5	0.816
Ireland	8	0.794
France	11	0.778
Germany	12	0.778
Denmark	14	0.776
United Kingdom	15	0.770
Switzerland	21	0.755
Spain	24	0.746
Belgium	31	0.739
Netherlands	32	0.737
Portugal	33	0.734
Austria	57	0.709
Luxembourg	59	0.706
Greece	78	0.692
Italy	82	0.692
Cyprus	92	0.684
Malta	93	0.682

NORTH AMERICA		
Canada	16	0.769
United States	49	0.718

* New countries in 2017

PART V
VIOLENCE

"The very first essential for success is a perpetually constant and regular employment of violence."
—Adolf Hitler

"Nonviolence means avoiding not only external physical violence but also internal violence of spirit. You not only refuse to shoot a man, but you refuse to hate him."
—Martin Luther King Jr.

"Violence is the last refuge of the incompetent."
—Isaac Asimov, Foundation

"It is the state of the heart within us that determines the nature of the triggers we will pull outside of us."
—Craig D. Lounsbrough

THE MATTER OF HUMAN VIOLENCE demands a thorough but focused inquiry. Researchers and scholars alike, across the entire spectrum of the natural and social sciences, have continually opined why we exhibit violent, destructive behavior. I will present some of the scholarly thinking relating to our species' proclivity for acting violently and its inevitability. We will also discuss opposing views so that you may glean more perspectives. Violence is at the core of our survival and concerns the ways and the whys of human inhumanity. It has been an obvious problem for our species. It is *more* than a problem and is an existential threat now that accidents, terrorism, and war can release the "e" from the "m" in $e=mc^2$.

SOME SAY VIOLENCE has been in our history for as long as we have been on Earth. Others believe it began about 6,000 EY ago, and some claim it has been diminishing over the past seventy-five EY; these are all true, depending upon the validity of ancient evidence and interpretation of the same.

The following chart is a record of some of the more notable damage we have wrought upon one another, to date, in just the past 2,000 EY.

The 20 deadliest events in human history

Death toll

Cause				
Genghis Khan, 13C				
Mideast Slave Trade, 7C-19C				
Xin Dynasty, 1C				
Timur Lenk, 14C-15C				
An Lushan Revolt, 8C				
Fall of the Ming Dynasty, 17C				
Fall of Rome, 5C				
Muslim Conquest of India, 11C-18C				
Atlantic Slave Trade, 15C-19C				
Conquest of the Americas, 15C-19C				
Second World War, 20C				
British India (mostly famine), 19C				
Fall of the Yuan Dynasty, 14C				
Taiping Rebellion, 19C				
Mao Zedong (mostly famine), 20C				
Thirty Years War, 17C				
Joseph Stalin, 20C				
First World War, 20C				
Congo Free State, 19C-20C				
Russian Civil War, 20C				

Axis: 0, 200,000,000, 400,000,000, 600,000,000, 800,000,000

Equivalent deaths today

Legend: Death toll at the time | Equivalent number of deaths today

13
LEMMING LUNACY

THE OLDEST KNOWN EVIDENCE of human violence begins with the uncovering of the 3.4 million-EY-old bones of the genus Australopithecus, species afarensis. Humans have increased their tool-making ability and developed more sophisticated hunting tools and weapons used not only for survival but for predatory offense and defense. Our facility for using our mindbrain-directed opposing thumbs made it easier to succeed at violence and is one of the main reasons we survived against larger species.

These skills, however, have not been necessary for some 10,000 EY, as we transitioned from hunter-gatherers to farmers by cultivating crops and domesticating and penning in nonhumans. In short, we no longer needed to be violent to survive. The male of our species has been dominant and unchallenged, for all but the last few decades of the past 5 million EY. During this period, from the cave to the luxuriously appointed abode and technological innovation, there has been one intermittent constant—human conflict and its resolution through violence. The medieval period was a particular killer, with human-on-human violence responsible for twelve percent of recorded deaths. But for the twentieth century, we have been peaceful, killing one another off at a rate of just 1.33 percent worldwide, in relative terms. And in the least violent parts of the world today, we enjoy homicide rates as low as 0.01 percent. Richard Wrangham, a biological anthropologist at Harvard known for his study of the evolution of human warfare, says these differences among primates matter.

Others call the twentieth century the bloodiest, cruelest time in history, fraught with endless wars and unprecedented cases of genocide, in absolute terms! According to the Polynational War Memorial, there were an astounding 237 wars between 1900 and today, starting with the Boxer Rebellion and continuing to the wars in Afghanistan and Syria.

So-called leaders using propaganda, prejudice, scapegoating, and claims of existential doom bleed into the all too receptive mindbrains of those they lead. It has led to the justification of and enablement of horrific acts of violence like rape and pillaging, genocide, the slaughter of those deemed unworthy or a threat to their authority, or all-out war. Hitler portrayed Jews as rats to justify their slaughter. Stalin condemned Russian "kulaks" (farmers) as lowly "profiteers" to confiscate their grain, land, and lives. These atrocities were dependent not only on propaganda and prejudice but upon the notion of the *hierarchy of intrinsic value* previously referred to. Humans driven by survival instincts, groupthink, and the desire for affiliation with a "winning" team have gone along to get along throughout history as gangs, supremacy and hate groups, various political and economic ideologies, etc.

In terms of *natural selection* and survival, it is safer to kill than be killed, and if the guns and power are in the hands of low AUQ leadership, we tend to either camouflage ourselves, accept the leadership, or just hope not to be killed. The devolution of our species, caused by the low AUQ leadership and the unfortunate support of those they lead, is the result.

WE CANNOT SEEM TO RESIST doing physical harm to one another, either individually or in groups. Oftentimes, we justify violence, and take it to the next level, as nations battle one another in a "death machine" called war. It spells trauma, deformity, death for soldiers and civilian casualties, and a *money-making machine* for the suppliers of war material. We have been quite proficient throughout history, driven by a *kill or be killed* mindset, continually finding a more efficient method of human destruction.

In his 1930 book *Civilization and its Discontents*, Sigmund Freud wrote, ". . . men are not gentle creatures who want to be loved, who at the most can defend themselves if we attack them; they are, on the contrary, creatures among whose instinctual endowments are to be reckoned a powerful share of aggressiveness." Hundreds of EYS prior to Freud, philosopher Thomas Hobbes had a similarly pessimistic view of humanity, believing all men could equally kill, and when two people or groups want the same thing, the inevitable outcome is war. I wonder whether he said anything about what women would do?

Winston Churchill experienced WWII as the leader of his nation and stated that "Little did we guess that what has been called the century of the common man would witness as its outstanding feature more common men killing each other with greater facilities than any other five centuries together in the history of the world."

D.L. Smith, a professor of philosophy at the University of New England, correctly shows that the thought of a universe that is hierarchically or vertically organized is a relic of a prescientific age and is at odds with the scientific Darwinian picture of a *horizontal* biosphere.

Yet he still suggests that humans, disregarding Darwin, cannot free their minds from the idea of a *hierarchy of intrinsic value*, wherein one species is ideated by humans as having morally higher value than another. Smith feels it is steadfastly entrenched in our psychology because of our being so-called "moral," and that morality would be inconceivable without it. [1] As concerns Smith's interpretation of morality, is it suitable to use the term "moral" at all, for those who would harbor the concept of any "hierarchy of intrinsic value," or are they mutually exclusive in the overall scheme of Nature? Would a truly moral person understand Nature enough to prevent thoughts of any hierarchy of life? Should we or should we not allow all species on Earth, most of whose true nature is unknown to us even as ours is to ourselves, to develop freely from that of a subjective human mindset?

Professor Smith believes we exhibit the same *coalitionary aggression* as do the chimpanzees, ants, and wolves, and feels that we cannot stop men from enjoying war; the best we can do is hope that men eventually revile it more than enjoy it. He describes our relationship with killing as ambivalent, an amalgam of pleasure and aversion, rooted deep in our nature, never to be eliminated.

Are we more worthy than any of the varied species on Earth, including those of our own or any other life forms in this universe? Could the term "hierarchy of intrinsic value," be an excuse used to dominate, control, and "do as we chose"—an excuse to remain violent, if you will? Violence has too many causes to ignore and may just be humankind's inevitable "curse" after all; or is the word "curse" just another excuse for our violence? Smith, to his credit, correctly shows that the thought of a universe that is hierarchically or vertically organized is a relic of a pre-scientific, pre-Darwinian age.

Harvard professor Steven Pinker authored the book *Better*

Angels of Our Nature: Why Violence Has Declined in 2011, which is a scholarly and thorough research of our past human intraspecies violence. Pinker explains that, contrary to widespread belief, modern people are much less violent than their ancestors. Amongst other things, he cites the decline in murder rates, a drop in capital punishment, and lower war deaths proportionate to the populations of the times. Though violence may be down, Pinker further explains, it is not out, and there are and will be upward blips on a downward trend. He has noted that slavery is all but gone and women and nonhumans are increasingly receiving better treatment. His research shows there are specific differences in societies that profoundly affect their behavior. People and societies with higher literacy, education, and public discourse commit less violent crimes, are less xenophobic and racist, and are more receptive to democracy.[2]

Populations with more abstract reasoning abilities (IQ) and universal thought increased in the twentieth century by three points over a ten-year span, and if it continues, it bodes well for the independence and freedom of thought, and a decrease in violence were it to continue.[3]

15
HERITABLE LEGACY?

WERE WE TO ANALYZE human violence from a heritable genetic perspective, it makes sense to investigate our own taxonomic family, the Hominidae/ape family. Humans are a family of eight species of primates. To enable focus on our purpose, only the closest three species—chimpanzee, bonobo, and human—will be discussed. This still leaves us with a conundrum, since humans share 98.7 percent of their DNA with both, and while chimpanzees have more of a propensity for violence, bonobos literally follow more of a *make love, not war* philosophy.

So, what kind of ape are we? Dr. Christopher Ryan, author of *Sex at Dawn*, thinks we have more in common with our cousin bonobos, who are a matriarchal run group; males are inclined to stay with their mothers, while young females go their own way. Ryan believes we would be happiest in a noncompetitive, sexually open society.[4]

Other researchers say we are more like our more aggressive, xenophobic, violent chimpanzee cousin than the docile, playful, sexual, bonobo. In the September 28, 2016, issue of the highly respected *Journal of Nature*, José María Gómez, having led a research team, authored a paper titled "The Phylogenetic Roots of Human

Lethal Violence," which reported that early humans were violent. They looked for evidence of killings *within* a species, whether by cannibalism, infanticide, or aggression. It should be noted that with chimpanzees and other primates that kill one other, infanticide is the most usual form of killing. Infanticide occurs for several reasons, the major one being when a new male leader instinctively wishing to mate with lactating females cannot do so while they are nursing their infants.

Gómez's sample size was 4 million deaths of more than a thousand of the 5,400 known mammal species, from shrews to primates. A history of human slayings was also tabulated. The pattern that emerged was that lethal violence had increased throughout mammalian evolution. While only about 0.3 percent of all mammals had died in conflict with members of their ownspecies, that rate is sixfold higher, or about an average of 2 percent, for several primate mammals. In line with those findings, they noted that early Paleolithic human remains had a two percent total as well[5].

Gómez and his investigative team also reported the species most and least likely to engage in intraspecies killing. They reported that the toll is 8 percent for hyenas, 10 percent for the yellow mongoose, and 17 percent for lemurs. The results also indicate that 60 percent of all mammal species do not kill one another at all, as far as anyone has seen. Very few of the more than 1,200 species of bats kill each other, and pangolins and porcupines get along fine.[6]

Famed and renowned primatologist and anthropologist Dame Jane Goodall states, "It is easy to get the impression that chimpanzees are more aggressive than they really are. In actuality, peaceful interactions are far more frequent than aggressive ones; mild threatening gestures are more common than vigorous ones; threats per se occur much more often than fights; and serious, wounding fights are very rare compared to brief, relatively mild ones."[7] If anyone understands our cousins, having devoted her life to that purpose for sixty years, it is Ms. Goodall.

An even broader research finding was that of the late Robert Sussman, a longtime professor of anthropology in arts and sciences at Washington University in St. Louis, who found that all *primates*, some of the most aggressive of all mammals, spend less than 1 percent of their day fighting or otherwise competing, and that more than 90 percent of their social interactions are cooperative rather than competitive or divisive.[8] Therefore, it may well be that it is misguided to believe our "family tree" is the cause of *our* brand of violence and destruction as a species; perhaps it is just another of our misconceptions waiting to be reasoned and researched away.

Richard Wrangham, a Harvard biological anthropologist, whose research has supported findings that infanticide is the most common form of intraspecies killing, found that very few primates kill adults of their own species. The "adult killing club is very small," he writes. "It includes wolves, lions, spotted hyenas, and humans," he finds. In the case of Wrangham's work, a point of main interest is his research into *why* we kill. He describes two types of killing aggression, either of which can lead nonhumans and humans to kill adults. One is the *hot* kind or *reactive*, which is more prevalent with nonhumans and involves the basic instinctual emotions such as the anger and fear caused by immediate threat. The other is the *cold* or the *proactive* kind, which permeates human activity and is fueled by a desired *goal*, leading to a calculated and deliberate murder, such as terrorism, bombings, school shootings, and war. Wrangham feels that "When it comes to murderous tendencies, humans really are exceptional."[9]

Marc Bekoff, PhD, is a preeminent researcher whose tireless effort to further the awareness and understanding of the world's populations for the need to foster the value for *all* life has spanned decades. His research and writing include the disciplines of animal behavior, cognitive ethology (the study of animal minds), behavioral ecology, compassionate conservation, human-animal interactions, and the protection of animals. He is the professor emeritus of ecology and evolutionary biology of the University of Colorado, Boulder, where he taught for thirty-two years. Bekoff is the multi-award-winning author of over thirty books, and the author of 1,000 articles as well as the co-founder with Dame Jane Goodall, of Ethologists for the Ethical Treatment of Animals in 2000.

As a key advocate and supporter of compassionate conservatism, the cornerstone belief is "First do no harm, and the life of every *individual* matters because they are alive and have intrinsic value, not because of what they can do for us. Treating every individual with respect and dignity is the decent thing to do."

Were you to become familiar with any of Bekoff's contributions to the literature in his disciplines, you would find that he takes great exception to, and feels a great amount of disdain for, any information that is heard or written in the media or texts which ascribe to the claim that human beings are acting like "animals" or "they're just animals," whenever they commit violent or murderous acts. What he does believe is that the biological science and research have proven this notion is totally bogus. He has spent his life with the hands-on study of nonhuman behavior and emotions. What Bekoff says is that "Murderous humans are *not* acting like animals. . . . Nonhuman animals are predominantly peaceful, and that just as some roots of violence can be found in our animal past, so too can roots of altruism and cooperation."[10, 11]

There is sufficient scientific evidence to acknowledge once and for all that we alone must take responsibility for our murderous ways and destructive behavior, and not *blame* nonhumans for it. The sooner we keenly understand and become aware of the fact that we alone, unequivocally, have complete mindbrain control over our choices, the better. We may then begin to educate our young to understand that all living and growing entities are a *family of life*, and we must take care of *our family*.

16

IS HUMAN VIOLENCE INEVITABLE?

"Chimpanzees have a dark side just as we do. We have less excuse because we can deliberate, so I believe only we are capable of true calculated evil. Some people say, therefore, that violence and war are inevitable, I say rubbish: "Our brains are fully capable of controlling instinctive behavior."
—Jane Goodall

WITH ALL DUE RESPECT to the voluminous studies, research, and records on our mammalian and primate heritage of violence, we should analyze other important views and subtleties before the completion of this most important matter. What may be most surprising is not how violent we are, but how much less violent in comparison to other primates we are. It is difficult to estimate how often nonhumans kill its own in the wild, but José María Gómez and his team, previously mentioned in their *Journal of Nature* September 2016 article, tabulated an excellent overview of the species most and least likely to kill their kind. Science shows that the role of instincts in determining the behavior of nonhumans vary from species to species. The more complex the neural system of nonhumans, the greater the role of the cerebral cortex, and social learning and instincts play a lesser role. For example, the comparison between crocodiles (reptiles) and lionesses (mammals) illustrates how altricial mammals are much more heavily dependent on social learning than precocial reptiles. Lionesses and female chimpanzees, both mammals, raised in zoos away from their birth mothers most often reject their offspring because they have not been taught the

skills of motherhood. Such is not the case with simpler species such
as reptiles.[12]

In full consideration of the results of his major research
project, José María Gómez, who led the study and published "The
Phylogenetic Roots of Human Lethal Violence," *unequivocally* states
that "Evolutionary history is not a total straitjacket on the human
condition, as humans have changed and will continue to change in
surprising ways . . . No matter how violent or pacific we were in
the origin, we can modulate the level of intraspecies violence by
changing our social environment. We can build a more peaceful
society if we wish."

As to whether violence is a fait accompli in the modern human
species, please familiarize yourself with the psychology of the
small but destructive group of ever-present paranoid, sociopathic
leaders and their sycophants, and the damaging divisiveness of
every style of early childhood ideological indoctrination. Add to
that the psychological understanding of what specific childhood
circumstances, be they familial or social, engender our mass
murderers, serial killers, and homicidal maniacs. You will find all
the answers you need therein, and you will come to understand it is
the deadly few who disturb the many who have a natural and rational
desire for peace. Violence is *endemic,* and the plan is to eliminate the
causes of its nascent germination prior to its consistently infective
pandemic contagion.

17
FEMME LESS FATALE

LET US NOW CONSIDER the 600-pound gorilla in this section, concerning aggression and violence. This would be the differing behavior of the female and the male of the species. There are genetic and historic reasons for these contrasts, and all originally had to do with survival. From all points of view, men were evolutionarily selected and honed for physical battle rather than women.[13] That males are more aggressive and more violent than women reflect their anatomy. Men are heavier and more muscular, have denser and heavier bones, a shorter reaction time, better visual acuity, a bulkier heart, and bigger lungs, and are thus better armed with the means of attack and defense.[14, 15, 16, 17]

Men also have testosterone which is responsible for inducing competitive and even criminal behavior. According to *evolutionary neurocardiogenic theory*, male sex hormones (androgens) correlate with the increased ability of males to gain resources, hierarchical position, and sexual partners.[18] The male—being the most muscular but not required for childbearing, nursing, and nurturing the progeny—was the designated provider of food, shelter, and predatory defense. Females took care of the children and the hearth. When males were no longer needed to scour the land for food, and defense became a task for police forces, the male role developed into that of *breadwinner*. The female has proved to be more than capable of not only childbearing and child-rearing—but they have also become the breadwinner. Because of economic necessity, higher education, their growing numbers, and powerful voices, 47.7 percent of all women worldwide took part in the labor force in 2019; the figure for males was 74.7 percent.

The findings of social psychologists have revealed that the social emancipation of women in recent decades has barely influenced or enhanced the expressiveness of aggressive behavior in women. This reinforces the established belief that the higher degree of masculine aggressiveness is primarily because of genetic factors. Sex differences predetermine, on a genetic level, the differences in aggressive behavior.[19] Women present verbal aggression in intersexual competition; rarely are there cases of physical assault. Women use language only in competitive strategies.[20] As the economic playing field continues to level in most parts of the world, remnants of a genetic and historical basis for behaviors that are no longer necessary for our survival remain, and are seriously detrimental to society.

The male of the species has always played the role of *warrior* and *soldier* when called upon. As a result, the struggles over treasures, land, and ideologies have left mountains of corpses throughout our history. Simply put, men are much more likely to engage in physical aggression and feel positive about it, viewing their aggressive acts as an exercise in control over others that challenges their self-esteem or integrity. One should note, however, the important fact that, throughout the history of war, soldiers have suffered from hysteria in the Civil War, shell shock in WWI, battle fatigue in WWII, and PTSD in the Vietnam and Middle Eastern wars (among others). Would these identical and crippling conditions of the mindbrain— brought on by the destruction, maiming, and killing many consider an inevitable part of normal evolution—ever occur if they were, indeed, *normal*?

Women view their aggression as often coming from excessive stress and a loss of self-control, and they feel more guilt and concern after being aggressive than do men.[21, 22, 23] These anatomical, hormonal, behavioral, and evolutionary factors show the biological and instinctual inclination of men to be more combative. Therefore, on an individual and social level, men engage in acts of violence and crime, and the social environment only cultivates and points out these predispositions toward fighting and aggression. [24, 25, 26] Though there is proof and a modicum of hope that violence is on the decline throughout the world, it is now opportunistic for our species to realize that the female and male must equally share management of this planet, keeping in mind the value of all life thereupon. The treatment of women as second-class citizens in many parts of this world is ongoing, and even in enlightened societies, their power is extremely limited.

Even if based upon one factor alone, we must give women equal or more sway in the vital decisions affecting life and death in a government's deliberations concerning an armed conflict—women have experienced the life-giving enterprise known as childbirth and the associated nurturing associated with it; men have not. Women, already given to resolving problems in a nonviolent manner, will certainly think exceptionally long and hard before committing to the sacrifice of their children's (or others') lives, if there are alternative means by which to avoid doing so. Males have not yet recognized their defenses, fears, and dogma, and they have not admitted that females may very well be even more than their equal.

PART VI
PARENTING

"If you bungle raising your children, I don't think whatever else you do matters very much."
—Jacqueline Kennedy

"Let parents bequeath to their children not riches, but the spirit of reverence."
—Plato

"Relationship with a consistent, stable, attuned, loving adult, within a predictable, stable environment, is what builds a healthy brain and develops a successful human, period."
—Marcy Axness, *Parenting for Peace: Raising the Next Generation of Peacemakers*

ALTRICIAL SPECIES ARE THOSE in which the young are incapable of moving around on their own soon after hatching or being born. The word derives from the Latin root *alere*, meaning "to nurse, to rear, or to nourish," and shows the need for the young to be cared for and protected, for a long duration.[1] A newborn human is essentially still a fetus for *another nine months* after birth, given the infant's protracted period of total helplessness. human parents must diligently attend to its needs far longer than any other parental primates do. Some evolutionary biologists propose that several of the last touches made to infants in the womb are cosmetic, turning the baby into something so cute the parents will feel compelled to care for it. Dr. Sarah Blaffer Hrdy of the University of California at Davis suggests that the "adorable" factor is one reason the human infant puts on layers of fat right before birth. Once the mother has fallen in love, she forgets the pain, she forgets the hassle, and she gladly accepts indentured servitude for the next eighteen EY.[2] Mindbrain growth is energetically costly, and postponing the greater part of this to the postpartum period conserves the energy demands on mothers, as well as enabling the cranial size to expand way beyond the dimensions of the pelvic floor and birth canal. Delaying most of the cortical mindbrain growth to the postpartum period has also ensured that it develops in a social environment that promotes social skills as well as provides for the alloparenting of the infant. Even more significant is the provision of an attachment figure, usually that of the mother, which provides a secure base from which to explore and develop other social relationships.[3]

Nature's cosmic unfolding has led to a variety and volume of life, as propagation goes on unabated across all species, whether or not the propagating parents have passed a *qualified to be parents* test. Qualification takes on another dimension when it involves the long-term needs of the newly conceived, most needy of all, highly altricial human species. The responsibilities of parents, in this case, to nurture and care for their offspring are essential to the well-being of not only their newly conceived life—but to a degree, this new life may contribute positively (or negatively) to the peace, socialization, unity, and overall well-being of our planet. *This process begins in the womb.*

Research shows the development of a fetus' organs and brain are more affected by a mother's environment, experience, and behavior than ever before realized. Conditions programmed through such non-genetic circumstances during fetal growth may not show up until decades later. Poor nutrition in early pregnancy can correlate with later heart disease and diabetes. Nature dictates that, while in the womb, our organs develop in direct response to our mother's current experience of her world, so we will be best prepared to survive in those same conditions.

If a mother consistently feels negativity, anxiety, or stress during her pregnancy, her fetus will respond to the messages "taught" by her stress hormones: it will adapt its brain and nervous system to prepare for the unsafe environment into which it perceives it will be born. Chronic stress in pregnancy is designed to sculpt her child's system to be suited for survival in dangerous environments: quick to react, reduced impulse control, and a limited capacity to feel serene.

By contrast, consistent joy allows for the optimal development of the organs, especially the brain, predisposing the baby to greater health and serenity. Both positive and negative traits make up the foundations of the personality/psyche.

Early development specialist Marcy Axness invites parents to be mindful of the ongoing question being asked by the fetus in the womb, and continually answered chemically and energetically through the mother's thoughts, feelings, and behavior: "What kind of world am I coming into, Mommy?" As Axness points out, this basic question and its nine months of answers drive foundational aspects of their baby's development. When parents understand this, they can recognize how important it is for the pregnant mother to feel support, love, and safety so that their baby can begin life ready to love and learn, not struggle and resist.[4]

The relatively new science of epigenetics offers proof of the effect that certain chemical processes can have on genes, responsible for marking them for expression or suppression. Epigenetics is effectively one of the basic mechanisms for health or disease throughout life, as it controls which genes operate and when. Without getting technical, the environment constantly affects the genome, especially in the formative period from conception through early childhood. The mother's diet, stress levels, and exposure to toxins all affect the fetus through the chemistry of the epigenome. Most significant is its influence during the childhood period up to the age of five years, wherein 85 percent of the mindbrain develops.

Neuroscience informs us that we can confirm what our ancestors took for granted, that letting babies get distressed is a practice that can damage children and their relational capacities for the long term. We now know that leaving babies to cry is a sure way to develop less intelligent, less healthy, but more anxious, uncooperative, and alienated beings who can pass the same or worse traits on to the next generation.[5] A view that is completely ignorant of human development, according to some behaviorists, is that the child must be taught to be independent. Though it is counterintuitive, we can now confirm that forcing "independence" on a baby leads to greater dependence, and giving babies what they need will lead to *greater* independence later. In anthropological reports of hunter-gatherers, parents took care of every need of babies and young children. Toddlers felt confident enough, and so did their parents, to walk into the bush on their own.[6] The fact is that caregivers who habitually respond to the needs of the baby before the baby gets distressed, preventing crying, are more likely to have children who are *independent* than the opposite. Soothing care is best from the outset; once patterns of distress get established, it is much harder to change them. We can state with a good deal of certitude that humans and many other altricial species are affected by prenatal conditions to a greater extent than ever before known.[7] It is also safe to say that current research debunks long-held beliefs that overly attentive care detracts from the future well-being and independence of the child.

Future ongoing research will give us more data as to the most beneficial ways to raise our offspring and will be one of the most important research projects ever undertaken. One hopes parents will understand the consequences of their eternal role and responsibility, which is to execute a plan of love that spans the conception of their child to the moral character and independent development of their child. This is the singular most important lifetime enterprise they will ever engage in. They should enable their child to develop a keen sense of self through being cared for, encouraged, respected, and loved in their formative EY. From that beginning, a child can develop an unshakeable core identity, gain respect for themselves and others, and be capable of integrating into and contributing positively to society.

18

CHARACTER: MORAL QUALITIES

"I would rather be a little nobody than to be an evil somebody."
—Abraham Lincoln

"You can easily judge the character of a man by how he treats those who can do nothing for him."
—Malcolm Forbes

"All cruelty springs from weakness."
—Seneca, *Seneca's Morals: Of a Happy Life, Benefits, Anger and Clemency*

"If you send out goodness from yourself, or if you share that which is happy or good within you, it will all come back to you multiplied ten thousand times. In the kingdom of love there is no competition; there is no possessiveness or control. The more love you give away, the more love you will have."
—John O'Donohue, *Anam Cara: A Book of Celtic Wisdom*

"It is curious that physical courage should be so common in the world, and moral courage so rare."
—Mark Twain

TWO WORDS THAT DEFINE the basis for what we commonly refer to as one's *character* are (a set of) *values* and *ideals*, which underpin a person's ideas and actions. The fullness of character develops over a lifetime, but the parental direction and influence during the child's early maturation seed its foundation.

Nature has produced a natural feedback loop when nurturing and educating a child, whereby the heartier the values and ideals sown, the stronger the character reaped, and vice versa. The role of parents is not only to take care of their child's physical and mental well-being, but to make certain that they prioritize the development of their child's character as well. Nature's design has provided a new life for parents, and the ideal way those parents show their appreciation and gratitude is by fostering and encouraging that new life to appreciate and respect *all* life.

The cultivation and promotion of character may begin with the seeds sown by parents and educators, but as a lifetime process, its continued development is the responsibility of the individual throughout their lives. "The chain is as strong as its weakest link" is an appropriate expression used to describe the passage of character from one generation to the next. Optimally, generational chains will have fewer weaker links and a greater number of stronger ones, as the underpinnings of character pass along to each one, building from generation to generation. Many psychologists have concluded that a child gains their socioemotional skills, including their fundamental sense of right and wrong, between the ages of three and five. A child's first experiences with their caregivers can shape their character and attitudes in later life and help lay the foundation upon which they build their adult value system. Given the spacetime children spend in school—and our school's ideal of holistic education—there is little doubt that teachers have the platform and influence to develop young mindbrains and characters.

It is important to emphasize that the larger onus remains with the parents to instill the proper values in their children from an early age and reinforce these as they mature. A child will pass through many classrooms and learn from different teachers throughout their formative EY. But parents and guardians remain constants throughout a child's life, and there are as many, if not more, important lessons to be taught at home as there are in schools. By understanding their child more intimately, parents are in a stronger position to instill values in their children—with one caveat. If the educators are instilling the right values, it is counterproductive for parents to ignore what a child learns in the classroom—or worse, contradict it. To better build moral character and impart positive values to our youth, it is best that parents complement and reinforce these lessons.[8]

If you want to raise a child with a keen sense of right and wrong, start by cultivating *your* morality, as well as *your* empathy. A new study from the University of Chicago suggests that the sensitivity of parents to another's feelings and injustice is a probable influence in the nascent moral development of their children.[9]

It is essential for children to "do as you do," as a basic protocol in developing their ethical credo. In Graham Music's book, *The Good Life: Wellbeing and the New Science of Altruism, Selfishness, and Immorality*, he draws on a large body of research from psychology, evolutionary biology, and neuroscience. Music believes that early childhood relationships take children down different paths, and that kids born into loving homes will form positive attachments with caregivers, which will help them trust the world, and feel safe enough to be kind and caring to others. Those born into stressful or abusive homes will form problematic attachments and learn that the world is not a safe place. They may have trouble being empathic and forming relationships, which affects their altruistic behavior later in life. In one study, people who had gone through an eight-week mindfulness class were four times more likely to get up and offer their seat to a person on crutches entering a waiting room than those who had not had the course. This suggests that we can still influence our prosocial behavior positively, even at that late stage.

Even adults who are empathetic and altruistic may shut off their prosocial tendencies when in negative social environments. We will all have less of an inclination to be kind and helpful toward others when we feel stress or duress. Contrarily, when we are in a good mood or inspired by the generosity of those around us, we are kinder and more generous toward others, making us happier, too. "Feeling good, being kind, and altruism seems to constitute some kind of virtuous circle, good acts fueling good feelings which fuel good acts," writes Music.[10]

In the competitive world in which we live, we emphasize what our children can do more so than who they are. To survive as a species, we will need to stress the equal importance of attitude versus aptitude, effort versus ability, and character versus talent. Rather than merely espouse these priorities, we should emphasize them from kindergarten through to the decisions made by college admissions departments. The first move in rethinking how we teach values in school is to impress upon parents that they, and not teachers, are their children's primary educators. If parents reach for deeper values, character, and purpose, so will their children. One way to do this is to make sure that while goals are being set for their children, i.e., course selection, extracurricular choices, etc., parents are also setting personal goals for themselves, such as exercise, community service, and cultural enrichment. Parents inspire children by their willingness to place themselves in the vulnerable position demanded by any process of personal growth, that they don't even care all that much about their parents' progress. Perceived as a catapult, one's character serves as the means to a fulfilling and inspiring personal destiny. A poem by the nineteenth-century writer Charles Reade captures this: "Sow an act and you reap a habit; Sow a habit and you reap a character; Sow a character and you reap a destiny."[11, 12]

In Darcia Narvaez's 2014 book, *Neurobiology, and the Development of Human Morality: Evolution, Culture, and Wisdom*, she endeavors to increase morality, empathy, and cooperation among adults through an understanding of the evolutionary, biological, and social bases of morality. By referencing Darwin, she argues we developed to connect, cooperate, and be moral beings, even as we have seen a decline in social interaction, health, and ethical decision-making in the US. It makes sense because these characteristics are some of the most necessary survival tools for our species. Only recently have we abandoned the wisdom our hunter-gatherer ancestors possessed about acting communally and cooperating. In our early years, she asserts that only with responsive parenting does one develop an *empathic core* that begins our understanding of ourselves as moral beings and our socioemotional potential. When raised by inattentive parents or in a dangerous environment, our social capacities suffer and shrink from their full development.

Not only is the influence of early social experiences observable behaviorally—but also the changes in people's mindbrains and physiology. She argues that morality is coordinated with our neurobiological and emotional development and that a person's moral architecture establishes itself early in life. Moral development emerges "bottom-up" from parenting, respect for moral authority, discipline, and lived experience. It is therefore essential that one's early experiences are indeed positive.[13, 14]

In her book *Parenting for Peace: Raising the Next Generation of Peacemakers*, Marcy Axness writes that "the adults in a young child's life have a responsibility to create an environment—

including themselves, their speech and actions—that is worthy of his unquestioning imitation," if they seek to raise an individual to be a positive force in society. Parents, please refrain from a lot of complaining and criticizing of others, and instead express mindfulness, gratitude, and a sense of wonder.[15] Character, unlike any other feature of our nature, is a quality of being that one will either develop, augment, and improve throughout their lifespan or not. It is helpful to experience and research as many facets of life as possible—to allow the "green shoots" of character sown by parents and educators to sprout. One must also navigate the "mind" fields of childhood, adolescence, and adulthood, and strengthen the core of their identity; parents, educators, and leaders should encourage, edify, and enlighten the child. Inevitably, the respect and concern for all life is the cornerstone of a solid and continuing growth of character, and without it, there is not a chance for human survival as we know it.

As we continue to learn through experience and science, what we should focus on as parents is reality, not ideality, gaining more knowledge as we, too, develop and improve our skills. The reality is that we are all flawed compared to ideal, and not only haven't we mastered our own AUQ to address the negative emotions, divisions, and violence that hamper us, other impediments to the essential task of parenting impede us as well.

19
EFFECT OF ECONOMICS AND EDUCATION ON PARENTING

BEFORE WE CAN MAKE genuine progress in parenting, one must address the effect of *economics* and *education* on the subject. Because marriage has always played such a critical role in the raising of children, one of the most devastating results of poverty and the lack of education is the proliferation of single-parent households. In most cases, the economic benefits of marriage are substantial. Marriage among families with children is an extremely powerful factor in promoting economic *self-sufficiency*, which is the ability of families to support themselves above the poverty line. The reason is straightforward, as two parents working together can support a child more efficiently than one.

The chart on the next page shows some 37 percent of single-parent families lack economic self-sufficiency and are over five times as officially poor, compared to almost 7 percent of married-couple families.[16]

CHART 1

In the United States, Marriage Drops the Probability of Child Poverty by 82 Percent

Source: Author's calculations based on data from the U.S. Census Bureau, American Community Survey, 2007–2009 data, http://factfinder2.census.gov/faces/tableservices/jsf/pages/prod uctview.xhtml?pid=ACS_09_3YR_S1702&prodType=table (accessed August 6, 2012).

PERCENTAGE OF FAMILIES WITH CHILDREN THAT ARE POOR

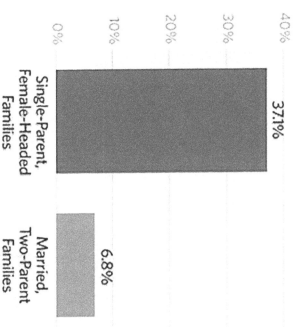

Single-Parent, Female-Headed Families	Married, Two-Parent Families
37.1%	6.8%

40%

30%

20%

10%

0%

The chart below shows a steady rise in the number of single-parent US households, from 1970-2019, and a leveling off in recent years. As more women enter the workforce at higher-paying jobs, men are increasingly taking over the chores of single parenting.

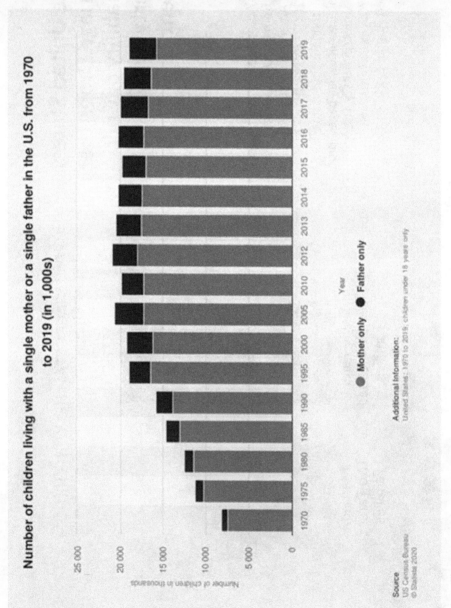

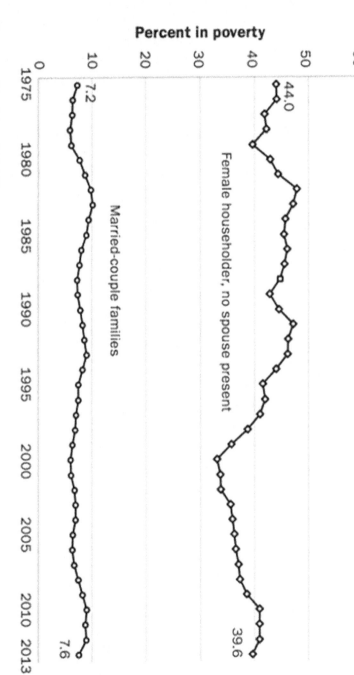

Figure 2. Poverty Rates for Female-Headed and Married-Couple Households with Children, 1975–2013

Percent in poverty

Female householder, no spouse present

Married-couple families

44.0

7.2

39.6

7.6

Source: Haskins (2015)

Of the world's 2.3 billion children, 14 percent, or 320 million, are living in single-parent households, about 80 percent headed by single mothers. In the US alone, the figure is 23 percent. Those children, from birth to eighteen years, and their single mothers and single fathers face special challenges, including economic hardships, social stigma, and personal difficulties that require society's attention and help.

The table on the next page, with *data*, shows that the average percentage of children living *outside* of the conventional two-parent families is 7 percent, or about 140 million children worldwide.

Almost a quarter of U.S. children live in single-parent homes, more than in any other country

% of children under age 18 in single-parent households

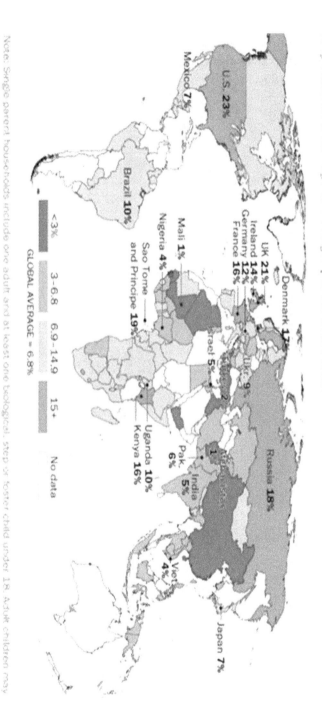

U.S. 23%
Mexico 7%
Brazil 10%
Denmark 17%
UK 21%
Ireland 14%
Germany 12%
France 16%
Israel 5%
Turkey 9%
Russia 18%
Mali 1%
Nigeria 4%
Sao Tome and Principe 19%
Uganda 10%
Kenya 16%
Pak. 6%
India 5%
Viet. 4%
Japan 7%

<3%   3 - 6.8   6.9 - 14.9   15+   No data

GLOBAL AVERAGE = 6.8%

Note: Single-parent households include one adult and at least one biological, step or foster child under 18. Adult children may be present, but no other relatives or non-relatives.

Source: Pew Research Center analysis of 2010-2018 census and survey data. See methodology for details.

"Religion and Living Arrangements Around the World"

PEW RESEARCH CENTER

The chart below shows the tremendous rise in unwed motherhood in the US steadily increasing during the 1950s and speeding up at an alarming rate from the beginning of the 1960s through today.

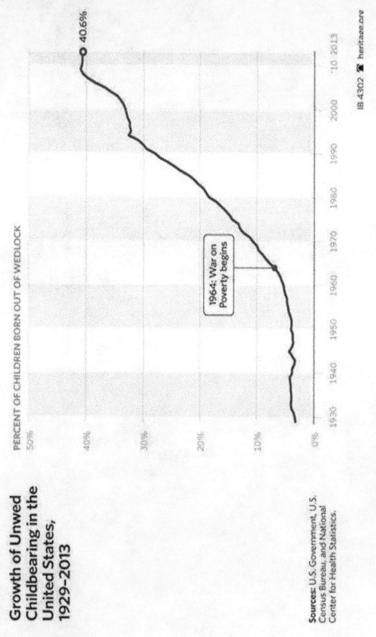

CHART 2

Growth of Unwed Childbearing in the United States, 1929–2013

Sources: U.S. Government, U.S. Census Bureau, and National Center for Health Statistics.

It suggests, with merit, that the steep rise has been because of a failure of the welfare system. Welfare seems to break down the habits and norms that lead to self-reliance, especially those of marriage and work, generating a pattern of increasing intergenerational dependence. The welfare state is self-perpetuating in the undermining of productive social norms, creating a need for even greater help in the future. As the war on poverty passes the half-century mark, it is time to rein in the endless growth in welfare spending and return to LBJ's original goal of reducing the *causes* rather than the mere *consequences* of poverty. Able-bodied, non-elderly adult recipients in all federal welfare programs must work or prepare for work, as a condition for receipt of benefits. Welfare programs should remove the anti-marriage penalties and take long-term steps to rebuild the family in lower-income communities.[17]

It is clear in the chart below that the educational level attained by a woman affects her state of wedlock and her number of births. Three of ten girls who dropped out of high school marry; six out of ten women who had some college marry; and over nine out of ten women who had graduated from college were wed. Educating young girls and boys about the disaster of early pregnancy and detailing contraceptive methods should be mandatory in all households and a part of school agendas.

This chart shows out-of-wedlock births worldwide:

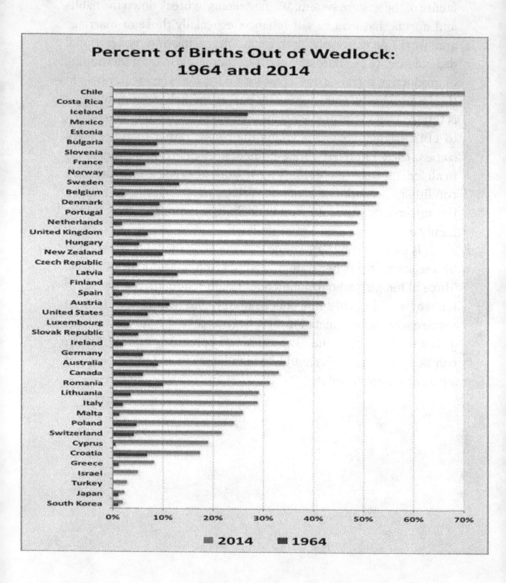

PART VII
GOVERNMENT: TO ORGANIZE AND SERVE

"How fortunate for governments that the people they administer do not think."
—Adolf Hitler

"Only when things are investigated is knowledge extended; only when knowledge is extended are thoughts sincere; only when thoughts are sincere are minds rectified; only when minds are rectified are the characters of persons cultivated; only when character is cultivated are our families regulated; only when families are regulated are states well governed; only when states are well-governed is there peace in the world."
—The founder of Confucianism, Master Kong (K'ung, Confucius, 551-479 BCE), excerpted and adapted from de Bary, Sources, I: 115-16. The Great Learning, "a section of the Classic of Rituals."

ONE OF THE MOST ESSENTIAL human endeavors to further our evolution is the way we have organized societies by the location of our parental birthplace or settlement. For living and cooperating in large numbers, people needed structure, order, and the means to develop culturally and economically.

20

LOOKS LIKE A NICE PLACE TO SETTLE DOWN

AN ANCIENT GEOGRAPHIC AREA, presently encompassing modern-day Iraq, Kuwait, Turkey, and Syria is the very first cradle of civilization. It was there that intensive year-round agriculture was first practiced, leading to the rise of the first dense urban settlements. What followed was the development of many familiar institutions of civilization—namely, centralized government and empires, social stratification, organized religion, and organized warfare. It saw the dawn of the first writing system and law codes, the development of astronomy and mathematics, and the invention of the wheel.[1] These socializing advances showed people could live and work together in peace within the confines of a common border, and go to war outside those borders as well.

Sumer was established in the region then known as Mesopotamia around 5000 BCE, the historical region of Western Asia within the Tigris-Euphrates River system. The Sumerians and the Akkadians, later known respectively as Babylonians and Assyrians, all flourished in this region. The first governments developed with the early dynastic civilizations of Sumer and Egypt, in approximately 3500 EY BCE.[2] They organized the area into what historians now refer to as city-states, most of which had hardened sunbaked, mud-brick walls around them. They were like independent countries all ruled as the kingdoms of Sumer by kings as the gods, assisted by priests who collected taxes and decided cases of justice, scribes who measured land into square units and decided taxes to be paid, and nobles.[3] Religious beliefs made the government more powerful because the Sumerian people believed the gods chose the kings, and they always obeyed the will of their gods. Sumer and the surrounding city-states lasted for about 1,000 EY, then were conquered and merged into the Mesopotamian Empire.

Early dynastic Egypt was amongst the first civilizations to define its borders and become increasingly large and prosperous. Only one pharaoh (king) was the Egyptian government leader, and the mantle passed to the eldest son of the king's chief wife. The government structure of ancient Egypt involved high-ranking political advisers or ministers known as viziers, army commanders, chief treasurers, the minister of public works, and tax collectors, all of whom answered directly to the pharaoh. At the local level, ancient Egypt's government was divided into forty-two provinces called nomes governed by officials known as nomarch. In each Nome, there were courts, and in the capital, there was a high court. The world population was stable at approximately 10 million in 3500 BC.[4] Egypt flourished for over 3,000 EY, until they too became controlled by militaristic empires. Boys will be boys; pass the sword, please.

Fast forward 3,000 EY from 3500 BC to about 500 BC, to a city-state in Greece. Keep in mind it has taken about 250,000 EY, or eight cosmic minutes, for *modern man* Homo sapiens to reach this place. The place is Athens, and there is about to be an implementation of governance, new and revolutionary, on planet Earth. It is *democracy*, from the Greek *demos*, meaning "the people" and *kratos* "strength/ rule," or "rule by the people." Many consider this to be the birthplace of Western civilization, and in terms of our progress on the road to the "realization" of our species, it is a most defining moment. Not that everyone is a citizen as only free males born in Athens, or about 25 percent of the populace, were citizens. However, it was one of the most powerful and space-timely ideas at the time, and it pointed humanity in the right direction.

21

THE CURRENT BURGEONING population growth makes it more urgent that we plan for an inevitable future strain on our resources, socialization, and management skills. This is particularly essential when we evaluate the AUQ of those whom we choose to organize and lead us, into whatever form they morph our governments.

The global population has risen steadily from 200 million to 7.7 billion over a mere 2,020 EY of civilization, or the past 4.6 cosmic seconds. We estimate it will require only thirty EY, or a mere 0.069 cosmic seconds, to increase the population by 2 billion people from 2020 AD to 2050 AD. See figures on the next page:

YEAR/POPULATION:
1/200 million
1000/275 million
1500/450 million
1650/500 million
1750/700 million
1804/1 billion
1850/1.2 billion
1900/1.6 billion
1927/2 billion
1950/2.55 billion
1955/2.8 billion
1960/3 billion
1965/3.3 billion
1970/3.7 billion
1975/4 billion
1980/4.5 billion
1985/4.85 billion
1990/5.3 billion
1995/5.7 billion
1999/6.5 billion
2009/6.8 billion
2011/7 billion
2025/8 billion
2043/9 billion
2083/10 billion

These numbers are not only staggering—they are imminent. As our populations increase geometrically, creating more individual voices for their governments to control or hear, the clock ticks. With staggering increases in population, it will be more challenging to succeed—because of the enhanced pressure on the government to organize and execute its protocols. This only points out another major danger if we delay the sea changes necessary to raise the AUQ of government leadership, parents, educators, and the generations to follow.

The sheer rise in population, combined with a mindset that has not yet reached the levels of *intra* and *inter* necessary to even cope with the current populations and resources of the world, will certainly further challenge the ability of our species to cooperate peacefully with one another and through our governments in the future.

As technology increasingly replaces our need for the services of unskilled human labor, governments will need to intelligently oversee future technological and biological advances and develop new ways of enabling the productivity of an ever-increasing and longer-lived population. We, the governed, must be ever more vigilant in identifying and evaluating those whom we allow to educate and govern us.

22
NATIONS AND NATIONALISM

"The patriot is proud of his country for what it does, and the nationalist is proud of his country no matter what it does; the first attitude creates a feeling of responsibility, but the second a feeling of blind arrogance that leads to war."
—Sydney J. Harris

"I am by heritage a Jew, by citizenship a Swiss, and by makeup a human being, and only a human being, without any special attachment to any state or national entity whatsoever."
—Albert Einstein

"All wars are civil wars because all men are brothers . . . Each one owes infinitely more to the human race than to the particular country in which he was born."
—François Fénelon

"Nationalism is an infantile sickness. It is the measles of the human race."
—*Albert Einstein, the Human Side: New Glimpses from His Archives*

OUR RACE, LANGUAGE, GEOGRAPHY, and culture divide us from the outset. A child learns there are many differences between the people of the world, long before they learn, if ever, of their similarities. The notion of *nation* or *government* has been with us since the beginning of civilization and has facilitated the organization of and service to the masses of people living within a specific area, culture, and language. Presently, there are 192 separate nations recognized in the world. The allegiance to a country has always been one of the most honorable values a person can possess. People unite under a banner and an anthem and are required to *protect and serve* when necessary. It is further testimony to our species' social and organizational skills that we have built large prosperous nations over the brief period of 5,500 EY.

We have met the challenges of living in proximity to one another without destroying one another and the planet and survived all means of cataclysm both natural and *man*ufactured to date. We have survived the destructive forces of warfare until the nuclear age. It was physically impossible until 1945 AD for warmongers, armaments manufacturers, terrorists, governments, or psychopaths to destroy life on Earth instantly. Even at the time of the dropping of the two atomic bombs by the USA on the empire of Japan, no nuclear weapons were remaining on Earth; both bombs were the only two in the US arsenal, and no other nation had nuclear technology. Those two bombs, brought to you by the collective genius of the brilliant physicists of the Manhattan Project and others, were a momentous change, ending World War II eight days later. It was not too long before all the nations on the block saw the beauty in that great store of energy.

The accompanying chart shows just how much beauty they saw and subsequently developed.

2021 ESTIMATED GLOBAL NUCLEAR WARHEAD INVENTORIES

The world's nuclear-armed states possess a combined total of nearly 13,080 nuclear warheads; more than 90% belong to Russia and the United States. Approximately 9,600 warheads are in military service, with the rest awaiting dismantlement.

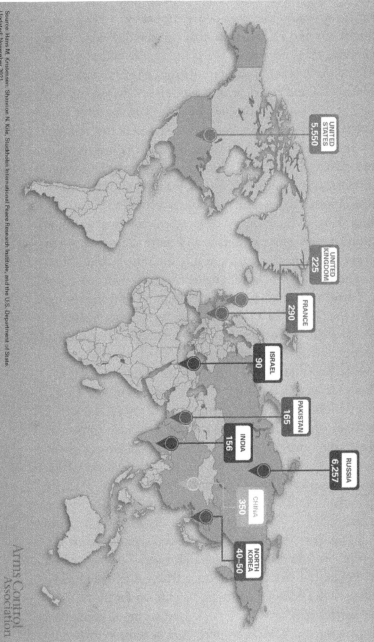

UNITED STATES
5,550

UNITED KINGDOM
225

FRANCE
290

ISRAEL
90

PAKISTAN
165

INDIA
156

RUSSIA
6,257

CHINA
350

NORTH KOREA
40-50

Arms Control Association

Source: Hans M. Kristensen; Shannon N. Kile, Stockholm International Peace Research Institute, and the U.S. Department of State.
Updated: November 2021

Perversely, the people in a position to profit most from war may be the staunchest supporters of nuclear disarmament. That would force governments back to the more conventional use of weaponry and defense systems and facilitate the "back in the day" long-term way of eliminating each other from the planet, more delicately and profitably. After all, one does not profit from losing all of its customers, including themselves, and a nuclear worldwide bomb fest would end the "business" of war and the "business" of life. A more acute look at nationalism will shed light on what we have faced in the past and what we can expect to face in the future, barring the intervention of an increasing AUQ. Jingoism is nationalism as aggressive foreign policy,[5] and refers to a country's advocacy for the use of threats or actual force, as opposed to peaceful nonviolent resolution to national matters. Then there is chauvinism, considered the most extreme form of nationalism. While patriotism and nationalism represent moderate pride, chauvinism is outright intemperate elitism in that the chauvinist harbors the belligerent belief that their own country is superior to all others. The individuals with this mindset form a group of people with the belief that a certain ancestry, intrinsic quality or worth, intellect, wealth, or other distinctive attributes affords them greater influence and authority to govern.

For example, in America, the term "elitism" often refers to the concentration of power on the Northeast Corridor and West Coast, where the typical American elite—comprising of lawyers, doctors, high-level civil servants, such as White House aides, businesspeople, university lecturers, entrepreneurs, and financial advisors—live.[6] History bears witness to the devastating results of these nationalistic attitudes and the imperialistic actions which followed them, culminating in the untold violence and waste of war, the acquisition of other nation's territories, and the colonial exploitation of those territories and people. In a nuclear age, extreme nationalism is a most dangerous brew and needs to be addressed for what it is, a divisive and existential risk to our species that, when taken to its extreme, will spell the end of humans and all life on Earth.

We once were a species waving sticks and stones around; now we are a species waving WMDs around. I am certain many would call that progress; what would you call it? We are at that point in spacetime where we should realize that national interference with one another, rather than national cooperation, may be deadly. Technology has now made ubiquitous communication available, and therefore provides the immediate and instantaneous sharing of information from mindbrains around the world. If a nation blatantly pursues self-interested actions at the expense of other nations, the entire world will know immediately and react accordingly within a forum of nations. In most cases, this is a welcome deterrent to these types of actions. In today's world, a nation's priority should be the accommodation and well-being of their populations, not the suppression of their freedoms. Governments should not force their people, because of internecine strife, to emigrate en masse throughout the world. Concomitant with that, the well-being of a nation should not be at the expense of any other nation.

Nations are like petri dishes, 192 of them and leadership should not enable policies that allow the wholesale infective interference of one nation with another, whether through aggression or wholesale immigration. The interference in the internal affairs of nations is unwise, because it is inevitably self-defeating. A nation is a creature of a culture that has taken hundreds to thousands of EY to develop and should be allowed to *thrive* or *dive* given their governing methods and culture. Let us allow them to either join the world of nations as responsible partners or collapse internally because of their leaders' ill-conceived notions of governance. The people en masse of any nation need to strengthen, united, be the determinants of their futures—not the elite power brokers, nor the military. They will need a groundswell of people to elevate the leadership necessary to allow this. An example would be the collapse of the USSR in 1989 because of their failures of governance, foreign incursions, and the failed communist system. Venezuela is the opposite model, wherein a once-thriving democracy collapsed under the weight of autocracy.

The attempts throughout history to force-feed colonialism, whatever type of economic/political systems, "puppet" governments, or the like on a nation merely retard the unhindered inevitable success or failure of a nation's systems and culture. Once a failed nation has no one to blame but itself for its failures, it makes the internal changes necessary to succeed in the growth of its citizenry and within its own culture. Rather than mass emigration in the future, the success of a nation to cultivate its garden through free trial and error will enhance the populations worldwide. Nations will need well-thought-out policies for their immigrating and emigrating populations in the future, and base them upon their mutual needs, so that the population of all nations accrues to the mutual benefit of the people.

Will we continue to be so emotionally and cognitively ignorant that we let our "differences" rather than similarities risk the future of thousands of unborn generations? It is time to rethink the meaning of nationalism and morph it into humanism, with the deliberate and focused development of universal awareness and understanding of all life. This does not mean the breakup of nations; it means the elimination of the divisions that anchor us to the past 10,000 EY of settlements/civilizations and 2.5 million EY of evolution.

23

LEADERSHIP: LED BY WHOM INTO WHAT?

"It is a curious thing, but perhaps those who are best suited to power are those who have never sought it."
—Albus Dumbledore (from J.K. Rowling's *Deathly Hallows*)

"The population is intelligent enough to understand the fundamentals of the issues, if they are presented with all the clear facts. The information must be presented by leadership fully and honestly, and reported the exact same way so as not to sway the people for political expediency."
—Carl Sagan

"I must follow the people. Am I not their leader?"
—Benjamin Disraeli

"Unthinking respect for authority is the greatest enemy of the truth."
—Albert Einstein

"The greatest leader is not necessarily the one who does the greatest things. He is the one that gets the people to do the greatest things."
—Ronald Reagan

People have always required leadership because of the sheer number of our species and our need for social order. We choose leaders or have them chosen for us based on democratic (and sometimes "allegedly" democratic) elections, conquest, bloodline, coup, and revolution. We have had one dictator, or another foisted upon us, and too often than not even the elected ranks of leadership are filled with self-interested alpha personalities. Those in leadership positions rarely have sufficient AUQ to be responsible for the well-being of their charges. In plain language, our leadership pool has been devoid of qualified high AUQ leaders throughout the ages.

We need to scrutinize our leaders carefully, prior to them

assuming power, and determine the common thread that makes them human or inhuman. This will be possible in the future with the scientific mapping discussed in the last Parts of this book. To adapt a quotation from Glad, "the interestingly deficient leaders are mostly dead; they have taken their Oedipus complex, authoritarianism, and power motivation with them."[7] Let us have a look at some of our serious mistakes and the petri dishes from which these misanthropic psyches have slithered out.

MISLEADERS

The following will give you a taste of what the toll has been in lives when some of the most self-interested, depraved, sociopathic, inhuman excuses for human beings end up in a position to lead governments and nations. They may have been "elected" or not, but that did not make any difference in their ignoble reaping of death and destruction. These numbers are so large that they cannot seem real, but the death toll is their legacy.

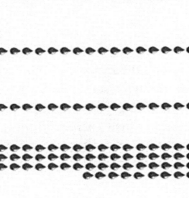

The structures of government which gave rise to these self-absorbed, power-hungry, monstrous personalities and their sycophants are never close to having democratic ideals nor should we ever mention them in the same breath. The governments which abide by these sociopathic misleaders have many names, but always end up in the hands of a few despots who control the nation's wealth and military, with no concern for their people. Be it through bloodline, autocracy, dictatorship, oligarchy, or coup, they are malignant forms of governmental structure that infect their populations.

It would be shortsighted to blame these demagogues as if they existed in a vacuum; they did not and never will. It would be much more palatable were we able to account for the horrors orchestrated by these excuses for leaders if they bore sole responsibility. That is never the case, however, because they need the support of many elites, sycophants, organizers, and enforcers to account for the resultant devastation they cause. Add to them the many nameless accomplices who helped to perpetuate these atrocities because they felt it was a matter of self-preservation or to their economic advantage to do so. Never forget that the main tinder necessary to incinerate the future comes as a fearful and floundering population, is fertile for "inspiration," and is an "uplifting," out of their malaise. The lack of AUQ which allows hate, bigotry, scapegoating, and whatever else one may "rationalize" to execute their misleader's every edict is a misleader's dream come true.

LEADERS

Keep in mind that despite the misleaders who have scourged our Earth, the human species did not survive to the present, nor will it into the future, without the likes of leaders and their supporters, who have improved the lives of their charges. Throughout history there have been those who have held up the mantle of leadership and inspired us, proved to be empathetic, rational, and very productive leaders.

Selfless leaders have united their people, stood firm for peace and freedom, and enhanced the human condition for everyone. The commonality of high AUQ found in hundreds of history's most enlightened world leaders has infused them with the humane, intelligent, and compassionate qualities they incorporated into their leadership styles. The takeaway is that the responsibility falls upon us to not only foster outstanding leaders but to take on elevating ourselves as human beings so that we allow no one of lesser quality to ever lead anyone again. In-depth study of how to select wise and humane leaders should always be a primary prescription for educational curricula.

Described here are several genuine leaders from a pantheon of talented women and men who have held themselves to an exemplary standard of service and human excellence. We can learn a great deal from the lessons of their navigation, especially in the boundless nuclear and technological ages within which we now live. Sometimes, especially in the ancient world, it was the codifying of laws and precepts to ensure fair treatment for all, like Hammurabi's codes. Hammurabi, the sixth Babylonian king, was a man of such ilk. His code dates to 1754 BC and comprised of 282 Babylonian laws of ancient Mesopotamia. The law's basis scales punishments, adjusting "an eye for an eye" depending on social status,[8, 9] as graded from slave to freeman.[10] Catherine II ("the Great") Empress of Russia, from 1762 until 1796, revitalized her country, strengthened its defenses, and adopted western European philosophies and culture. The Hermitage Museum opened during her reign, beginning as part of her personal collection, was to be shared with the people[11].

Mohandas, Mahatma, or "great soul" Karamchand Gandhi was born and raised in a Hindu merchant caste family, and led British-ruled India to independence, and thereby inspired movements for civil rights, and freedom across the world. He resisted the British colonization in India with his sagacity and sense of patriotism, making "ahinda," nonviolence, his mantra. Gandhi believed that truth and equality should prevail without blood-shedding and practiced civil disobedience movements and boycotts of foreign goods to further his cause. Nelson Rolihlahla Mandela was imprisoned for twenty-seven EY (1963-1990) for standing up against the Afrikaans apartheid abuses against black South Africans. He was a militant, much the same as Israel's sixth Prime Minister Menachem Begin was, and went on to pave the way for the abolition of apartheid in 1994. As South Africa's first black president elected that same year in a fully representative democratic election, he turned it from a

British colony into a powerful state. The Truth and Reconciliation Commission was his creation and proved to be a most astounding accomplishment after personally suffering years of abuse, focused on healing the country's wounds from human rights abuses using truth-telling and forgiveness.[12]

Winston Churchill, "the British Bulldog," during and after World War II, inspired his country after a bloody and crucial time in the history of the world, helped hold back Hitler, and ushered in peace and prosperity. In the campaign for equal rights, Martin Luther King Jr., ignoring severe risk to himself, led the way and succeeded in seeing to it that the laws were changed to effect greater equality for minorities.

Having glimpsed the gamut of historically inferior and superior leadership qualities, it will edify one to glean the current state of leadership in today's world. In the words of Stephen Hawking, "We are at the most dangerous moment in the development of humanity, having the technology to destroy the planet on which we live, but not yet the ability to escape it en masse." He goes on, "We need to break down, not build up, barriers within and between nations, and the world's leaders need to acknowledge that they have failed and are failing the many. With resources increasingly concentrated in the hands of a few, we must learn a measure of humility. We face exceptional environmental challenges: food production, overpopulation, the decimation of other species, epidemic disease, acidification of the oceans. We are going to have to learn to share far more than at present."[13]

Joseph Nye Jr. is a university distinguished service professor emeritus, and former dean of the Kennedy School of Government at Harvard University; his government service includes positions as assistant secretary of defense for international security affairs, chair of the National Intelligence Council, and a deputy undersecretary of state. He is a good contemporary subject to look toward as one whose character, dimension of thought, and leadership skills would qualify him as the type of leader to lead us toward realization. He originated the term "soft power" which rests on three of a country's facets, the desirability of a country's culture, the ability to be true to its political values at home and abroad, and the legitimacy and moral authority of its foreign policies. *Soft power* policies use persuasion, example, and rely heavily on international institutions to get others to want what they want. *Hard power* utilizes coercive diplomacy, economic sanctions, military action, and aligning militarily for deterrence and defense. *Hard power* policies use coercion, force, and aggression, to order others to do what they want. A s*mart power* policy will combine both the hard and soft power of skilled leadership, driven by the particular situation.[13.5]

MAD DEBUNKED

In political parlance, there is the common belief amongst our so-called "rational" political leaders, relating to the nuclear age and its proliferation of weapons, that a built-in deterrence labeled mutually assured destruction, *MAD*, will save us. In other words, *if I die, you die.*

This may very well be a fatal mistake as it assumes that those who have the power of leadership, and the sheer number of worldwide terrorists, are all graced with rational mindbrains. The fallibility of human nature dictates otherwise. New realities have cracked the veneer of MAD, as humans have once again reared their ugly heads, and put into question MAD's core concept. The results are a game-changer.

Enter Ayatollah Ruhollah Khomeini, the supreme leader of Iran from 1979-1989, who is just one example of what modern-day leadership can look like. The most significant legacy of Khomeini internationally is a broader definition of martyrdom to include Istishhad, or "self-martyrdom.[14] Khomeini believed martyrdom could come not only from *inadvertent* death but *deliberate* as well. While martyrdom has always been celebrated in Islam and martyrs promised a place in heaven (Q3:169-171), the idea that opportunities for martyrdom were important has not always been so common. He not only praised the large numbers of young Shia Iranians who became *shahids* (Muslim martyrs) during the Iran–Iraq War, but he also asserted the war was "God's hidden gift.[15] One scholar of Khomeini put it this way, "War is a vital outlet through which Iran's young martyrs experienced mystical transcendence."[16]

During the Iran-Iraq war (1980-1988), flames of religious

devotion fanned, and put piety into action. Iranian children, ages twelve to sixteen, were roped together and forced to stumble across Iraqi minefields in human wave assaults, to clear the way for the Iranian infantry. Each one of the estimated 100,000 killed, however, had a plastic key around their necks, to open the gates of paradise, as the Iraqi infantry mowed them down.[17]

Khomeini and all his kindred spirits throughout history had major psychological problems, were religiously maniacal, egomaniacal, some of the above, or all the above. They possessed no consideration nor understanding of life other than a bloodlust for the satisfaction of their own warped "ideologies." One thing is certain—they were supported by a well-paid military as well as their citizens, who were their inadvertent accomplices in allowing such inhumane leadership to initiate and perpetuate such insanity.

We must not forget the isolated incidents of terrorism such as the World Trade Center destruction, brought to you by suicide bombers on their way to virgin-filled heaven. Considered as well must be the myriad terrorist acts of individuals and those that are state-sponsored. And do not think that it has only been only the autocratic leaders of nondemocratic countries or terrorists that have cornered the market on death and destruction. Elections in democracies have resulted in leadership whose policies can and do lead to unpredictably unsettling and violent outcomes. No one should be at all surprised that countries with a democratic leadership in concert with their political, military, and industrial power have produced a great deal of death and destruction as well.

THE FEMALE TOUCH

This brings us to the female role in leadership and the future paths and possibilities to new and different outcomes. Women are given to problem-solving, rather than focusing on the unilateral imposition of solutions. A study examining all the countries involved in international conflicts around the world over the last fifty EY found that the more women were involved in the leadership of a society, the less militarily aggressive that society was. This lowered the probability of their being in a violent conflict with other countries.

Researchers Mary Caprioli and Mark Boyer argue that their

study in the *Journal of Conflict Resolution* is compelling evidence for the proposition that, in general, women work for peace and men wage war. Psychologically, at a profound level, the authors suggest that men tend to engage in power struggles for personal egoistic gain, whereas women tend to attempt to minimize power differences, share resources, and treat others equally. Yet despite these advantages of female leadership, Caprioli and Boyer found only twenty-four countries around the world, by the time the study had been completed in 2001, had placed a female leader in office since 1900. The study found only 16.6 percent of these countries led by a woman were involved in international crises at any point during the period of female leadership, and none of these female leaders initiated the crises.[18]

Eight current women leaders are their country's first

Current female heads of state or government (March 2017)

✓ country's first female leader

Head of state or government	Country	Years in office
PM Sheikh Hasina	Bangladesh	13
✓ Pres. Michelle Bachelet	Chile	6
Pres. Kolinda Grabar-Kitarović	Croatia	2
✓ Pres. Kersti Kaljulaid	Estonia	<1
✓ Chancellor Angela Merkel	Germany	11
✓ Pres. Ellen Johnson Sirleaf	Liberia	11
✓ Pres. Dalia Grybauskaitė	Lithuania	7
Pres. Marie-Louise Coleiro Preca	Malta	2
✓ Pres. Hilda Heine	Marshall Islands	1
✓ Pres. Ameenah Gurib-Fakim	Mauritius	1
✓ Pres. Bidhya Devi Bhandari	Nepal	1
PM Erna Solberg	Norway	3
PM Beata Maria Szydło	Poland	1
Pres. of Swiss Confederation Doris Leuthard	Switzerland	1
PM Theresa May	United Kingdom	<1

Note: Figures are through March 8, 2017. President of the Swiss Confederation Doris Leuthard is a member of the Swiss Federal Council, which serves collectively as head of state and head of government.
Source: Britannica, BBC, World Economic Forum, Pew Research Center analysis.

PEW RESEARCH CENTER

The number indicated in the chart is a paltry 7.8 percent, or 15 of the 192 officially recognized nations.[19] As of 2022, the number of female leaders remains fifteen.

The then Vice President of the US, Joe Biden, suggested that "foreign policy is a logical extension of personal relationships, and women are widely acknowledged to be canny at conducting them. It follows that female leadership in international affairs would produce more empathy and collaboration between countries. To the extent that global problems like violence and inequality are failures of empathy, the global influence of women would produce a genuinely different, better world.[20]

Until such spacetime that our or another species' AUQ is ubiquitous—and at a sufficient level for realization—women will have to forge their rightful positions in society.

24

TO BE FREE OR NOT TO BE FREE;
IT IS IMPERATIVE TO BE FREE

TO REITERATE, one out of three human beings on Earth, 2.5 billion of us, are presently living under the thumb of an authoritarian regime. These several billions of people are still restrained from living with the most basic forms of independence. The restraints imposed by the few who control the many result in the inability of the many to express free movement, free action, and their true thoughts, either through speech or by the written word. This is the exact form of government structure that gives us the type of entrenched and suppressive leadership and systems that die hard.

And it does not help that in some of the more democratic systems we find leadership who find it easier to flex their military power, rather than their mindbrain power, which leaves us with an unfortunate dichotomy. It cannot be stressed enough that there must inevitably be an enlightened populace if we are to ever incubate a higher number of high AUQ leaders—democratically elected to serve not themselves and the elite few, but the many.

To reiterate, one out of three human beings on Earth, 2.5 billion of us, are presently living in nondemocratic countries.

25
WAR AND OTHER INSANITIES:
ORGANIZED AND SANCTIONED DEATH
AND DESTRUCTION

"Every gun that is made, every warship launched, every rocket fired signifies in the final sense, a theft from those who hunger and are not fed, those who are cold and are not clothed. This world in arms is not spending money alone. It is spending the sweat of its laborers, the genius of its scientists, the hopes of its children. This is not a way of life at all in any true sense. Under the clouds of war, it is humanity hanging on a cross of iron . . . I hate war as only a soldier who has lived it can, only as one who has seen its brutality, its futility, its stupidity."
    —Dwight D. Eisenhower, Leader of Allied Forces against Hitler in World War II; President of the United States of America.

"It is forbidden to kill; therefore, all murderers are punished unless they kill in large numbers and to the sound of trumpets."
    —Voltaire

"This topic [the importance of individuality] brings me to that worst outcrop of the herd nature, the military system, which I abhor . . . This plague-spot of civilization ought to be abolished with all possible speed. Heroism by order, senseless violence, and all the pestilent nonsense that goes by the name of patriotism—how I hate them! War seems to me a mean, contemptible thing: I would rather be hacked in pieces than take part in such an abominable business. And yet so high, in spite of everything, is my opinion of the human race that I believe this bogey would have disappeared long ago, had the sound sense of the nation's not been systematically corrupted by commercial and political interests acting through the schools and the press."
    —Albert Einstein, (1879-1955) Physicist and Nobel Laureate

WE DEFINE WAR as an active conflict that has claimed over 1,000 lives. Of the past 3,400 EY of recorded history, humans have been entirely at peace for a mere 268 EY, or just under 8 percent of that spacetime. During the remaining 3,132 EY, wars have killed at least 108 million people, in the twentieth century alone. Estimates for the total number killed in wars throughout all human history vary from 150 million to 1 billion.[21] That is a broad range, but even one life lost in a war is one too many. War is the best proof that human beings are still prisoners to the dictates of mindbrains that use less cognitive than emotional energy. We accommodate the information broadcast by the media as fact, though it is merely describing the fallacious "intel" of its masters, marching us to the tune of trumpets, over the cliff. Fear, pride, self-interest, impulsiveness, and blatant ignorance are the major contributors to our failure to use reasoned and rational thought to solve our differences. The lies, innuendos, and obfuscations promulgated by the power players when readying its "sheeple" to sacrifice themselves and their children for the "cause" know no bounds.

As a recent example of a war-minded demonic, to show that this plague remains virile, we need to go no further than Ayatollah Khomeini, who gave a speech during the Iran-Iraq war on Muhammad's birthday and said, "War is a blessing to the world and for all nations . . . The wars that the Prophet led against the infidels were a blessing for all humanity . . . A prophet is all-powerful. Through war, he purifies the Earth.[22] Khomeini was the political and religious leader of 55 million Iranian people from 1979 to 1989, speaking about death as a cleansing for

any one or group on Earth that did not share his views of an Islamic-run world. This kind of

rhetoric is as anti-life as it gets, and as the Ayatollah was not the creator of life, no one gave him

nor anyone else the right to end it. Regardless of his charisma, power, religiosity, education, intellectual prowess, or whatever other attributes he possessed, he was just another figure who rose to the position of *chief honcho* by dint of circumstance. With these types of warmongers, the conditions are always toxic to enlightenment and the affirmation of life. The populations that were led by sociopaths were mostly helpless to counter the stronghold of the power and control entrenched against them. What life-denying ideology/ characteristics allow anyone of this low AUQ level to rise to the height of power? Khomeini was not the only hominid who thrived when the path was death to "whomever," as you will note from the chart in part VII, subsection "Misleaders." Men have historically had control of economic, political, and military power. Those who assume a dominant role in such endeavors usually possess a psyche determined to control. If they succeed in the economic realm, they create or manage businesses, but success in the political-military realm results in the control of a nation. Juxtapose that against the productive and focused person with no aspirations to hold positions of power, for whom the measure of success is a lifelong pursuit of a honed skill or solution to problems that tax their mindbrains. The sole interest of those with that mindset is that they remain free to solve the problems that interest them. That type of highly motivated mindbrain may change the world for the better, and at the least, will not harm others, whatever the outcome of their efforts. One of the great ironies of life on Earth, plaguing civilization from the outset, is the fact that those of the human species that possess the highest AUQ mainly wish only to control or lead themselves and not others. A fine example of such a person is Albert Einstein. When David Ben Gurion, in 1952, gave him an offer to lead the new State of Israel as its first president, he replied, "I am deeply moved by the offer from our State of Israel, and at once saddened and ashamed that I cannot accept it."

Even democracies fall victim to unfortunate leadership. We do not eliminate the chance of war merely because a government is "democratic," with its assumption of free, fair elections. Many times, democracies start wars not because of any direct aggression targeting them, but because of the perception that there is a threat to their way of life or by others' actions or ideologies. A prime example of this is the fact that communism and capitalism have been the basis for many a major conflict, rather than allowing the survival of any ideology to succeed or fail of its own merit. Shouldn't the test of any system be its long-term utility? The peaceful self-dismantling of the USSR in 1991 is a perfect example.

BLOWING UP THE DOMINOS

In 1952, some forty EY prior to the self-implosion of the USSR, the US National Security Council presented a paper on US governmental policy which espoused a *domino* theory involving all Southeast Asia, or Indochina as it was then known. This was a theory that reasoned that if one country in the region adopted communism, each of the surrounding countries would follow. Thereafter, we could expect Cambodia, Laos, Vietnam, Myanmar (Burma), Thailand, and Brunei (on the island of Borneo), to embrace communism. Having won World War II, both the US and Russia could now turn their attention to the business of whose system of government and economics would proliferate. However, placing the nose of one nation's missile in another nation's business has been a bad idea throughout history. The next case is a prime and most destructive example of such a scenario and should be scrutinized for the lessons we have yet to learn from it. Vietnam is a country made famous for all the wrong reasons. I do not intend to rehash the events of a tragic saga, which, to understand fully, goes back at least 350 EY. Instead, a brief history will suffice as a window through which to view its tragic but predictable course. Ideologies of the religious and political flavor and the hunger for and use of power by self-interested cabals are the themes pervading the history of this region. Many of the habitable regions we hominids have lived in throughout our 2.5-million-year sojourn on Earth have suffered similar fates.

The French Jesuits took a foothold in Vietnam in the early seventeenth century with their zeal for converting the world to Catholicism. Two hundred EY later, Minh Mạng, Emperor of Vietnam in an 1825 *edict against Christianity*, wrote, "The Westerner's perverse religion confuses the hearts of men"; "many Western ships trade with us and introduce Catholic missionaries into our country destroying our beautiful customs . . . a great disaster for our land."[23] In today's Vietnam, only 6.8 percent of the population is Catholic; they spilled much blood for that number.[24] The region's serious wars began in the mid-1800s and did not end until almost 200 EY later; the total number of years of conflict and war were sadly 400 EY. Whether it was the French versus Vietnamese, French versus Chinese, US versus Vietnamese, etc., none of these participants could engage in dialogue nor agreement that prevented a war, while it was possible to do so. The Vietnamese got embroiled in a war with whoever wished to extend their influence over them and were not in control of their destiny as one country until 1976, as the Socialist Republic of Vietnam. There were internecine wars as well, between the North and South Vietnamese, which were proxies for Russia and the USA, and then the US involved itself in the affairs of the Vietnamese in 1955 big time following the defeat of France and the splitting of the nation into the North and South. The US was the greatest economic and military power the world had ever known; Vietnam was *rice paddies*. Lives squandered, not to mention the suffering and wounded, in that region between all warring parties from 1955 to 1975 alone were 4 million military and civilians.[25]

In 1964, when the USA was minding Vietnam's business in the Gulf of Tonkin, faulty radar signals became proof of strikes on US vessels by North Vietnamese gunboats. The facts are that the US had been aiding the South Vietnamese in shelling and provoking North Vietnamese coastal and island outposts. Following the presentation of "selective intelligence" to Congress, the House of Representatives voted unanimously, and the Senate 88-2, to give carte blanche to President Johnson to do whatever was necessary to protect US *interests*. Never asked are two questions. First, if Vietnam engages in communist ideology, will the surrounding countries ascribe to it as well, like "falling dominoes?" Second, were we to embroil ourselves in a war by supporting the South Vietnamese, would we be victorious?[26] There is no asking of these questions because the answers were a foregone conclusion, considering the mix of egos, arrogance, and self-serving alpha males deciding. They were in control of the US, the greatest power on Earth aside from Nature, and Nature was not deciding.

Communist leader Ho Chi Minh of the North, however, was not a pawn of the communist giants Russia and China. He sacrificed having his own family for the sake of the people of his country. Ho was their father figure, and the populace were his "children." The fact was that the North Vietnamese, who had finally defeated the powerful French colonial administration of Vietnam in 1954, wanted the unification of its people under a single independent communist regime modeled after those of Russia and China. Ho's desire was not the proliferation or prevention of the spread of communism to other countries, as that was always the work of the great powers who could afford it. The corrupt South Vietnamese puppet governments fought to preserve a Vietnam more closely aligned with the West's money, if it flowed. VP Lyndon Johnson had already decided to expand the war before assuming office on November 22, 1963, but stated, "We seek no wider war" during the next 1964 presidential campaign.[27] This included plans to bomb North Vietnam well before the 1964 election. He had been dishonestly outspoken against doing so during the election campaign and claimed that his opponent Barry Goldwater, who honestly and openly supported bombing, was the one who wanted to bomb North Vietnam.

During the war, his military advisors gave LBJ a choice: add 200,000 more American soldiers to the forces already in Vietnam, with only a *one in three* chance of a military victory, or negotiate peace in Vietnam. Johnson chose to continue and indeed escalate the war. In his book, *Choosing War: The Lost Chance for Peace and the Escalation of War in Vietnam*, Fredrik Logevall looks at the decisions of Kennedy and Johnson most carefully from every angle to understand their logic. What he continually finds is that they do not base their reasoning on the significance of Vietnam for American national security, nor working out of a US commitment to Vietnamese self-determination, nor in any good or honorable intention whatsoever. It is that their ruling premises were domestic politics, and they were aggressive and politically savvy, surrounded by advisors of the same ilk[28]. They, unfortunately, lacked sufficient AUQ to be ruled by sanity and not vanity.

This memo from the Defense Department under the Johnson Administration listed the reasons for American persistence in Vietnam:

70 percent–To avoid a humiliating US defeat.

20 percent–To keep South Vietnam and the adjacent territory from Chinese hands.

10 percent–To permit the people of South Vietnam to enjoy a better, freer way of life and emerge from the crisis without unacceptable taint from methods used.

0 percent–To help a friend.[29, 30, 31]

Because of the few people in key posts making poor decisions, the US were stationing over 500,000 US military personnel in Vietnam by 1969. Meanwhile, the Soviet Union and China, not to be outdone, were pouring weapons, supplies, and advisers into the North, which provided military support, political direction, and regular combat troops for the campaign in the South. At home, the costs, casualties, and *protests* of the growing war were too much for the United States to bear, and the US withdrew all combat units by 1973. In 1975, South Vietnam fell to a full-scale invasion by the North. In his 1995 mea culpa, *In Retrospect: Tragedy and Lessons of Vietnam*, Robert McNamara, at the age of seventy-nine, cleared his conscience. As Secretary of Defense and chief architect of the war in Vietnam, he is unsparing in blaming himself and his government colleagues, including President Johnson, for a series of blunders that led to tragedy. "We were wrong, terribly wrong," writes former Defense Secretary Robert S. McNamara.[32] Robert, we trust you felt cleansed after that—twenty EY better late than never—abreaction, but it was best told first to the families of the estimated 1,353,000 civilian and military war victims, from 1965 to 1974. This includes 59,000 US soldiers, most of whom were seventeen to twenty-nine years young, etched in stone, memorialized on black granite slabs in Washington, DC. This does not include all the wounded soldiers and civilians on all sides.

In *The Fog of War*, a documentary released at the time of the 2003 invasion of Iraq, McNamara said, "We are the most powerful nation on Earth . . . I do not believe that we should ever apply that economic, political, and military power unilaterally. If we had followed that rule in Vietnam, we would not have been there. None of our allies supported us, not Japan, not Germany, not Britain or France. If we cannot persuade nations with comparable values of the merit of our cause, we'd better reexamine our reasoning. Our judgment, our understanding, are not adequate. And we kill people unnecessarily . . . war is so complex, it's beyond the ability of the human mind to comprehend," he concluded. He had thought for a long time that the United States could not win the war. In retirement, he listed reasons: a failure to understand the enemy, a failure to the limits of high-tech weapons, a failure to tell the truth to the American people, and a failure to grasp the nature of the threat of communism. "What went wrong was a basic misunderstanding or misevaluation of the threat to our security represented by the North Vietnamese," he said in his Berkeley oral history. "It led President Eisenhower, in 1954, to say that if we lose Vietnam or if we lose Laos and Vietnam, the dominoes would fall."[33]

WEAPONS OF MASS DELUSION

Brewed and served from the very top of government to the world at large is a more recent *violation of life disaster*. It represents another victory of human animus, power, and ego, over reason and critical thinking. This reference is to the US precipitation of the wrong war against the wrong enemy.

On September 11, 2001, the terrorist group Al-Qaeda used four planes, as weapons, on four US domestic targets, and killed 2,977 people. The US under President G.W. Bush, in concert with seven allies, invaded Afghanistan in December 2001 to dismantle al-Qaeda and deny it a base of operations by removing the Afghan-based Taliban terrorist group from power. This war against the group that attacked us was unfortunate but justified, lasting until January 2019, the longest in US history. Vexed by these incidents, and the Iraqi dictator Saddam Hussein's alleged plot to kill his father, G. H. W. Bush, President G.W. Bush started a war against Iraq in March 2003. Bush publicly repeated the CIA claim that "there was slam dunk data proving that Iraq was securing the means to produce nuclear weapons." The information was bogus and the war it caused did not end until over seven EY had elapsed, in August 2010. Estimates of 125,000 military and civilian Iraqis dead and the US military 4,500 dead and 32,000 wounded are conservative.

As part of the endnote to this section of the text, one would think that by the end of the twenty-first century, humankind would be free from the unprovoked, unmitigated disaster of purely aggressor wars. We should be beyond that kind of insanity. Yet as I write today, the psyches of Vladimir Putin and his oligarch associates who control the federal republic of Russia's industry, the military, and their population have ordered their war machine to invade the independent, no-threat, sovereign country of Ukraine and engage in the mass slaughter of innocent democratic Ukrainian citizens by the thousands. Why? Do not ask those directly responsible. They could not give you a rational answer, because they have the characteristics of group 4 on the part III chart: CHANCE OF SPECIES SURVIVAL BASED UPON LEVEL OF INTER AND INTRA AWARENESS AND UNDERSTANDING.

The Putin psyche—rooted in a *me above all,* street thug, KGB, *resurrect me as the Czar of an Empire* mentality—is merely one form of cancer that is alive and well today. There are many other leaders with a cancerous recipe rooted in their own, personal, primary psyche need.

Most people believe that war, violence, and conflict will forever be a part of the fabric of human life. Shocking news sells whether it is war, murder, natural disaster, crime, conflicts, or anything like it. They inundate the people ingesting the news with the most negative examples of human nature so that it is not surprising that the fears, anxieties, and negativities of the public grow. The fact remains that only death is inevitable, and it affects stars, planets, and all living entities at present. The thought that anything else is inevitable is nothing more than a person having convinced themselves of a nonexistent reality. Everyone has an expiration date, though it will extend in humans as we genetically engineer our own "miracles." The date will remain finite, however, androids excluded, and it is therefore exigent upon us to see that war expires before we do.

People worldwide have an ever-increasing opportunity to understand and learn from one another as communication becomes instantaneous and ubiquitous. Are we not the embodiment of endless possibilities because of the infinite capacity of our mindbrains for thought? Aren't we naturally designed to be free to think and feel as we wish so long as we consider the thoughts and feelings of others and follow just and societal laws? As new generations replace past generations, we make available an ever-increasing historical record of our triumphs and failures.

Our history is a road map to a more enlightened future—if we study it and learn from it. Anyone who attempts to change the genus Homo's history does not care that it is an indispensable, unchangeable part of the evolution of our thinking and behavior. A genuine record of our history is the only unwavering guide we must use to enable the understanding and awareness of who we were, and therefore who we might become. Those who wish to change, redact, or alter in any way those records have a self-serving, self-interested motive to do so, and it is essential that the truth counter them—else we will devolve from a repetition of the errors we have historically made.

No one with an understanding of the connectivity of all human beings and nonhumans seeks the destruction of any life as the solution to any situation. This is exactly why the focus on raising our AUQ is so essential to our survival.

PART VIII
EDUCATION

"Children must be taught how to think, not what to think."
—Margaret Mead

"If the traditional Rs (reading, writing, and arithmetic) are the basics that we want our children to master academically, then reverence, respect, and responsibility are the three Rs that our children need to master for the sake of their souls and the health of the world."
—Zoe Weil

"Universal education is the most corroding and disintegrating poison that liberalism has ever invented for its own destruction."
—Adolf Hitler

"The aim (of education) must be the training of independently acting and thinking individuals who, however, find purpose in the service to the community their highest life problem."
—Albert Einstein, Address, October 1936

WE SHOULD TREAT the mindbrains of *all* life on Earth with reverence. Nature has taken 14 billion EY, the age of the universe, to develop the human mindbrain, and each passing generation presents our species with the latest model. Normal birthing is possible only because a newborn baby's head is small, and only ninety days from birth, the infant's mindbrain is already approximately 65 percent larger![1]

An infant is thinking from the moment it egresses from the womb, and begins to perceive to make sense of the unfamiliar environment it finds itself in. A two-year-old's mindbrain is already about 80 percent the size of an adult's, and it does not cease to shape itself to fullness until twenty-five to thirty EY later. The term "altricial" takes on a new meaning. We may therefore conclude that since the life expectancy at birth worldwide by 1900 was thirty-one

EY and forty EY in the US[2] few of the over 100 billion people[3] who had ever existed until then knew what it was to be fully mindbrained until their old age, if ever.

Once Nature has modeled it, a devoted parent will see that their child's mindbrain develops properly, and care for their child's health and welfare. It is imperative that leaders and educators, as well, consider it their profound responsibility not only to help nurture the nascent mindbrain of our highly altricial offspring but to study and constantly broaden our understanding of it. The current scientific knowledge of mindbrain is not even in its infancy at this current spacetime. Longer term, if we are to realize our potential as a species, future generations must be in-depth explorers of the mindbrain and any other areas ripe for exploration. Their ability to be a positive or negative force will determine humanity's future. At the core of this work is the mindbrain and the various milieus within which it has functioned in past ages. How will you use your thinking in the future, given the knowledge you have culled from the most reliable, factual historical records of the past? Will you allow yourself and your children to devolve, or help to develop plans for the realization of the mindbrain's optimal function, expansion, and expression? It should begin with the most beneficial parenting, education, and leadership of our children. Should we choose errant leadership and paths of education that do not strengthen—or even worse, interfere with attention to increasing the AUQ—species failure will be the result.

Many a devoted, skilled, and well-intentioned teacher has become an unintentional pedagogical tool of the state because of the shortcomings of the curriculum mandated by the institutions they work within. And even assuming that the intentions of many educational institutions are worthy, there will need to be a sea change in the content of our education and a keen understanding of why it must change. If we are to have a robust understanding of a subject so essential to our species survival as education, we should begin with its origins.

THE HISTORY OF EDUCATION begins with the activities of our hunter-gatherer ancestors 2.25 million EY ago. Adults in hunter-gatherer cultures allowed children almost unlimited freedom to play and explore on their own, recognizing those activities to be a child's natural way of learning. They would groom the children to adulthood by socializing and exploring with their peers and older children. They would learn how to survive through their everyday experiences of interacting with others, solving problems, thinking, and concluding for themselves.

With the growth of agriculture 11,000 EY ago and of industry 250 EY ago, children unfortunately became forced laborers. The suppression of play and exploration began, and willfulness which had been a virtue became a vice that had to be beaten out of children. For several thousand EY following the introduction of agriculture, the "education" of children was to a considerable degree a matter of crushing their will to make them good laborers. A "good" child was obedient and suppressed the urge to play and explore and dutifully carried out the orders of adult masters. Such treatment was never fully successful because the human instincts to play and explore are so powerful that they can never be fully beat out of a child. However, the philosophy of "education" throughout that period was the opposite of the philosophy that hunter-gatherers had held for hundreds of thousands of EY earlier.

As most industries progressed through automation, there was a decline in the need for child labor, and the idea spread that childhood should be a time for learning. This allowed for the development of schools for children. For several reasons, some religious and some secular, the idea of universal, compulsory education arose and gradually spread, beginning in Europe from the early sixteenth century through the nineteenth century. Its supporters all had their agendas concerning the lessons that children should learn, and a good deal of the impetus for universal education came from the then-emerging Protestant religion. Martin Luther's declaration that each person should learn to read, because the Scriptures represented absolute truths and salvation, promoted public education as a Christian duty to save souls from eternal damnation. By the end of the seventeenth century, Germany, which led to the development of schooling, had laws requiring children to attend school under the Lutheran church, not the state's control. Schooling was an indoctrination, through the implanting of certain "truths" and ways of thinking into children's minds. The only known method of inculcation, then and now, is to force repetition and then to test its recall from memory. It began in America in the Massachusetts Bay Colony from 1642 through 1648.[4]

The concept that schools might be places for nurturing critical thought, insight, creativity, self-initiative, or the ability to teach oneself was the least of their concerns. To them, willfulness was the sinfulness they had to drill or beat out of children and was not to be encouraged.[5] With the rise of schooling, people thought of learning as a child's obligatory work. The same power assertive methods that had been in use to make children work in fields and factories were naturally transferred to the classroom. Repetition and memorization of lessons are tedious work for children, whose instincts urge them constantly to play freely and explore the world on their own.

Just as children did not adapt readily to laboring in fields and factories, they did not adapt well to schooling. This was no surprise to the adults involved because, at this time and place, a child's willfulness had zero value. Everyone assumed that to make children learn in school, the children's willfulness would have to be beaten out of them, and punishments of all types were part of the educational process. In some schools, children had permission for certain periods of play, a recess, to allow them to let off steam, but play had no place in learning. And in the classroom, they considered any play the enemy of learning.[6]

We should not allow our modern mindsets, competitively and technologically driven, to allow for the nonchalant belief that our ancestor's children, having nothing better to do, were uninhibitedly playing. They were, in fact, learning how to survive in their world at that spacetime.

27

LEARNING:
THE TALE OF "WORK AND THE THREE RS"

DECADES OF RESEARCH show that a foundation in a strong core curriculum and playfulness are compatible. It also found that both academic and social skills are important for children's success. The improvement in modern education might be in delivering the correct curriculum in a playful and meaningful manner, but we need more quality research to examine the interaction of play and learning. It is plausible, however, to suspect that is just what we may need to help children be engaged learners, and become more independent, responsible, and thoughtful adults.[7]

Throughout the history of formal education, we have had mostly devoted and capable educators who have done their jobs well and uplifted their students both academically and emotionally. Modes of education currently run the gamut from authoritarian repetitive indoctrination, in a madrasa, for example, to the Sudbury Model, which is a worldwide K-12 protocol. Students at Sudbury schools have the complete responsibility for their education and a direct democracy in which students and staff are equals having no authority other than that granted by their consent.[8] Sudbury students individually decide what to do with their time, and any freely formed groupings are independent of age. Learning becomes a byproduct of ordinary experience rather than through any prescribed coursework or testing, none of which exist there.[9] Those are the two extreme examples of the educational models in use today. Today's methods of education run the gamut between these two extremes and offer what their adherents believe to be the best possible means of education. At one extreme, you will find the rejection of free-thinking, inquiry, and expansive mind-stimulating methods, which instead base learning on exclusionary "faiths" and self-interest. At the other extreme, you will find the interaction of students through hands-on activity, having ideas leading them to discover through experimentation. The focus is on world events and social progress, and issues of controversy to develop the means to a more enlightened world.[10]

Many of these types of education provide an atmosphere in which people are free from fear, pressure, coercion, and comparison with one another. The freedom to grow, understand, think critically, and live is supreme so that the mindbrain does not function robotically. These latter methods help the mindbrain become very active in critical inquiry, the search for what is real, and the discovery of what is true. The hope is that the mindbrain's creative power grows and breaks away from all habits and traditions, so it is free from the very beginning to the very end, understanding what is and could be, in a new way.[11]

Zoe Weil, the co-founder of the Institute for Humane Education, believes that the world becomes what we teach. Ms. Weil feels that what we universally believe is the goal of education, and that preparing students for jobs in our economy is too narrow and outmoded a vision for today's world. Weil believes that we must also teach students to be conscious choice makers, "a generation of solutionaries" who can cope with the challenges of our changing, seemingly perpetually, imperiled world.

We can all agree, education that leads one to become gainfully employed as an unskilled or skilled worker, or a professional, has helped to ennoble mankind. Education has raised the standards of living throughout the world and enabled many of its population to rise from poverty. Some of the finest colleges and universities have grown in quality and size throughout the centuries and have succeeded in fostering a more knowledgeable populace. We have modern library systems and the internet, which make information both ubiquitous and inexpensive. The modern human has proven capable of utilizing the knowledge and skill sets necessary to engineer the progress we have witnessed in business, arts, science, medicine, and technology to date. The human mindbrain is equipped for exactly this type of learning, and the human body is built for the motion and dexterity necessary for it to be applied.

If we as the sole survivors of all the species collectively believe our continued progress and growth is well in hand, then we may as well proceed with the same syllabus we have. We need only continue the same path and elicit the most capable people and best methods to fill the ranks of public and private workers and professionals and raise our standards of living. We can then continue our competitive race with one another academically, economically, and militarily. Have we not made "progress" in those areas since appearing as a new species some 250,000 EY ago? If we wish to tack that way into the future, we need only create more innovative technology and allow our driving competitive spirit to do the rest. That will be easy-peasy. Let us take this path to its conclusion and see if we can predict its effect.

Let us assume we have survived with the same educational mindset that has produced the current situation we live with today. Assume we have more national pride, more technology, stronger militaries, more wealth, higher standards of living, and less poverty than ever before. We must also assume we have leaders and educators who have the same vision and goal for their people that facilitated all of this "progress." Given this scenario, why change the major thrust of education? We can patch any problems that impede progress and keep on progressing. There will be no shortage of new educational philosophies, methodological approaches, techniques, and innovations periodically introduced, as they have been since formal education began. Our institutions of learning are as great in variety as they have ever been before. We now have public, private, charter, boarding, religious, special education, magnet, and language immersion schools; then there are all the global colleges and universities. We should be well on our way to Shangri-La with no need to effect any major changes in our children's education, other than to tweak it to be increasingly more efficient and progressive.

Some modalities of education currently in vogue have worked well and have grown and adjusted to our needs right up to our current milieu, have they not? However, a major caveat must justifiably give us pause. Despite the progress formal education has brought humankind to date, there remains our inability to eliminate the real and significant possibility that, despite our current educational curricula and methods, we may yet destroy ourselves. All the advances of humankind have yet to equate to our en masse ability to live in a less self-centered, self-interested world, though we have had at least 2.5 million EY to do so. This is an indication that the current methodology and curriculum of our present formal education systems need careful and critical reassessment.

Human beings require a sea change as it applies to the education of parents, educators, and leaders, and by doing so, the education of our future generations. There are significant improvements and specific changes that need to be made concerning the future of worldwide education. Whether it takes the form that will be presented here or another, it must eventually address a global, nuclear, interconnected world that continues to vacillate between belligerence and amicability, war and peace. The reality is that we are not currently, nor have we ever been, at a place in spacetime wherein we have had enough cooperation and a sufficient AUQ of leadership to affect an educational sea change.

At one time or another, from our beginning, approximately 115 billion of our species have existed on Earth. There has not once been a fertile enough bed in which to sow the seeds for the evolutionary "realization of our species." It may be fair to say that we have not yet had the cosmic time. Homo sapiens are a mere eight cosmic minutes old, with no roadmap with which to do so. However, the chasm between our present reality and our goals should not deter us from planning to undertake the most essential of all human enterprises. And that is to achieve a peaceful and productive setting for all life on this planet to prosper, to their fullest potential, unimpeded by low AUQ mindbrains. We need to begin yesterday.

28

WHO WILL INFORM?

THE SCHOOLS OF THE FUTURE may be ubiquitous, public, and organized by districts within regions, within continents. To start a program of this magnitude, exceptional women and men of the highest AUQ must be available in concert, at one spacetime. There will be a need for choosing administrators and educators who have, as their primary self-interest, the support and facilitation of an en masse path for the realization of future generations, one generation building upon the next.

They will decide the curriculum, when to teach it, who teaches it, and the resources necessary to support the effort. Each decision will be equally essential to the success of the enterprise. They would be the modern-day equivalent of an eclectic combination of influential thinkers, educators, statespersons, and healers of the past. People such as Confucius, Buddha, the great Greek thinkers and educators, Susan B. Anthony, Jonas Salk, Albert Einstein, Simone de Beauvoir, Mohandas Gandhi, R, Buckminster Fuller, Clara Barton, Martin Luther King Jr., Krishnamurti, Rosalind Franklin, Richard Feynman, and great business minds/philanthropists with records that indicate successful managing of innovation and motivation.

Without fail, those qualified for teaching positions should at the least include all among us who have shown through their vocations that they have a high regard for life and are interested in this enterprise. Individuals such as physicians, nurses, veterinarians, first front-line workers, and proven health administrators would be a worthy population. There would be AI testing for all others interested, to see if they are viable possible contributors.

Citizens should choose the administrators democratically and all will possess a deep respect for Nature, having reached the highest levels of AUQ and distinguished themselves by word and accomplishment. They will also have knowledge of the latest mindbrain science and technological educational enhancements, to set an essential and impactful curriculum by consensus and debate. Those duly elected as leaders in education would administer their districts, regions, and continents, and choose those who did not garner enough votes to assist them in administration.

Those qualified as teachers, with the proviso that they have the skills to communicate the curriculum—as well as *live* it—will directly interact with the children. They will understand the all-important differences between the processes of thinking and the processes of learning. When they require more educators, selections will come from amongst those who graduated, with the desire and aptitude to teach. They will first be interns and thereafter informed as to the skills necessary to educate their charges, as they themselves had learned. Their key work will be to convey a well corroborated essential but flexible curriculum, to facilitate the education of children, with a universal perspective.

29

WHAT, HOW, AND WHEN TO INFORM?

THIS SECTION IS ONE EXAMPLE of a curricula and a method of its implementation that the consensus of administrators and educators might decide upon. It is only one of several paths that may find widespread use. A general overall description of the educational system's underlying foundational principles will precede the more specific descriptive content of the curricula.

The curricula might comprise a first language; extensive in-depth awareness of all other than self-courses (*inter*), in-depth awareness of self-courses (*intra*) following *inter*, and incorporating within both an *extensive* curriculum in Nature continuing throughout one's entire education. It may include problem solving, critical thinking, logic, the humanities, evidentiary-forensic-based history (warts and all), all sciences, mathematics, economic, government, and elective coursework based upon individual choice and aptitude.

This will not happen overnight, nor can we predict it to ever happen quick enough to avoid the disappearance of Homo sapiens. We are, after all, the last extant of the seven species of the 2.5 million EY evolution of our genus, and the first species having nuclear capabilities.

The possibility exists in the future, for the compression of the spacetime needed to execute any plan. Using enhancements to the energy and capability of the mindbrain biologically, genetically, chemically, medically, or electronically, we may enhance our chances of survival.

At its very core, all subjects will de-emphasize divisive instruction. There should be no nationalistic, religious, political, or ideological content in any school other than that of the truthful and thorough forensic revelations of our collective histories. Indoctrination has no place in the education of children, especially during the most formative early years of their lives—period. There simply should not be any.

They may communicate the curricula to the students in a give and take exchange. Classes should emphasize inquisitive, critical, and collaborative thinking, to enable the thorough analysis and evaluation of all evidence, arguments, claims, and beliefs made by the educators or students. Our children may then learn the value of inquiry, how to make judgments and decisions based on all points of view, how to interpret information, and how to draw their own conclusions.[12] These types of exchanges—*greasing the mindbrain's wheels*—are the kind of thinking that expands a child's mental horizon to embrace insight, intuition, and creativity. By educating them on how to think things through, with a healthy dose of skepticism, the hope is that this will fortify all students' natural curiosity and serve them well for the instruction they encounter.

Children may begin school by the age of three or four EY and might playfully and musically learn two languages, at first spoken, then written. The *first language* will be ubiquitous, and the second will be the language of the continent of their residence. This should reduce the 7,000 languages spoken as of this writing to 9. People can have the freedom to learn as many languages as they wish in the future, but their need to do so will become mostly academic. The way we communicate will change, as we will all be able to communicate and understand all speech everywhere. By applying the *delicate touch* anywhere and everywhere, we will be more likely to understand one another's intimate feelings and thoughts all over the Earth and realize our existential similarities. Ever since the advent of speech, groups and families learned to communicate with one another in a first learned language—as do the inhabitants of every country. Isn't it time we personally communicate with all the families and nations on Earth in the same way?

Assuredly our technology will allow the "virtual" commingling of classes on different continents ubiquitously. We will integrate holographic images of many classes using virtual reality, sans headsets, with many other classes enabling them to experience one another, holographically, virtually, simultaneously, and seamlessly. Each educator and student will interact directly with one another, share ideas, and learn together. This type of commingling, beginning at age four, may continue for any subject when useful, up to graduation at seventeen. We should use the most modern technological modes of communication available in every class which teaches their first language. In the first language class of their early years, they can learn, play, sing, and dance together, always in a highly interconnected, intercontinental setting.

As students progress in their education, they can interrelate on higher levels by holding meaningful collaborative workshops and debates on integral, timely, and pertinent world matters. This early intercontinental experience with their first language should segue nicely into introducing the next phase of their education.

A priority following a child's proficiency in learning their first language is a playful, concentrated emphasis first on the *inter* phase of their schooling and followed by the *intra* phase, with both continually underpinning their education through to graduation. *Inter* education, to be most effective, should precede the inception of the *intra* education. The order of presentation does not show the relative importance of *inter* vis-à-vis *intra*, which it precedes, as they are both equally essential to the process. The placement of these phases of education in this order has to do with timing only. I base it solely on the natural maturation and development of the nascent human psyche and the subtle evolution of the child's identity and ego that follows. I make the rationale for the order of placement clear as we proceed through this section.

All classes convened during the next portion of the curriculum, which are the introductory phases of *inter*, should proceed in a holographic environment, using virtual reality, not only bringing children together but enhancing their lessons using the latest artificial intelligence videos and auditory technologies. The transition into this phase should be a seamless one as the children have already experienced their first language class with peers who are different in appearance and have differing cultures.

The introductory *inter* educational concentration should convey to children that arrogance, prejudice, bigotry, scapegoating, bullying, racism, etc., and their destructive consequences are the greatest barriers to *inter*. The courses in Nature, soon to be discussed, will present children with a broader awareness of all life and things other than themselves.

Students should realize by this stage that we have a high functioning mindbrain capable of realization when we think freely, critically, positively, and fearlessly. Likewise, we are devolving when there are restrictions to our free exchange of ideas and access to facts, and we think negatively and fearfully. They will learn that Homo sapiens are a sociable and communicative species, who know how to work together toward extremely difficult goals and succeed. They will see that petty differences and divisiveness hamper, impede, and destroy our interdependence as social beings. Students will also glean that we all have unique talents and capabilities, which we should celebrate, whilst respecting the fact that every life is significant. Having worked successfully together learning their first language with children from other continents, they will have had a first-hand *experience* in what working together in real-time truly means. Parental encouragement, support, and affirmation of this curriculum will be essential to their children's continuing success at this important educational stage.

After the exposure to the introductory phases of an *inter* curriculum, a child's first formal exposure in the classroom to Nature may follow, and will be incorporated into the *next* phases of the *inter* curriculum. The benefit of informing the student of the *inter* will be useful in integrating and socializing with one another, discovering the wonder of the *all* and *everything* of Nature. All the same "interconnected," intercontinental, high-tech settings will be in use throughout this phase as well. Nature, beginning with the first known creation, that of the universe, will include information relating to the birth of myriad living entities, from cells to complex life forms, emphasizing their symbiosis. Informed that Homo sapiens are merely one species of the over 8.5 million on Earth proliferated by Nature, children should gain an understanding and respect of all life forms, breathing and otherwise. Students will know we are not superior to any other life form, but that we all share a place horizontally, not vertically, on this planet.

Their education will incorporate the fact that higher *inter* involves an understanding that we are the stewards of other life forms, not their superiors. They will realize that many species such as mammals, primates, dolphins, orcas, wolves, bees, ants, and hyenas also work together to accomplish tasks that not one of them alone can do, and have functioning mindbrains.[13] They will learn of our interconnection with all the species of Nature, expanded to reveal our understanding down to the acute molecular level in more detailed coursework in the future.

Following the introductory Nature curriculum incorporated into *inter*, a child may begin their introduction to *intra* curriculum around the age of eight. This would be a time when one is naturally developing an identity and moral compass. The reason for beginning the *inter* programs before the introductory *intra* program is because children should be more supportive, less bullying, and more understanding of one another and the world of Nature by then. Exposure to the introductory first language course and *inter*, incorporating Nature curriculum, the children should develop a more pliant social and inclusive mindset. This will allow for a child's psyche to develop more healthfully and creatively, less hampered by the negativity of division, derision, and bullying.

As a part of *intra*, the areas of thinking, emotion, behavior, the selfish and selfless mindsets of personality, and an in-depth examination of the psyche should begin. Parental awareness and support are of fundamental importance at the initial stages of the psyche development of their children. The most advanced scientific knowledge of the psyche (mechanisms of cognitive-emotional function), continually updated, should enable an awareness level of oneself and others. And the *inter* and *intra* curriculum should continue to thread throughout the entire educational cycle onto graduation.

Once a student has reached the age of about sixteen, having completed the projected general curriculum, they will have the psychological and technical tools necessary to make a flawlessly informed determination of their future path. Based upon their ability, conflated with their desire, they will choose specialized curricula with the flexibility to change course at any time.

PART IX
Artistic Expression, Inventiveness,
and Scientific Investigation

"The thing that makes science so effective is the simple idea at its heart: It matters what's true. The scientific method is a mechanism for weeding out the lies we tell each other and ourselves."
—Ann Druyan

"An artist, under pain of oblivion, must have confidence in himself, and listen only to his real master: Nature."
—Auguste Renoir

"Science and art belong to the whole world, and before them vanish the barriers of nationality."
—Johann Wolfgang von Goethe

"Art is not what you feel, but what you can make others feel."
—Degas

"The greatest unsolved mysteries are the mysteries of our existence as conscious beings in a small corner of a vast universe."
—Freeman Dyson

"Curiosity, observation, intuition, inquiry, insight, creativity, and discovery offer us a glimpse into the mindbrains's highest mental function, and should be recognized as one of the keys to our optimal realization and long-term survival."
—Symmetrias

WE BASE OUR OPINIONS on possibilities, beliefs, conjectures, notions, and faith. The arts, invention, and the sciences require the focused and disciplined use of our higher cognitive abilities and have led to vastly greater productive results. They are intense human activities requiring curiosity, inspiration, imagination, personality, passion, and style.[1] This is not to imply that one should consider any other focused, intense mental endeavor—when compared to an artistic, inventive, or scientific one—lacking. Another point to consider is the fact that an individual's artistic, inventive, or scientific prowess is a sign of the level of their AUQ. They are mutually exclusive.

In the 14-billion-year evolution of its many mindbrained species, Nature has peppered some of them with *curiosity*. It is the natural need and capacity for a sentient species to investigate, both mentally and physically, the frontiers beyond their familiarity or current understanding. Simply put, it is the motivation for a species to explore or investigate to learn something, just for the sake of learning. It is a feature of our survival and progress—as much as oxygen has been. It is also the hallmark of many other species' learning activities.

Einstein suggested, when queried, that he owed his outstanding success in the mindbrain business to his unquenchable curiosity. Naturally, his humble nature prevented him from also stating that besides his curiosity, it was *how* he thought that led to that success. Our curiosity has been essential to our survival and, whether working alone or collaboratively, the fruits of the innovative mindbrain have been an essential characteristic of our success as a species. Some of them will be referenced in this section.

The hallmark and essence of the arts are their truth and beauty. Whatever form it takes, art speaks of the artist's success or failure to either engage and "move" the viewer—or not. Science, too, has its truth and beauty, as the intrepid ranks of scientists have always attempted to uncover those underlying qualities in Nature. The greater the scientific discovery, the simpler its expression as an exquisite formula or revelation.

In recognizing the named and famed contributors to art, invention, and science, there are many more whose works, however noteworthy, will forever be unknown. Depending upon the spacetime within which many highly focused and fully productive people lived, they remain nameless for the credit they deserve. There are many reasons for this unfortunate circumstance, amongst them being gender, class, prejudice, timing, or sheer bad luck. The curious thing is that fame and power did not mean much to the people who helped change humankind for the better; their contribution was enough.

30
PREHISTORIC TO MODERN, MOTHERS AND FATHERS OF ART AND SCIENCE

WITH THE APPEARANCE of Homo habilis, the first of our genus 2.5 million EY ago, stone tools were the invention of the day, and a need was met by the inventive mindbrain. A major thrust into the world of gastronomy was evidenced by the containment of fire and the use of open fires and hearths about 800,000 EY ago. Dietary choice began about 500,000 EY ago when wooden spears were made to bring down large prey.

The idea that tools could be formed from bone, ivory, or antler was realized approximately 400,000 EY later in 100,000 BC. Then the human mindbrain conceived the bow and arrow around 65,000 EY ago, and their targets were never the same, be they nonhuman or human foe.

FROM THE CAVE . . .

Some of our forebears lived in caves as early as 170,000 EY ago or six cosmic minutes ago, to as recently as 10,000 EY ago. They included Neanderthals, 200,000-40,000 EY ago, and Cro Magnons, 45,000-10,000 EY ago, both of which were physically like the people inhabiting our world today. Neanderthals were eventually driven from their European homeland and to extinction by the Cro Magnons.[2]

It was an unawareness infected by a dose of arrogance that led the most recent species of our genus, Homo sapiens, to believe that our ancestors were incapable of producing permanent art. It had been thought that the abstract, symbolic, and creative thinking necessary to produce enduring rather than ornamental body art was our exclusive domain. To sum it up, the thinking was that we may not be perfect, but we are certainly more perfect than any of our predecessors. This is the same self-aggrandizing thought— reminiscent of the geocentric theories of Ptolemy and the relegation of our ancestors and all brethren nonhuman kingdoms—to an inferior-to-us status on Nature's evolutionary life-giving path. Thankfully, art and science have rescued us from our illusions, and combined in a way that provides proof as to who the first known artists were. Several major discoveries have yielded unequivocal testimony that it was not us.

Our bubble originally burst with the1940 Lascaux cave discovery in Montignac in southwest France. Within the cave, there were a few thousand 17,000-EY-old Cro Magnon paintings and engravings of horses, bulls, deer, etc., rendered with significant artistic skill. The artwork followed the contours of the cave walls and incorporated perspective, shadowing, highlighting, stenciling, and pointillism to express the artist's thoughts. Many handprints found in the caves reveal that males and females of all ages crafted the works with the use of powdered colors, brushes, and stumping cloths. There were twenty-five more caves and 150 rock shelters in that region found to contain paintings and engravings as well. After Picasso visited the Lascaux cave, he emerged and exclaimed, "We have invented nothing." Miró once said, "Painting has been in a state of decadence since the age of caves."[3] These great artistic minds were truthful enough to recognize the facts, as humbling as it may have been to do so. Fifty-four EY later, in 1994, again in France, the discovery of the Chauvet cave in the southern town of Pont-d'Arc was made. This time, radiocarbon dating showed paintings, also made by the Cro Magnons of nonhuman figures, 35,000 EY ago.

Lascaux horse.

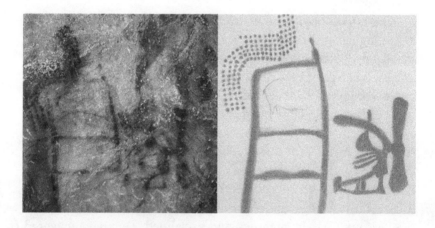

Cave wall paintings from La Pasiega in northern Spain. The ladder shape, composed of red horizontal and vertical lines, dates to older than 64,000 EY, made by Neanderthals.

A real humbler came with the definitive proof of dating even older art. The discovery of symbolic, nonfigurative artwork in Spain in the caves of Ardales in 1821, La Pasiega in 1911, and Maltravieso in 1951 were all thought to be the work of the same anatomically modern Homo sapiens as those of the French caves, the Cro Magnon. That was the general belief of archaeologists during the 200 EY since the discovery of the first cave in 1821, and then it all changed. A process known as uranium-thorium dating was used to determine the age of the calcitic crusts that had formed over these paintings.[4]

Following the verification in several labs, the findings showed a minimum age for the artworks of 67,000 EY and, in fact, could be much older, depending on the age of the drawings prior to the formation of the calcite that covered them. It is undeniable, therefore, that the Neanderthal was the ancestor responsible for the works. The Neanderthal artists show thoughtful planning in that the paintings needed light, pigment prep, and the decisions on where to place the work.[5]

Neanderthal Male

"What we've got here is a smoking gun that overturns the notion that Neanderthals were knuckle-dragging, stupid cave dwellers," said Alistair Pike, professor of archaeological sciences at the University of Southampton, who co-led the study. The scientific evidence supports the fact that the world's oldest known cave paintings are the artistry of Neanderthals, not modern humans. This suggests that our relatives were far from being uncultured brutes and were possibly *cognitively indistinguishable* from early modern humans. Joao Zilhao of the University of Barcelona believed the new findings demanded that the search for the origins of human cognition needed to go back to the common ancestor of both Neanderthals and modern humans, or over 500,000 EY ago. It was therefore realized that Neanderthals living in the same land, who would one day give birth to Diego Velazquez and Pablo Picasso, had the intellectual ability to think symbolically, like modern humans.[6]

TOWARD THE WAVE . . .

Hunter-gatherers as late as 10,000 BC began farming and domesticating cattle, goats, sheep, and pigs in the so-called Fertile Crescent, a region now covering eastern Turkey, Iraq, and southwestern Iran. This enabled the settling in one area of a people who eventually organized and formed city-states, beginning with Sumer in Mesopotamia, around 5000 BC. This began the division, because of timing and geography, of the globe into separate cultures. Once human beings could group en masse in one place and collaborate, civilization took firm hold. Artisans were first using the potter's wheel around 3500 BC, before transforming it into the tool that would change the world, the wheel. Within decades, the recording, accumulation, and transmission of knowledge began with the first texts written and would have a profound impact on the future of life on Earth. Warfare ignited throughout human history over the need for land and resources.

The Medieval period, a.k.a., the Dark Ages, was a period between 500 and 1000 AD that was especially marked by frequent warfare and the virtual disappearance of urban life. The Renaissance followed this bleak period and ended the years lost in the Dark Ages. For 200 EY, from 1400 AD through 1600 AD, we witnessed the rebirth of the classical art and intellect of Ancient Greece and Rome. This was a most hopeful sign for humanity and proved that we did not lose everything in the prior, wasteful 1,000 EY. High Renaissance art flourished for about thirty-five EY in Italy from the early 1490s through 1527, powered by the legendary and giant talents of Leonardo, Michelangelo, and Raphael, all worth mentioning here. Leonardo da Vinci (1452–1519) is the *universal genius* or *Renaissance man*, an individual of unquenchable curiosity and inventive imagination.[7] He is one of the most diversely talented human beings to have ever lived. To characterize Michelangelo (1475–1564), then thought to be the greatest artist of his time, now seems to have been shortsighted, as we now consider him to be one of the greatest of all time.[8] Raphael (1483–1520) illustrates his excellent artistry in the harmony, beauty, and majesty of his subjects as he brilliantly mastered the purity of composition.[9]

The cathedrals, museums, and libraries of the world are the repositories of the great art, literature, and science of humankind. Not only are these sanctuaries a place to preserve treasured works, but they are an everlasting tribute to the experts in their craft who created them. They are a tribute to the value human beings place on the high-minded time and energy spent to realize these creations. They are the gifts to future generations, of some of the most beautiful forms of human emotion, expression, and aspiration of human creation.

APPROACHING THE WAVE . . .

The teacher and philosopher Aristotle (384 BC-322 BC) is the first to argue the importance of empirical evidence, which is the belief that one gains knowledge only through observable sense-experience, and by building upon what one already knows. His concepts were the cornerstone for the gradual building of the Scientific Revolution, toward the end of the Renaissance and through to the late eighteenth century (1600-1800) in Europe. This period gave birth to the scientific method, and by utilizing it through reason, experimentation, and observation, we have successfully differentiated between opinion, speculation, and illuminated fact.

The central theme of the scientific method and modern science is that all proof must be verifiable through experience rather than speculation or logic. Trust in facts and proof is imperative, especially when one is trying to survive on a nuclear-armed planet. Copernicus (1473-1543), Johannes Kepler (1571-1630), and Galileo (1564-1642) were the first "modern scientists," and each emphatically stipulated that the search for explanations of natural phenomena must have at its base terrestrial examination, and that the laws of Nature are the same in all places, always. Issac Newton (1643-1727) built upon Kepler's formulae of planetary motion, and with the use of the calculus co-invented with Leibnitz, he planned the laws of motion and universal gravitation. These scientists laid the groundwork for contemporary science to develop a consistent picture of the universe and have been essential to the theories of its formative origin through to the present.[10]

Revolutions are wont to be bloody. When a motivated populace forcibly acts to change the status quo and give birth to a new societal system and nation, violence ensues. Occasionally, revolutions can be bloodless as with the so-called Industrial Revolution which spanned almost 100 EY from 1760 to 1850. The profit of all goods-producing businesses has always depended on the speed of production and transportation of materials and goods. This revolution saw the meteoric advance of both. It was a time when necessity met the cumulative knowledge of the mind and burst into myriad creative industrial inventiveness. It began in Britain where the textile industry burgeoned with advances in automation that spun and wove cloth, prompting the invention of the cotton gin in America to automate raw cotton production. The improvements to the steam engine that J. Watt (1736-1819) made, that revolutionized land and sea transport when adapted to boats and trains, was the greatest contributor to industrial growth. By the mid-nineteenth century, industrialization had spread to France, Germany, Belgium, and the United States. The period was a prime example of nations working together, while surreptitiously commandeering one another's technology.

This widespread automation and industrialization, when given government support, began the growth in the wealth of some nations and their empowerment over others. People in industrialized countries produced manufactured products, and people in less industrialized countries possessed the raw materials necessary for that production. This division of circumstance led those who needed the raw materials to commandeer it through colonization of those who had it, which led to the beginning of a clear delineation en masse, between the haves and have-nots of the world.

DISCERNING, DEFINING, AND RIDING THE WAVE

The Danish physicist and chemist Hans Oersted (1777–1851) discovered that electric currents create magnetic fields, and he was the first to make the connection between electricity and magnetism.[11] He ran a current through a wire in 1820 and, without touching a nearby compass, watched as the current caused the compass needle to jump. That was indeed a magic moment, and it eventually led to magical changes in our world. A decade later, Michael Faraday (1791-1867), with his knowledge of Oersted's findings, took an opposite approach than Oersted and induced electric current in a wire by manipulating a magnetic field. This led directly to the production of the modern electric motor, generator, and transformer, which were the true backbone of the industry.

Building upon Faraday's work, James Clerk Maxwell (1831-1879) theorized from 1861 to 1864 the mathematical equations that formally unified electricity and magnetism and their speed. He found that the self-propagating oscillating waves of electric and magnetic fields were electromagnetic wave radiation and traveled close to the speed of light. He then inferred that light itself must comprise those propagating disturbances, ie., radiation, in the electromagnetic field. These insights, experimental proof, and formulations led to the discoveries from 1887 to 1903 of the entire spectrum of electromagnetic wave energies. They existed from low to high energy radiation such as radio waves, microwaves, light (infrared, visible, and ultraviolet), X-rays, and gamma rays.[12]

The technology that followed from the scientific mindbrained includes many of the products we take for granted today—wireless transmissions, television, satellite communication, medical screening, instrumentation, radar, thermal imaging, GPS systems, and more. It is important to note that Einstein had on display three pictures in his Princeton home study, images of Newton, Faraday, and Maxwell. He felt particularly inspired by these scientists, and it was also his way of giving them their deserved credit.

31
"I NEED TO UNDERSTAND
HOW THE UNIVERSE WAS MADE"

IF EVER A PERSON in their essence exemplified a humanistic view and a nonviolent hope for humanity, in combination with a mindbrain that saw through to the "ground" of space, time, gravity, and energy, it is Albert Einstein (1879-1955). Einstein was a humble, unassuming, witty, and playful physicist thrust into fame by the direction and energy of his fiercely powerful independent mindbrain and limitless curiosity. His work product was first recognized by Max Planck, the most renowned German physicist of his day, who had theorized the energy quanta. In 1905, at only twenty-six years of age, he published four major papers, one of which won him the Nobel Prize in Physics. His theories of *special* and *general relativity*, 1905 and 1916 respectively, revolutionized the thinking of the influential thinkers of that age, and every age that has followed and will follow. His contributions are profound, and his legacy is indisputable. The sheer majesty of his thought is so piercing, it ennobles and enriches us all.

A portion of his masterful work product was the exact formulation of gravity, proof that time and space were not absolute, proof of the existence of atoms and some of their properties, proof of the equivalence of matter and energy, and proof that the photon is the basic particle of electromagnetic emission. Any of those insights would have been sufficient for a legacy. He never ceased working toward a theory that would unite the four known forces of Nature, and he died while still attempting to do so, in 1955.

32
DEVOTED HEALERS

IT IS A CREDIT to world character for members of our species to devote their time and energy to the preservation and improvement of the life and health of other living entities. These individuals have spent long hours for many EYs in academia, learning a craft which requires them to pass stringent licensing exams before ever applying their skills in their chosen fields of endeavor. They are, mostly, a motivated and devoted subsection of any population, and the type of person who has determined that life is worth fostering, healing, sustaining, and saving.

The people who elevate themselves positively to life, and who possess the talent for that contribution, have unquestionably enabled us to enjoy longer and healthier lives for the past few centuries. As the breakthroughs in medical research and science expand, we can expect that new talents will be available to meet the challenges of those advances. The breakthroughs in the medical sciences that most people take for granted today had their origin with the critical and insightful thinking of many a known and unknown innovator. Their areas of endeavor were microbiology, chemistry, virology, research, and practitioners, i.e., physicians and surgeons. Edward Jenner

(1749-1823) saved more lives with his smallpox vaccine, the first vaccination ever developed, than any other human being in history. Why isn't his name at least as well-known as Mao, Hitler, Stalin, and Pol Pot? If one gives this question some thought, the reason is not surprising. These demons, disguised as human beings, sear into history and our mindbrains because of their heinous actions. It is the same as a normal pleasant day compared with a historically damaging act of nature, such as a devastating tsunami, hurricane, or earthquake. History only records the destructive ones.

Louis Pasteur, Joseph Lister, Heinrich Koch, Alexander Fleming, and Jonas Salk may be unknown to the latest generations of human beings, but those generations may never have been born were it not for the work of the preceding names. Pasteurization, antiseptics, bacteriology, antibiotics, and the eradication of polio followed from the thinking of the aforenamed. There could be hundreds of millions of names added to this group—the type of person who devotes their life to helping heal and care for the sick and less fortunate. Of all the healers, stealers, and wheeler-dealers, which group do *you* think has the mindset to educate, lead, and propel us toward realization—or contrarily, lead us to devolution?

33

THE CODED SPIRAL STAIRCASE

CHARLES DARWIN PROPOSED that all life had its origin in "one primordial form," and implied that our species and every other were relations of even the simplest and evolutionarily oldest organisms. This was one of the greatest scientific thought concepts ever recognized at that point by a human being, and it still is. What it meant was that all living things shared the same basic materials and the means of propagating them to their offspring. There is a list of people who have set out to detail the exact molecular mechanisms that facilitate Darwin's theory of biological evolution (1859). It includes the toil of people in the trenches and laboratories searching for the *stuff* of hereditary transmission. The *stuff* is the ingredient that contains the chemicals for the conveyance of life, going from parents to offspring throughout every single generation in the history of every living species on Earth. This was unproven until the collective and collaborative thinking of many researching microbiologists, geneticists, and physicians combined their findings.

There are a few names worth mentioning, all of whom contributed and paved the way to the definitive description of DNA. Once the following legion of contributors had gleaned the *what* and *where* of the *stuff*, the exact description of it was a fait accompli to a great extent. Whose energies helped to find the *what* and *where* of it all? Gregor Mendel, the "pea" man, discovered, in 1865, that heredity transfers in discrete units; Johannes Miescher isolated DNA from a cell in 1869, calling it "nuclein"; W. Sutton, in 1902, observed that the segregation of chromosomes during plant cell division matched the segregation pattern of Mendel's; W. Johannsen, in 1909, first used the term "gene" to describe a Mendelian unit of heredity and the terms "genotype" and "phenotype" to differentiate between the genetic traits of an individual and its outward appearance; T. Hunt Morgan, the "fruit flyman," in his 1911 discovery determined that genes are portions of the chromosome. O. Avery determined that DNA, not proteins, transformed cells and also defined its chemical nature, in 1944; in 1952, Alfred Hershey & Martha Chase showed that only the DNA of a virus needs to enter a bacterium to infect it and suggested that genes comprise DNA.[13]

Almost 100 EY had elapsed between the publication of *On the Origin of Species* by Darwin in 1859 and the actual modeling of the spiral double helix DNA molecule by F. Crick and J. Watson, in 1953, based in part upon the expert X-ray crystallography of Ms. Rosalind. Franklin. Research continued robustly as humankind was on the doorstep of deciphering the keys to the creation of every living entity. During the ensuing period, many more details concerning the actual chemistry and mechanisms that were part of Nature's work. known as "life," became known. Discovered were how messenger RNA ferries nuclear DNA to the cell's cytoplasm and encodes to protein; how an alteration of genes caused disease; that polymerase was the enzyme responsible for DNA replication; the sequencing of the genomes of various species of bacteria and nonhumans, including that of human beings by 2003; and gene-splicing techniques were vastly improved.

In 2017, the discovery of fossilized bacterial microorganisms—or microfossils, in hydrothermal vent precipitates in the Nuvvuagittuq Belt of Quebec, Canada, that could be 4.28 billion EY old—took place. This would be the oldest record of life on Earth and suggests "an almost instantaneous emergence of life" in geological time, after ocean formation 4.41 billion EY ago, and not long after the formation of the Earth 4.54 billion EY ago.[14] Its name is Luca, the *last universal common ancestor*, and it shows that all life on this planet comprises the same formative molecular structure. Nature has woven a continual thread through all of her life forms. Finally, Darwin's supposition that all species share the means of hereditary transmission was definitively and scientifically proven.

HOPE SPRINGS

Technology is the application of established scientific laws and theories to the production of the products and conveniences of the world. The scientific mindbrain produces the machines, computers, robots, artificial intelligence, etc. that have freed us from the drudgery of routine tasks. It is this model of innovation that offers us the unlimited possibility of developing our mindbrains by freeing up our bodies, and we should always encourage and accommodate the future development of the artistic, innovative, and scientific mindbrain. We trust these contributors will inspire those who wish to follow their course and help the genus Homo, and all the developing genera and species that follow, to progress in the mindfulness necessary to countermand the forces that rend and devolve us.

The people pursuing their artistry, inventiveness, and scientific exploration through their independent or collaborative work have *no interest in controlling or being controlled by anyone but themselves.* They have not been available to follow our misleaders. These creators and discoverers focus and control their mindbrains laser-like on their chosen and challenging tasks, or they could never have achieved them. They are on a highway toward realization.

PART X
Your Treatment of Nonhuman Life:
A Major Signpost on Your Way

"Dominion does not mean domination. We hold dominion over animals only because of our powerful and ubiquitous intellect. Not because we are morally superior. Not because we have a 'right' to exploit those who cannot defend themselves. Let us use our brain to move toward compassion and away from cruelty, to feel empathy rather than cold indifference, to feel animals' pain in our hearts."
  —Marc Bekoff

"Speciesism, is a prejudice or attitude of bias in favor of the interests of members of one's own species and against those of members of other species."
  —Richard D. Ryder, 1970

"We patronize them for their incompleteness, for their tragic fate of having taken form so far below ourselves. And therein do we err and greatly err. For the animal shall not be measured by man. In a world older and more complete than ours they move finished and complete, gifted with extensions of the senses we have lost or never attained, living by voices we shall never hear. They are not brethren, they are not underlings; they are other nations, caught with ourselves in the net of life and time, fellow prisoners of the earth."
  —Henry Beston, *The Outermost House: A Year of Life On The Great Beach of Cape Cod*

HAVING EXTENSIVELY ADDRESSED the subject of human life in this writing, it is most important to view our past and present relationship with nonhumans. Several causative factors have influenced the way we interact with all species of life, key amongst them the human psyche, economics, the quality of both parental and educational guidance, and leadership. The way we have treated our nonhuman co-travelers is a microcosm of the meandering continuum we have been on toward human awakening and understanding.

Insects first appeared on land 400 million EY ago, vertebrates 360 million EY ago, and the genus Homo 2.8 million EY ago. The fact is that many millions of species have preceded us as inhabitants of this planet by hundreds of millions of EY. The survival and evolution game of nonhumans has therefore had a far longer history than that of the genus Homo. Would it not serve us well to learn from each of Nature's profligate progeny as models of long-term survival, and to recognize them as a gift to appreciate and steward?

As social beings, we possess an innate need to interrelate to others of our species, and other life forms as well. Nonhumans brings out the caring in some, and this is especially so with domesticated home-boarded nonhumans whose needs are those of an infant or child that never grows up. They never argue, are not prone to misunderstandings, trust is never an issue, and love is unconditional. Fine, warm, and fuzzy.

There is another reality of our interaction with Nature's nonhumans, throughout history to the present, that is not positive, and we will examine it here. In doing so, you may well understand how to progress and increase the expanse of your mindbrain's understanding, appreciation, and care for all life. You may not, but that is, unfortunately, at our peril.

Will our values, which are slowly strengthening toward more humane treatment of nonhumans, be sufficient and timely enough to enable a countermand to existing and entrenched policies? When reading the following sections of this part, please keep in mind the *values* that were, and at most times still are, the causative factors influencing and determining our treatment of nonhumans.

34

PATHS OF ELIMINATION

WHEN IN ROME

SOME THINGS the Romans did for fun were horrible. In ancient Rome, the destruction of human and nonhuman lives morphed into an entertainment form. One need only reset their clock back 2,000 EY or five cosmic seconds to spend a day in the Colosseum or many amphitheaters throughout Rome for "entertainment." Who was to blame? The misleaders who controlled the populace, courtesy of the Roman legions, and promoted violence that became endemic to the culture.

There were about fifty amphitheaters in Rome alone and 230 throughout their Empire so that most of the wider populace outside the locus of Rome could attend the events. The largest amphitheater was the Colosseum in the center of the city of Rome, built by eighty AD, seating 50,000, treating the people for its 100-day inauguration, to the slaughter of 9,000 nonhuman species. The slaughtering *for sport* of 400,000 human beings and 1 million nonhumans took place in that one locale alone.[1] There are no metrics for the *Empire-wide slaughter*, lasting 400 EY from about 50 AD through 450 AD, though one can extrapolate out the unimaginable number of humans and nonhuman carnage. The number of elephants, lions, jaguars, and tigers plummeted across the globe, absolutely devastating the wildlife of North Africa and the entire Mediterranean region, wiping some species off the map entirely.[2] They starved nonhumans purposely and pitting them against each other in savage fights or dispatched them in wild beast hunts by highly trained hunters.[3]

With the birth of the first nonhuman program, they achieved a milestone. This was the point at which a human being faced a snarling pack of starved beasts, and every laughing spectator in the crowd chanted for the big cats to win. This was the point at which the Republic's obligation to make a man's death a fair or honorable one was outweighed by the pure entertainment value of watching him die.[4] Given the Roman mindset, it is easy to understand that any nonhuman that survived were, of course, likewise dispatched in future games. Waste not, want not.

LESS THAN HUMAN

The rise to power of Adolph Hitler, the misleader of misleaders, is proof that even modern civilization has an extremely thin veneer.

This did not take place in ancient times, but in early twentieth-century Germany, then a giant modern cultural center known for its beneficial development of science, philosophy, and music. This is an example of diabolical forces driving devolution, intending to eliminate the possibility of realization from the face of the Earth. Besides passing laws legalizing the denial of human rights, the Nazis began a press and radio propaganda campaign to portray their intended victims as rats, vermin, and *untermenschen*, or subhumans. They listed inmates of concentration camps as *stuecks* (German for pieces), with assigned numbers, rather than being permitted the dignity of a name. If a German were to give these victims any thought whatsoever, it was to think of them as nonhuman.[5] Devolution occurred because of the convenience of groupthink, scapegoating, and sculpting the mindset of a population fertile for a leadership that would restore German dignity at whatever the cost. Human insensibility allowed the degradation of segments of human populations to be considered nonhuman and thus fodder for elimination through unspeakable crimes led by the Nazis.

INTENTIONAL DEPRAVED CRUELTY

A child with a normally functioning mindbrain in an attentive, engaged, and loving home, who is receiving a reasonable education, should mature into having a neutral feeling at worst, and a caring feeling at best toward nonhumans. This is not always the case, and when conditions are such that they produce a severely impoverished and damaged psyche, it drives some of our species to destroy helpless nonhumans.

Cruelty in this area may be an early manifestation of the subgroup of children developing conduct problems associated with traits of low empathy and callous disregard.[6] The intentionally malicious treatment by youths is usually a harbinger of future psycho-sociopathic behavior. The preponderance of rapists and serial killers who have a childhood profile of violence toward nonhumans is statistically significant.[7] Children who torture or kill squirrels, birds, cats, and dogs—without showing remorse—have a higher probability of being sociopaths. Many serial killers, when young, kill to control others' lives, and small nonhumans are the only lives they have the power to control.

Arnold Arluke, a professor of sociology and anthropology at Northeastern University, studied twenty-three school shooters from 1988 to 2012 and found that 43 percent had abused nonhumans; 90 percent of them committed cruelty in an up-close and personal manner.

The young Jeffrey Dahmer killed his neighbor's pets, impaling a nonhuman head on a stick. As an adult, the Milwaukee Cannibal decapitated some human victims and raped, murdered, and ate parts of seventeen people. John Wayne Gacy, as a minor, set turkeys on fire using gasoline-filled balloons. As an adult, he killed thirty-three boys and men.[8] We may say with certainty that this type of behavior has been going on for millennia, but there are no substantive records to support it. Considering the treatment of nonhumans and humans in ancient Rome, one may logically surmise that the societal mindset preceding and succeeding during that time wouldn't have presented as a red flag or been aberrant behavior. Yet today, modern society allows the insensitivity for the lives and well-being of nonhumans to continue in many forms.

POACHING

Some of the most precious and endangered nonhumans remain in the gun sights of the human being, though it is all illegal. The destruction of the elephant, rhino, tiger, sea turtle, lemur, gorilla, and many others shows a blatant and callous disregard for other nonhuman species—for the sake of profit. These species are in danger of being eliminated from the face of the Earth, and we have not yet reached a point in our history wherein fines, felony convictions, and jail are sufficient deterrents. We should finally recognize universally that making a profit or a living by engaging in the illegal destruction of nonhumans is murder. Kenya has enacted the death penalty for poachers, and that is a sign that, for whatever reason, they will not tolerate it.[9] Some might call it a sign of progress, but others are vehemently against the legislation. How *you* feel about this is the proper test of your mindset concerning your devolution or realization.

The next groups are woefully more damaging than the depraved and the poachers. The following activities are even more dangerous to nonhuman in that they have been culturally and socially accepted and commercially driven, up to the present, despite the controls and laws that allegedly outlaw many of them.

THE HUNT: WARFARE IS MORE FAIR

Two million EY ago, long before there were establishments where one could purchase food, clothing, and shelter, we hunted, but we possess no hunting gene; it is not in our DNA. Hunting was simply a rational decision made to survive, and we adapted enough to make weapons, form hunting groups, and hunt. Somewhere in between, it became more than the work of survival, and at some moment in our consciousness, hunting became something else. It fed our psyches, not our stomachs. It had become a so-called *sport*. A sport whereby some of Nature's most beautiful creations have become the innocent bounty of our desire for a thrill, adventure, show of status and wealth, or all of them combined. The overt aim of sport hunting is the collection of an experience, thrill, trophy, or prize, but its motivation is certainly not the drive to survive. This is another form of nonhuman elimination in our culture and a rite of passage in some areas of the United States and other areas around the world. Some people may still hunt for sustenance, and that is more understandable in the present-day meat-eating world. But sport hunters in the USA alone, currently estimated at 19 million, handle the elimination of about 100 million nonhumans annually, according to wildlife agencies reports, which don't include the millions more which go unreported.

Simply stated, *sport hunting* is a misnomer. A sport requires that both sides are playing, but in this situation, the hunted are unaware that they are playing. You cannot hide in a deer blind or the African bush and shoot your prey and call it a sport. Lions stalk and ambush their prey, but at some point, the prey knows they are being hunted. The lion doesn't hide in the bush, shoot a claw at the prey, and exclaim, "Bang! You're dead." To call it a sport, one must come out of the bush and fight their prey with a spear—that would at least be fair.[10]

The sport hunting aficionado known as the "trophy hunter" is a striking example of arrogance and elitism, all twisted into one low AUQ mindset. The killer of big game for a set of horns or tusks, a skin, or a taxidermy body[11] is in a self-indulgent class.

The same machination of the psyche that drives serial killers to keep mementos from the encounter with their victims motivates the trophy hunter. In the first case, the illegal souvenir is to be hidden, and in the second case, the legal souvenir is to be displayed. Both canonize death by a collector. That may be an outlandish notion to some, but when viewed from the psyche need of both, the source is identical. Unfortunately, in both cases the event results in the senseless death of innocent life. The lure, in this case, is the hunter's interest in killing *only* endangered species. That they are contributing to the extinction of a species does not enter their psyche; it only enhances the value of their trophy. Nonhuman life, such as elephants, lions, rhinos, leopards, and the cape buffalo, are all on the list of the nearing extinction. They have become commodified, part of a new consumerism, marketed and sold. Their very existence is now a question of human demand, whim, and calculation. Wild game is the African continent's version of crude oil, and it too will run out someday[12] if we do not take measures to stop the killing. Canada, Mexico, New Zealand, and Argentina also allow *controlled* and *restricted* trophy hunts and the import and export of parts of the kill.

A trophy hunt can cost from $15,000-$100,000 and, considering all the other recreational options available to those with the discretionary disposable income to afford one, its choice is heinous and unjustifiable. Today's technology has taken a quantum leap forward, with drones, video of the hunt, and high-powered rifles equipped with laser range finders.[13] This makes the hunted easy prey and more of a sure thing—murder, not sport. Collectively, the trophy toll of American hunters alone is over 1.2 million nonhumans killed during the past fifteen EY; that represents 220 destroyed every day.

The head and skin of a lion, prepared for display by a taxidermy shop in South Africa, are boxed for shipment to those who killed the animal in 2010. In response to dwindling numbers of lions in the wild and doubts about the conservation of hunting them, the US has since made it harder for hunters to import lion trophies.[14]
David Chancellor, *National Geographic.*

These facts are worth a thousand words: fact 1, most American voters are against trophy hunting 5:1,[15], and fact 2, the US imports more "trophies" than any other nation on Earth. This is a constitutional democratic republic, so how can that be? The reason is simply that these issues are not on the ballot, and public opinion does not translate into action unless activism and political pressure accompany them. The circumstance is such that those who benefit from seeing that trophy hunting continues to put their money where their mouths are and wield all the organizational will and power. The NRA, Sportsman's Alliance, and Safari Club International are merely a sample of the groups represented and supported by weapons owners and manufacturers. These groups promote their interests to the state and federal legislators and the wildlife agencies, through well-paid lobbyists.

The International Union for Conservation of Nature, which monitors nonhuman populations, reports that the number of lions in five populations in Tanzania fell by two-thirds from 1993 to 2014.[16] Many more species are in the same decline. The public is always feeding on a consistent misinformation barrage, as the populations of our endangered species have continued downward. The public hears only that all the tax revenues from the sale of hunting material, licensing charges, and fees that accrue to the conservation and wildlife management agencies and governments are used to promote the preservation of nonhumans and their habitats all over the world. The worldwide sport hunting contingent, and specifically the US Fish and Wildlife Service, have long heralded the notion that conservation and wildlife management is a *user-pay, user benefit* system.

These assertions are far from reality in that the American taxpayer, including the firearm-owning, *non*hunting segment of the public, has increasingly been providing enormous and mandatory subsidies to the hunting industry for decades.[17] The pro-hunting community never fully acknowledges the vast number of nonhunting, firearm-owners who value living nonhumans and would never support recreational killing if given a voice or choice. "The Growth of Sport Shooting Participation," an article in *The Wildlife Society*, put out in March/ April 2017, states that the conservation community acknowledges the "downward trend in the national hunting rate." According to the authors, "sport shooters who do not now hunt make up an increasingly important segment" of the shooting population. Many of these may also believe that truly conserving wildlife is incompatible with killing or growing wildlife populations for satisfying hunter demands. It is time to recognize that the hunting industry's assertions that hunters pay for everything is an absolute falsehood. Most of the public and sport shooters are not hunters, nor users of wildlife resources, and they deserve a voice in how we manage wildlife—one that is proportionate to their majority status.[18, 19]

Setting aside publicly owned lands for wildlife habitation and taxing weapons and ammunition sold to defensive nonhunters contributes overwhelmingly to nonhuman protection. This is being done without a single nonhuman being eliminated. When one puts the value of federal land programs into the mix of wildlife conservation today, the killer hunters' contributions diminish to a mere 6 percent of funding nationwide.[20]

"ENTERTAINMENT"

Dogfighting: The dogfight has been a worldwide diversion for at least 200 EY, though it is no longer legal in most of today's world. A common denominator within the continuing plague of any fights and abuses involving nonhumans is that money trumps rights. The exploitation of dogs began a few decades before the Civil War with the import of the bull terrier from England and got a foothold in US culture in, of all organizations, the United Kennel Club. Most states made it illegal by the 1860s, yet it thrived as a pastime for seventy-five more EY, until the Kennel Club rescinded its endorsement and the 1930s and 1940s, which drove it underground.

It took another seventy-five EY to make it a felony in all states and territories as late as 2008. This type of bloodlust continues in America because of the chronic apathy and denial of the legal system[21] and, sadly notable, by the demand for it even as of this writing.

Wayne Pacelle, president of the Humane Society of the United States, estimated that the industry involves at least 40,000 people (about twice the seating capacity of Madison Square Garden) domestically,[22] forming a secretive network of trainers, breeders, and owners who have avoided scrutiny from lax law enforcement.[23] Pacelle calls today's dogfighting the modern-day equivalent of the ancient Roman Colosseum battles.[24] It is both depressing and sobering to know that the barbaric remnants of that time exist even now, a few thousand EY later.

In the brutal and secretive world of professional dogfighting, operators place starving pit bulls in a ring, accompanied by the goading and cheering of their owners and the crowd, and they watch as the dogs tear at each other's faces and throats.[25] It is still legal in Japan, Russia, and Afghanistan, and legal or not, it remains popular as fights are still held openly in parts of Latin America, Pakistan, Eastern Europe, and clandestinely in the United Kingdom.[26]

By replacing canines with roosters, then breeding and conditioning them for increased strength and stamina, and placing them in a pit to destroy one another, the cockfight is born. It seemed logical to some, since roosters possess congenital aggression toward all males of their species, to let them rip each other apart for our viewing pleasure. To heighten the "excitement" of this blood sport, strapping razor blades to the rooster's legs seems to have worked out well for business.

Cockfighting is now illegal in all fifty US states and the District of Columbia, with Louisiana the last to outlaw this cruelty in August 2008. One can still find the cockfight as it continues to thrive underground in Texas, Nevada, Oklahoma, Louisiana, Hawaii, New Jersey, New Mexico, and others. As regards the rest of the planet, where it is legal in the Philippines, Dominican Republic, Puerto Rico, Mexico, and Thailand, this blood sport is part of their culture and attracts large populations of followers. Puerto Rico has cockfighting stadiums and televised fights in the Philippines arenas that reach 20,000 seat capacities.[27] The World Slasher Cup is the Super Bowl of cockfighting, a five-day series of 648 matches held in a stadium in downtown Quezon City in metropolitan Manila. Outside the sleek chrome entrance, a thirty-foot-high inflated rooster sways in the tropical breeze, next to a poster featuring two cocks in combat.[28]

Killing bulls by matadors is still with us, and each year approximately 250,000 bulls suffer and die in bullfights. Under the guise of "entertainment," the bull is stabbed multiple times before suffering slow, agonizing deaths in front of an audience, including children. There are too many countries throughout the world where this practice is still sacred, including Spain, France, Portugal, Mexico, Colombia, Venezuela, Peru, and Ecuador. Bullfighting is a cultural event in which the crowd identifies with and lives vicariously, in the safety of the arena stands, through the machismo of the bullfighter, at the expense of the torture and destruction of the bull. There are laws in many US states and nations making these types of planned destruction and cruelty illegal, and thankfully it is difficult to take it underground. It is both a national pastime in the countries noted, and a sad commentary that it is still alive and well as of this writing.

Most people have never been to a rodeo in person, but they have witnessed one on television at a distance. Unless otherwise informed, one grows up thinking a rodeo is a competitive event displaying a cowboy's skills, for the chance to secure recognition and monetary prizes. It is an action-packed high paced "show" which has bred a modicum of the Wild West culture of America into the hearts and mindbrains of generations past and present. Underlying the visuals and excitement evoked by the presentation of the event are the hidden facts that are lost on generations. Larson has been a farmer, a bareback rodeo bronc rider, a state veterinarian, a large animal veterinarian, a medical researcher, a meat inspector, and a prosecutor. She was featured on the *Hard Copy* 1996 investigative report on abuses and public lies by the Professional Rodeo Cowboys Association (PRCA) in which she remarked, "There is no way that one can create a humane rodeo, and as a veterinarian, having participated in rodeo and having cared for rodeo animals, rodeo is an organized and systematic abuse of animals that has been marketed as family entertainment." She further states, "Animal abuse is one side of the issue; the other side is that some people enjoy watching other sentient creatures in pain and fear. Events like the rodeo produce and perpetuate cruelty in daily life."

We expose children to the sanctioned abuse present in a rodeo with the spurs, cattle prods, and the ropes all used by riders in pursuing prizes. This abuse can become acceptable to these nascent mindbrains, especially since the authorities sanction these events.

Make no mistake, nonhumans are tormented, abused, injured, and killed in rodeos.[29] Calves, steers, and horses suffer the crippling effects of broken necks, ribs, backs, and legs, and if they manage to survive, they continue the circuit until they no longer can, and then it is on to the slaughterhouse. As of this writing, few laws protect nonhumans forced to perform in rodeos, as the Federal Animal Welfare Act exempts rodeos from the protections it may otherwise provide to them. The Animal Legal Defense Fund fights in the courts for better protection, to little or no avail.

FOR SCIENCE'S SAKE

Using over 100 million nonhumans for experimentation is customary practice. These procedures range from lessons in biology, medical training, and curiosity-driven experimentation, to testing in the chemical, cosmetic, drug, and food industries.

The usual suspects such as mice, rats, frogs, hamsters, guinea pigs, rabbits, and monkeys are subject to torturous treatment and end up dead. Also included in the mix are fish, birds, dogs, and cats. We will eventually find a way through technology to duplicate this testing using modeling, super quantum computer simulations, and the use of AI programming. That would be a step toward our realization, and that day cannot come soon enough.

FOR TASTE'S SAKE

"You have just dined, and however scrupulously the slaughterhouse is concealed in the graceful distance of miles, there is complicity."
—Ralph Waldo Emerson

"At present, in most of the world, it is accepted that if animals are to be killed for food, they should be killed without suffering."
—Peter Singer

"Evidence seems to be building that the shoe's on the other foot now; that those who want to kill animals and eat them ought to justify their view. It shouldn't be the other way round."
—Gary Comstock

The killing of nonhumans for food began with the hunter-gatherer societies which hunted nonhumans for sustenance alone, beginning 1.8 million EY ago. Recent evidence shows this went on until 10,000 EY ago in Mesopotamia when large-scale farming began.

However, the Native American Plains Indian, as late as the nineteenth century, hunted buffalo for the provision of food, shelter, tools, and spiritual guidance, from a population estimated to be 60 million—close to extinction, on the Great Plains.[29.1] We kill a worldwide total of 56 billion farmed nonhumans each year for food, not inclusive of fish, which are measured in tons.

Producers, noticing the demand for plant-based products versus meat-based, have innovated and are making meatless "burgers" and "sausage" from genetically modified soy, potato protein, pea protein, and beets. The texture and taste are almost identical to those containing meat, so perhaps this will eventually stop the slaughter of millions of livestock.[29.2] There will not be a problem with an overpopulation of cattle, as there will no longer be an incentive to grow the herd.

DEATH FOR DOLLAR$

Demand is to business as a vacuum is to Nature; there will be an entity to fill it. That is the basis of economics. As we have become more "civilized," it has been a slow slog toward the elimination of the trade-in free human labor, illegal drugs, or sex slaves. It only makes sense that it has been a much slower slog when it involves and their legal protection. The greatest depletion and extinction results from the elimination of habitats lost to agriculture, logging, mining, commercial fishing, and urban growth.[30] The actions we have taken in the name of growth and progress, at the expense of nonhumans, leads one to recall an earlier time when, under the guise of Manifest Destiny in the early to mid-nineteenth century, America treated Mexico and the Native American Indian with the same mindset.

Whalers have been in business since the 1600s, as nations competed with one another for the *catch*. Fast forward to the period from 1900-2000, when the killing of 3 million whales[31], thirty-one or eighty per day, respectively, for 100 EY, steadily increased as the method of capture went from men in rowboats to men on industrial processing ships. Blubber produced oil, the meat was eaten, the bones were made into many products, and all produced revenue. In 1986, the International Whaling Commission (IWC) banned commercial whaling and trade in whale products because of the extreme depletion of the worldwide whale stocks, and its status as an endangered species.

Despite the ban, the killing of 40,000 whales has occurred since then by the several countries named here that continue to excuse themselves from the wisdom and humanity of the enacted law. Japan and Norway have recently raised their annual quota by 28 percent to 1,278 whales,[32] and the Soviets and Iceland currently kill over 1,500 whales collectively, per annum. This is after the entire world has studied the whale, agreed that whaling is cruel, unnecessary, must stop completely, and that it is a destructive and inexcusable way to behave.

It is still the misfortune of 300,000 dolphins, porpoises, and smaller whales per annum to be the bycatch of tuna fishers around the world with the use of sophisticated and advanced netting methods. Even in captivity, dolphins live shorter lives than they do in the sea. This is most significant because keeping them in an environment that is free of predators, pollution, and other threats that they face in the wild still shortens rather than lengthens their lives. And because they are highly intelligent and social, they are virtually in prison when in captivity, taken away from their social systems and natural roaming habitats.

Fur trapping and trading began in Russia and Siberia long before the discovery and colonization of North America, and whaling was an essential form of commerce as well. It began in North America in the 1500s with Native Americans bartering pelts for weapons, tools, etc. with the French, Dutch, and British in precolonial times, up until the 1850s. The fur trade played a significant role in the pre-industrialization period of the United States and Canada for over 300 EY, and that is why it proliferated. After that period, the Canadians began breeding.

We cannot tolerate the trading in the misery of small fur-bearing nonhumans as they continue to suffer incredibly at our human hands. Yet each year, worldwide, we raise on fur farms or trap in the wild over 1 billion rabbits and 50 million other nonhumans, including foxes, seals, mink, chinchilla, beaver, raccoon, dogs, etc. We kill them purely for fashion. Today it is one or the other—the *deplorable inhumane farm* or the *torturous inhumane trap*, and both mean misery, torment, and premature death at human hands. The traps crush them in a vice-like grip as the trap's jaws slam shut onto a limb or paw, cutting them to the bone as they struggle in pain to get free. If it does not kill them, the ones who survive the trap—and the predation in agony—struggle for hours or even days, some even attempting to chew off their limbs to escape the horror before the trapper returns to kill them. Back on the farm, it is no better.

After being cooped up and immobilized in crowded cages their entire lives, the methods used to kill them for their fur include gassing, electrocution, and neck breaking. The industry's bottom line is, if it is living, it is worthless, but if it is dead, it is priceless.

Since 2000, sales worldwide have soared to record highs fueled by technology and a sharp rise in disposable income in China and Russia. This growing demand has led to the development of extensive fur farming operations in China and Poland. Buyers of fur are unaware or do not care that it requires many nonhumans to make a single garment. The cost in innocent lives is one hundred chinchillas or up to sixty minks to make one full-length fur coat and, depending on the type, up to twenty-four foxes. Mandatory labeling laws showing how many go into producing each garment will emphasize the cruelty; the buyer should know these facts and be dissuaded from future purchases.

Signs are pointing in the right direction, in that there are fur farming bans in Germany,[33] Austria, [34, 35] Croatia,[36, 37] the United Kingdom,[38] the Czech Republic (effective in 2019), and ten other countries to date. The state of California is the first state to prohibit, by law, fur trapping, sales of crocodile and alligator skin, and the sale and manufacture of fur products, effective January 2023. Several major California cities have already banned fur sales and so has Sao Paulo, Brazil,[39] and over sixty countries have bans on certain types of traps.

Seal destruction is the clubbing, shooting, or impaling of two-
to three-week-old baby seals on sealing vessels. The photographs
or videos, that are publicly on display, of this monstrous practice
are much too incredibly dehumanizing to look at. Canada and
Greenland take the most baby seals, followed by Scandinavia, Alaska,
and Russia. Since 2002, the records show that in Canada alone the
slaughter of 2 million seals has taken place, making it the site of one
of the largest exterminations of marine mammals on Earth. "Europe's
citizens have made it quite clear they do not wish to buy fur and
other products from hideously cruel seal slaughters," Joanna Swabe,
the European director of the Humane Society International has said.
A ban by thirty-five countries, including the US, Russia, and Taiwan,
on the products that result from these killings is a step toward our
realization.

In the normal course of the evolution of the genus Homo, it is not
difficult to understand the inevitability of having engaged in all these
activities. Our evolution as a genus is analogous to the growth of a
child to adulthood, and we cannot expect a child to grasp the value
of all life until the adult population educating them has first grasped
that value themselves. When we view the past 400 EY, or about a
second of CT, it is understandable that our food, clothing, shelter,
and commerce at one time comprised the necessity to capitalize on
the availability and vulnerability of nonhumans for our very survival.
That is no longer the case.

Only when the wanton and inexcusable abuse ceases will we
eliminate another obstacle toward our realization. Do you believe it
is long past the time when all the people of this world who wish to
preserve the lives of Nature organize themselves and their economic
power to end the cruelty, torture, and destruction of what we should
ennoble and preserve? Is the human drive for the almighty coin going
to continue until it overtakes whatever progress we have made to
date to preserve the gift of Nature—both human and nonhuman?
This has prompted Peter Singer, acclaimed as the father of the animal
rights movement, to write, "In short, the outcome so far indicates

as a species we are capable of altruistic behavior for other beings; but imperfect information, powerful interests, and a desire not to know disturbing facts have limited the gains made by the animal movement."[39.1]

"We conceive of the individual creature as a small world, existing for its own sake, by its own means. Every creature is its own reason to be. All its parts have a direct effect on one another, a relationship to one another, thereby constantly renewing the circle of life; thus we are justified in considering every creature physiologically perfect."
    —Goethe

"All animals, including humans, have a right to lives of dignity and respect, without forced intrusions."
    —Marc Bekoff

"The realization of the genus Homo, can only be accomplished when accompanied by a mindset accommodating all life."
    —Symmetrias

"Science has shown that animals are very much like us; making that acknowledgment is the first step toward a kinder treatment of animals."
    —Caen Elegans

WHAT CHANCE DO NONHUMANS have to survive the genus Homo, considering our treatment of them to date? If we humans steadfastly continue to destroy one another, how may we engender an empathetic feeling in ourselves for the ant to the zebra?

Speciesism is the assignment of different values, rights, or special considerations to any living beings solely based on their inclusion in a particular species. Nonhuman rights advocates argue it is a prejudice like racism or sexism. They claim that the basis for the maltreatment is because nonhumans possess irrelevant physical differences that have no moral significance.[40] Is it not the height of arrogance, ignorance, or gross unawareness to believe that, of all of Nature's creations to date, it is we who have *carte blanche* to destroy whatever and whenever we care to? Could it be possible that the best use of our species on this planet is to grow our AUQ to the point of recognition that we are simply another living species amongst the many who all have different purposes, abilities, sensibilities, and possibilities? It is apparent by deduction that once Nature has provided life to a species, it has built into that species a *need* and *desire* and the ability to live.

If we are to survive as a genus in the future, we will have to cease killing one another and nonhumans as well. A belief in the power and control over a life other than its own, rather than regard for its growth and well-being, is a straight path to devolution. If ever there is a species of our or any future genus which views nonhumans with no commercial interest or food source in mind, it will be definitive proof of a higher AUQ. We, as the genus Homo, have cared for our dear pets like family, for millennia; it is time to expand the family.

OUR CONNECTION TO NONHUMANS

". . . then animals, our fellow brethren in pain, diseases, death, suffering and famine—our slaves in the most laborious works, our companions in our amusements—they may partake our origin in one common ancestor—we may be all netted together."
—Charles Darwin

In the everyday jargon of the layperson, evolution may mean progress or improvement; however, in biological terms, it is merely *adaptive change across generations; horizontal, not vertical.* Nature does not recognize higher or lower, only that all living things must be adaptive to survive and to reproduce.[41] It has been our convenient disregard for this "natural" fact that has precipitated most of the devolutionary actions and consequences described throughout this writing.

In his 1871 publication, *The Descent of Man, and Selection in Relation to Sex*, Charles Darwin asserts that we inherit both human character traits and mental characteristics the same way we inherit physical characteristics. He then argues against any mind-brain-body distinction concerning evolutionary theory.

He then provides evidence for similar mental powers and

characteristics in certain nonhumans, focusing especially on apes, monkeys, and canines. The ongoing harvesting of scientific data confirms the likeness in the genomes of nonhumans and humans. This not only supports the insight and acumen of Darwin; it cannot help but unveil the mental and physical similarities that may underpin all life. Concerning the mental function of nonhumans vis-à-vis humans, Darwin, using the limited science and technology of the mid-nineteenth century stated, "The difference in mind between man and the higher animals, great as it is, certainly is one of degree and not of kind." This was a fearless statement for a man of his time, and one which is proven both definitively and scientifically. Darwin opened the hereditary door with his original and insightful thinking, and the science of genetic experimentation and discovery took humankind through it. His insights into the descent of man were genius.

To be more specific, we share the following percentage of genes with the following:

NAME OF NONHUMAN/PERCENTAGE OF SHARED DNA WITH HOMO SAPIENS

BONOBO, CHIMPANZEE/.987
CAT, TIGER/.90
MICE/.90
LION/.85
DOG/.84
COW/.80
CHICKEN/.65

The terms we used to describe the taking of human life because of the action of another human, outside of war, justice, or accident, are murder and manslaughter. The laws punishing such action are written by human beings who understand what it is to be deprived of one's life. A major problem for nonhumans is that they do not yet write laws, nor may they ever.

For them to receive the same benefits of the law that protects humans, human beings must legislate to preserve nonhuman lives by becoming more mindful of them, despite any subsequent economic loss. As described in the earlier sections of this part, despite the legislative efforts to preserve nonhumans to date, we are far from there.

NONHUMAN LIFE HAS VARYING DEGREES OF CONSCIOUSNESS AND EMOTIONS

"Even insects express anger, terror, jealousy, and love, by their stridulation."
—Charles Darwin, *The Expression of the Emotions in Man and Animal,* 1872

"You shouldn't even have an expectation that because some animals are closely related to humans, that they're going to be more intelligent than others."
—Culum Brown

"There are certain things some animals specialize in for which their minds are uniquely adapted. In some ways you could say they are 'smarter' or more functional than us at performing these tasks."
—A. Josef

We may never fully understand the molecular and chemical complexities that lead to the well-being and behavior of our species, let alone those of nonhumans, but that is not the problem. The problems arise if we do not spend the resources and energy needed to progress along both paths, through spacetime, until we do. Forging ahead to understand ourselves does not prevent us from studying nonhumans to understand them, and our connection more robustly with them. The study of all life is one of our privileges and duties if we are to understand how to proceed on this planet rationally and successfully. We will require the sensibility and sensitivity to succeed in our attempts to understand all life on both the micro and macro levels. One of the major benefits of understanding the consciousness and emotions of nonhumans is the awareness we will gain in our own nature.

Most children learn antisocial behavior from those around

them, and the best way to prevent it is by teaching by example. Here, parenting is the key. Prosocial behavior by parents and other role models, such as removing ants and insects from the home humanely, feeding birds, and treating pets as members of the family, has the potential to make a positive lasting impression on children.[42] Aside from the unique capabilities of nonhumans, discussed in the following sections, the increased study of their mental, emotional, and pain functions is a righteous path to follow toward our enhanced understanding of their beings. Research dealing with the tiniest to the largest of nonhumans shows that we are using our energy and resources to increase our knowledge of them, and that is a most positive enterprise. Rather than presenting the abstruse details of experimental and investigative studies to date, using modern imaging techniques and technologies, a presentation of the results follow.

Amongst nonhumans, the research shows that complex mindbrains and high intelligence have developed. The notable and incomplete list includes insects such as termites, flies, beetles, ants, and bees; birds such as parrots, ravens, crows; cetaceans, elephants, and primates. The driving forces for high intelligence may vary amongst distinct species according to their need for spatial learning, foraging, social learning, and instrumental learning.[42.1]

It was not until July 7, 2012, that distinguished scientists in their relevant fields of expertise gathered in Cambridge University at the Cambridge Declaration on Consciousness. They thereupon signed a document that states, "The absence of a neocortex does not appear to prevent an organism from experiencing affective states. Convergent evidence shows that nonhumans have the neuroanatomical, neurochemical, and neurophysiological substrates of conscious states along with the capacity to exhibit intentional behaviors." They also agreed that consciousness did not have a firm and definitive boundary, but more of a moving range. Consider the substantiation of Darwin's determinations concerning nonhumans, even amongst the smallest of creatures (albeit, there's a 140-year delay here). Indeed, scientists say we should broaden our conception of the word *conscious* to include the awareness, feeling, thinking, and self-awareness of nonhumans. We should also be careful not to anthropomorphize them when attributing specific traits to the growing number of species studied.

Scientific studies have provided an abundance of evidence establishing the fact that marine and land mammals, birds, and fish possess varying degrees of consciousness, self-awareness, empathy, innovative tool use, cooperation, mourning behavior, etc. heretofore unbeknown to us. We learn that they have a range of mindbrain and emotion once thought to be our exclusive province and that we have had many misconceptions concerning them throughout our long history together. Many have complex thoughts; they are capable of some things that may awaken in us a true understanding of their beings. We are learning it is not the size of a nonhuman mindbrain that is significant in presupposing their capabilities, but its weight compared to their total body weight; the other major factor is the development of the areas of their mindbrains, enabling memory, communication, problem-solving, planning, etc.

It is the determination of the research studies that nonhumans and humans are composed of similar systems and have the same kinds of sensations and emotions, inclusive of hunger and thirst, heat and cold, pain and pleasure, fear, stress, and anxiety—not at all surprising considering the similarities in our DNA composition. Nonhumans do not always feel or react in the same way we do, and that makes it challenging at present to decipher their precise experiences.[43] There is, however, little doubt that as we learn more through science, we discover that we have underestimated the depth of their internal lives and range of their abilities.

––––––––––

Our "kissin' cousins," the chimps and bonobos, and our other close relatives, the gorillas and orangutans, all have *nonhuman person* status. They have long been known to be amongst the most sentient, conscious, highly functional, and social of all nonhumans and I will not go into detail on these well studied species. In his book, *The Emotional Lives of Animals,: A Leading Scientist Explores Animal Joy, Sorrow, and Empathy—and Why They Matter*, Marc Bekoff's decades of animal research proves that the higher primate nonhumans exhibit wide ranging emotions. These include compassion, joy, empathy, happiness, grief, anger, resentment, and embarrassment.

He finds that many animals have extreme intelligence, and sensory-motor skills that are superior to ours. His work is supported by his psychological, behavioral, and neurochemical studies and shows how they relate biologically across all mammals, as evolution has increased the complexity of emotions, and thereby social interactions, to aid in our survival.[44]

THE ONTOLOGY OF STUDIED SPECIES

As a preface to this subsection of text, a key element is the current research into the *independent evolution* of the mindbrains of many varied species. Prior to the advances in the studies being made today, scientific researchers had been looking for a highly developing cortex as a sign of higher cognition in nonhumans. Current findings indicate that complex brains and high intelligence have evolved independently in some insects, vertebrates, birds, cetaceans, elephants and primates.[44.1] One might say we had been looking for "higher cognitive faculties in all the wrong places.

Entomologists who study bees in their hives, ants in their colonies, spiders in their webs, etc., have long recognized those species' purposeful, complex, and life-sustaining behavior. Lesser known are the findings which verify that the smallest nonhuman's mental, emotional, and pain functions go through different neurological pathways than ours.[45] There have been studies whereby researchers provide food-deprived fruit flies with food access as they cast a shadow over them, simulating the approach of an overhead predator. The flies seemed to have entered a state of fear, anxiety, or whatever other interrupting emotions, and ignored the food for many minutes; considering the flies live for only thirty days, we may see this a sizeable length of time.[46, 47] The mapping of the neural circuitry that underlies the fear-like behavior in flies, anger-like behavior in bees, or empathic-like behavior in woodlice brings us closer to understanding insects' experiences of feelings with our own. The insect mindbrain is surprising even to entomology experts in its similarities with ours, and despite markedly different physicalities, the similarities in output may be more profound than we have ever thought possible.

———————————

A friend once mentioned a pet parrot that was driving him to heightened anxiety by calling his name out frenetically and incessantly. He said that he had to return the bird to the store from which he had purchased it, or he would fly out the window. I told him I thought parrots were highly conscious, and he said to me, "Haven't you ever heard of the term bird brain?" After that, I took it for granted that the term "bird brain," based upon the bird's small brain size, shows low intelligence. I fell into the lazy, close-minded trap of not doing my own research. It turns out that birds lack a cerebral cortex, which allowed scientists, for decades, to assume they were incapable of any higher thinking.

However, researchers now know that a part of the bird's mindbrain, the nidopallium, has developed to do many of the same tasks as our cerebral cortex.[48] How, with such small mindbrains compared with those of most mammals, including primates, is that at all workable? Presumably, because of the high density of their pallial neurons, they have a remarkably high informational processing capacity. Even though their nidopallium exhibits anatomy and architecture that differs from our neocortex, they achieve high intelligence because of a different neuronal architecture in their mindbrains.[49] Large parrots, ravens, crows, and jays have the same or greater number of neurons in their forebrains than do monkeys with much larger mindbrains. Avian mindbrains thus have the potential to provide much higher cognitive power per unit mass than do mammalian mindbrains.

A new study found that African Grey parrots were the equivalent of human three-year-olds on a test of mental acuity.[50] Parrots, crows, and ravens may well be amongst the most intelligent nonhumans on Earth, based on their ability to problem solve, make tools, and consider both possible future events and other individuals' states of mindbrain.[51] Parrots exhibit characteristics and tendencies consistent with that of a person's traits, such as intentionality, creativity, and symbolic communication. "Bird brains?" NOT!

In a different "family" than the parrots are the corvids, a family of birds that includes magpies, crows, ravens, and jays. Along with parrots, they are among the most intelligent groups of birds. Helmut Prior, PhD, a natural scientist, researcher, and educator at the Universities of Münster, Oxford, Düsseldorf, Bochum, and

Frankfurt, found the first evidence of *mirror self-recognition* in a nonmammalian species. When provided with a colored mark on their bodies, magpies showed spontaneous mark-directed behavior. His research suggests that the essential components of human self-recognition have evolved independently in diverse vertebrate classes with a separate evolutionary history.[51.1]

Haven't you ever looked at people with pet pigs as if they were a bit quirky? *Pig*—the word evokes an association with a filthy, grunting, dumb, *rolling around in the mud,* voracious nonhuman. This has led to the linkage in our lexicon to the terms pig, greedy, dirty, unpleasant, and gorger, among others. You get the picture. We should add this notion and *bird brain* to another of our historic misconceptions of what is real and what is not. The skinny on pigs is that they are amongst the smartest, cleanest domestic nonhumans known, more so than cats and dogs if some experts are to be believed.[52]

Filthy? Pigs love to wallow in the mud. But pigs have no sweat glands, and the mud not only cools them, but it also cakes their bodies for protection from the sun's UV rays while dislodging parasites they cannot reach with their short legs. Besides, pigs are fastidious and have dedicated areas where they eliminate waste, and it is never where they eat or sleep. The more we learn, the more we see pigs are sentient beings who experience joy, loneliness, frustration, fear, and pain, just like the nonhumans with whom many of us share our lives.[53] Pigs are currently considered the fifth-most intelligent nonhumans in the world and, in experiments performed as early as the 1990s, found to play video games with at least as much focus and success as chimps![54]

Cetacea is an order of marine mammals comprising the whales, dolphins, and porpoises who are very social and live in groups or pods. They descend from a four-footed semiaquatic mammal, which thrived about 50 million EY ago. The scientific research into whale and dolphin life proves they command a mindbrain function that rivals all higher primates, including ourselves and the elephant.[55] Both cetacea are capable of self-recognition, a precursor to self-awareness, which implies knowing themselves and the world around them.[56] This is highly unusual in nonhumans and rare in non-primates.[57] They both have human-like cultures and societies supported by sophisticated social and cooperative behavior traits. And concerning emotions, they grieve, mourn, show joy, and communicate proficiently with one another.

Robin W. Baird, a research biologist with Cascadia Research Collective, told *National Geographic* that a dolphin was trying to keep her dead calf up on the surface for a week by balancing it on her head and retrieving it when it fell below the surface. In other instances, a killer whale mother and her offspring may spend their whole lives together, and when one of them passes away, the survivor goes through a period when they're experiencing the same emotions we feel. Established belief is that the dolphin mindbrain is more structurally complicated than ours, and that, had they developed on land, they may have progressed in more ways than modern man has. The accumulation of evidence is leading governments to consider the whales and dolphins a placement in the category of *nonhuman persons*. This is a status reserved for nonhumans who possess reason, language, emotions, complex social structures, etc.

The large, lumbering, loveable pachyderm known as the elephant is worthy of acknowledgement as one of the most intelligent on the planet. Their mindbrain has a more complex number of patterns and folds than do higher primates, including human beings, and in tests with mirrors, when one places a mark on their skin, they can recognize themselves as they touch the mirror to groom themselves.[58]

Elephants are known to have complex visual/tactile, acoustic, and olfactory communication systems. As do we, elephants have large mindbrains, and are slow-growing, long-lived mammals having all the necessary attributes that favor the evolution of empathy. The elephant can detect and respond appropriately to the emotions of others and can recognize when a herd mate is upset, as they caringly offer gentle caresses and chirps of sympathy to them.[59] Empathetic behaviors among them are observed when they form coalitions to assist others in need of help or food, and to protect young or injured elephants. They will babysit calves when they separate from their mothers, retrieve a calves' natal family, and assist individuals who have fallen, require physical help, or become immobile.[60] Female elephants remain highly bonded to their close relatives for life, and caring for another relative's offspring is common and important for the survival of calves. They react to the dying and dead in a variety of ways, touching the bones or tusks with their trunks and feet, lifting and carrying the body or bones, body guarding, covering, and burying.

Elephants use and even manufacture simple tools using their prehensile trunk with its finger-like tip to execute movements like those performed by primates with their fingers and thumb. The sensorimotor specializations of their trunks are extensive, allowing the gross manipulations of logs and rocks and the delicate "handling" of small objects. They, amazingly, even help other species. We consider them *nonhuman persons*.

THE CONTINUING SLOG TO PROTECT NONHUMANS

"The deeper minds of all ages have had pity for animals."
—Friedrich Nietzsche

"Now that scientists have belatedly declared that mammals, birds and many other animal species are conscious, it is time for society to act."
—Marc Bekoff

Nonhuman rights is the concept that states, "some or all *nonhuman animals* are deserving of the possession of their own lives and that their most basic interests, such as the need to avoid suffering, should have the same consideration as similar interests of human beings."[61, 62] The concept that nonhumans have as much of a right to life as we do is not new, but it is not a universally ingrained one. *Ahimsa* is the respect for all living things and the avoidance of violence toward others. Hinduism, Jainism, and Buddhism have taught it for thousands of EY. Many adherents of these religions have learned to forego meat-eating and sacrifice, and take great precautions to avoid injuring all nonhumans.

While Judaism, Christianity, and Islam are less comprehensive in their concern for nonhumans, they include some provisions for humane treatment in their teachings.[63] In fact, many ancient Greek and Roman philosophers advocated for vegetarianism and kindness toward nonhumans several thousand EY ago.[64] Considering the dearth of scientific knowledge and lawlessness present several thousand EY ago, it took a very impressive mindset to guide any philosophy to value all life.

This was before the rise of the *almighty dollar*. People did not bear the burden of the ever progressing mechanized, industrial, and commercial world of the past three centuries. The lack of early education for nonhuman inclusion and the powerful magnet of business interests have always subdued the advocates for nonhuman welfare. The continuing efforts of legislators and organizations worldwide, such as World Animal Protection, Institute for Ethics and Emerging Technologies (IEET), The Humane Society, People for the Ethical Treatment of Animals (PETA), the ASPCA, must continue. Work like theirs has driven Ringling Bros. and Barnum & Bailey Circus to remove elephants from performances and thereafter disband. SeaWorld stopped the breeding of orcas because of these agencies' continual pressure. Besides the wildlife organizations, it is the public's growing awareness and increasing rejection of harming nonhumans for human entertainment that has brought about these changes.

More recently, artificial intelligence has offered a most significant way to improve the welfare of, in this case, the elephant. Paul Allen, a co-founder of Microsoft, funded a 2015 census which found that poachers killed almost a third of the African elephant population between 2007 and 2014. Allen wanted a high-tech solution to these wanton killings, and he founded a company to create a program called Earth Ranger using AI. The data input into the programmed computer contained all the information that park managers knew from EY of experience, and the paperwork park rangers fill out, to find the patterns and to learn the rhythms of the elephants in the park. In the past two EY, poaching in Liwonde National Park, Malawi, has plummeted and hasn't lost a single high-value animal in three EY.[65]

The following is a report card of sorts regarding concern that various countries of the world currently exhibit toward the suffering of consumed nonhumans.

The rankings from worst to best consider a composite of the following factors:

1. The *producing cruelty* category ranks countries based on the number of farms that have slaughtered nonhumans for food each year, on a per capita basis, considering the fact that nonhumans receive different care and treatment in each country.

2. The *consuming cruelty* category ranks countries based on their consumption of nonhumans by looking at the ratio of plant-based protein to farm protein consumed in each country on a per capita basis.

3. The *sanctioning cruelty* category ranks countries based on their societal and cultural attitudes toward nonhumans, as reflected in the quality of the regulatory frameworks that are in place to protect them. Unfortunately, the use, misuse, and exploitation of farms continues to be rationalized by cultural and social norms.

VOICELESS NONHUMANS
CRUELTY INDEX, <u>WORST</u> TO BEST:

50th	Belarus	23	France/Denmark/Poland
49	United States	22	Egypt
48	Venezuela	21	China/United Kingdom
46	Russia/Iran	19	Algeria
45	Canada	18	Vietnam
44	Australia	17	Pakistan
43	Brazil	16	Chile
41	Myanmar/Malaysia	15	Japan
40	Argentina	14	Romania
39	Netherlands	13	Italy
37	Ukraine/Morocco	12	Sweden
36	Azerbaijan	9	Indonesia/Ethiopia/Niger
34	Thailand/Spain	8	Austria
33	Turkey	7	Germany
31	South Africa/Uruguay	5	Nigeria/Switzerland
30	New Zealand	4	Philippines
29	Peru	3	Tanzania
27	South Korea/Colombia	2	India
26	Mexico	1	Kenya

World Animal Protection delivered its own comprehensive assessment of fifty countries around the world according to their commitments to protect nonhumans and improve welfare in policy and legislation.

They designed the Animal Protection Index in collaboration with various protection NGOs, academic experts, law firms, and the World Organization for Animal Health (OIE). They created a comprehensive assessment of fifty countries worldwide by utilizing several indicators to address the key issues relevant to improving global welfare. They assessed each country on fifteen unique indicators, then grouped into five general themes:

1. Recognizing nonhuman protection
2. Governance structures and systems
3. Welfare standards
4. Providing humane education
5. Promoting communication and awareness

The analysis is available online for further review under Animal Protection Index.

The general assumption amongst human beings is that there is this vast difference between the behavioral and emotional experience of humans and nonhumans. This is another of the misconceptions discussed throughout this text and has allowed us to presume dominance over them, rather than what should be our stewardship with relation to them. This lack of AUQ limits our energies to offer them the care and protection that we should afford them. Were it not for our systemic disregard, we would suddenly hold ourselves accountable for the host of injustices, past and present, the likes of which overshadow many in the history of human civilization.

Inflicting pain and suffering is easier if one considers the victim as inherently different, as this makes mistreatment easy. Science has shown that nonhumans are very much like us, and making that acknowledgment is the first step toward a kinder treatment of animals.[66] All of this has especially important implications, of course, because if we gradually bring nonhumans into the same moral and legal circle as ourselves, then we cannot exploit them as our slaves or of lesser value. We must stop the abuse of millions upon millions of nonhumans for the sake of science, education, food, clothing, and entertainment. We owe it to them to use what we know of them, on their behalf, and to factor compassion and empathy into their treatment.[67]

Jane Goodall and Marc Bekoff are the co-authors of the 2003 book titled *The Ten Trusts: What We Must Do to Care for The Animals We Love*. At the time of their book, they had a combined seventy-five years of dedicated service for which they became not only famed for being experts in their fields but also as tireless activists for the animals, both human and nonhuman, whom they cherish. The essence of the work outlines what our species needs to do with respect to animals—in order to secure a world at peace. Woven into their personal experiences with chimpanzees and other primates are their values and principles, "to respect all life, the need to educate our children with those principles, our need to be stewards of the animals and do them no harm, and a 'do unto others' mindset."[68]

URGENT: IMMEDIATE RESPONSE REQUESTED!!

All nonhuman and human life comprise an extremely brief span of spacetime in the vast cosmos, and it should therefore awaken one to the precious and frail nature of every living entity. Human beings are a species whose 14-billion-EY evolution has resulted in the capacity to understand, empathize, and mold and shape both our inner and outer environments. We also kill one another and nonhumans. Is our belief in the superiority of the human species a major part of what has led us to ravage and raid the Earth like parasites, and to downplay the value of nonhuman life?

Were we to educate and properly guide our children from childhood to adulthood, would it not follow that a greater sensitivity to the well-being of all life would grow? Will our realization depend upon how we come to respect and treat all of Nature's eloquent designs? Will our thinking suffuse enough understanding and respect for all life to enable the survival of all the biodiversity on this planet?

How we answer these questions will show our intent to either sustain or destroy the life forms that Nature has naturally selected, including ours. Is it not the same fount that feeds an elevating AUQ that feeds our sensibility toward nonhumans?

———

And as implausible as it may now seem, we—or a future higher AUQ species of our genus or another—may leave this planet Earth to the myriad nonhumans and move on. They were here long before us, and we could leave the Earth to what remains of them, with our blessings. As a gesture of our wise stewardship, respect, and understanding for their beings, we might consider the restoration of their natural habitats as a parting gesture of goodwill.

Crazy ideas? Whatever the outcome, if we cannot respect, effect harmony, and coexist with *all* life on this planet, however long it takes and by whatever means, we will deservedly devolve and disappear. Our extinction would seem to be the unfortunate, ultimately ironic, finale to Nature's *natural selection* of the species Homo sapiens, and all of the other species we bring with us, since it is *we* who will have consciously selected it.

PART XI
MISSION: INNER SPACE

"If the brain were so simple we could understand it, we would be so simple we couldn't."
—Lyall Watson

"We don't see things as they are; we see them as we are."
—Anonymous

"Awareness of an objective truth about anything, is a process that proceeds more often than not, from that which we thought we knew but never did, to the instant we wake up to the fact that we did not know that which we thought we knew, based upon the evidence of a scientific proof."
—Symmetrias

THE PURPOSE OF THIS CHAPTER is to introduce the reader to the research and findings that can lead to quantum sea change in our evolution.

We know precious little—not only of our being in a vast universe but the elemental processes that enable us to be highly productive—interactive beings in this universe. Until now, we have been looking all around us. Now is a propitious time to look within and determine exactly how and why we are who we are, and why we do what we do, both individually and collectively. This should lead to a detailed understanding of all life forms and may in time awaken us to an awareness of a *similarity of being* heretofore unknown. The resolution of this long-term research will be one of the most dominant contributing factors whether we realize, or devolve, our beings—and whether we forge this continually revealing new knowledge into a radical elevation in our social and self-awareness (*inter* and *intra*), parenting, education, and leadership acuity.

Ninety-five percent of the universe comprises unknown matter that neither astronomers nor particle physicists can detect or even comprehend! We refer to 25 percent of it as *dark matter,* which is inferred to keep galaxies intact, and refer to 70 percent as *dark energy,* inferred to be pushing the universe to expand and create more spacetime.[1] The remaining 5 percent of the universe is the matter which we can identify, but of unknown function. The most essential portion of the 5 percent of identified but unknown matter is the *inner space* of all conscious life. If we are ever to cohere life on Earth, it will be through the essential studies and lessons learned from research into the area of consciousness itself in all beings, beginning with our species. And as a pause for thought, when one thinks about what we have wrought on Earth with only a small fraction of what we know of our inner space, one can only imagine what we might accomplish as we go through spacetime with a more profound knowledge of it.

36

ROCKETS FOR THE JOURNEY

POWERFUL OPTICAL IMAGING technologies and data processors now dominate the modern neuroscience lab, much of which were not available until the end of the presidency of Bill Clinton in 2000.

Concerning the mindbrain, a sea change has taken place since the beginning of the twenty-first century. It has been the ability of research scientists across all fields, engineers, and information technologists to entwine their ideas in collaboration, to produce the pictures and analysis of the mindbrain as fully and intricately as ever. Combined with the power of modern computers specifically programmed to capture, categorize, and analyze terra-bytes of data,[2] we have developed an arsenal to address the intensity of the work.

To understand in exacting detail how approximately 500,000 miles of neurons operate in the mindbrain, a structural map that will take many EY to complete is being assembled, which will serve several purposes. One is to develop and record parts of the neurons and their synapses in between all neuronal circuits and the entire mindbrain three-dimensionally from all its regions, lobes, and centers, down to the bundled tracts that connect the parts.[3]

Another is to describe each mindbrain center by its function, with accuracy and detail never achievable before. The development of our knowledge of the mindbrain is just a whisper now, but the revelations that it will engender as we move forward are certainly within our purview today.

A major point to keep in mind is that many of the key technologies used in the mindbrain's study are being used on living, mindbrained species. Many studies are being conducted in vivo, which is why the progress accelerates measurably. In many human studies, researchers can communicate with all subjects for the entire duration of the process.

Electron microscopy, developed in the third decade of the twentieth century, offers mostly black and white imaging of both inorganic and nonliving biologic specimens. An electron microscope can view nanoparticles and atoms because it is about 500 times more powerful than a standard light microscope.

The major drawback, aside from being very costly and large, is that every electron microscope needs a vacuum to avoid the scattering of electrons by the particulate matter in the air. This alone prevents the imaging of any living matter; and so, it has little value for in vivo mindbrain research.

VARIETY IS A "SLICE" OF LIFE

The development of Standard Magnetic Resonance Imaging, or MRI, in 1977, noninvasively and without radiation imaged 2D slices of soft body tissue by making use of magnets and radio wave sensing of the protons in our bodies. Although it has been a workhorse in the detection of many medical disorders and abnormalities, we did not use it for the studies discussed here. Because of the major enhancements made to the standard MRI concerning the live study of the mindbrain, a few of the more significant ones are worth describing.

A functional MRI (fMRI, as we know it) was first developed in 1990 and has gone through modification and improvement since. It colorizes real-time pictures, showing the increased activity of neurons and specific mindbrain regions. Its detection of the increase in oxygen's magnetic properties makes this possible, as oxygenated blood courses through the body to those specific mindbrain areas in use.[4] We will discuss the significant applications for this technique later in this section.

A second innovative use of the MRI, called Diffusion Tensor Imaging (DTI), is its detection of the strength of the magnetic field caused by the motion of water molecules in the white matter of the mindbrain. The field is stronger toward signal carriers known as axonal fiber bundles, the interconnecting highways of our mindbrain, which are then mapped. To illustrate this, an example of this phenomenon is presented.

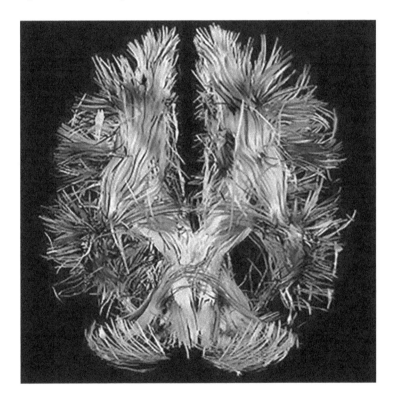

Diffusion tensor imaging (DTI), a variation of MRI, tracks the movement of water molecules along nerve cell connections revealing the brain's pathways. The image shows fiber tracts in the adult human brain. Tyszka, et al. *The Journal of Neuroscience*, 2011.

The final MRI modification described is the Optogenetic Functional MRI (ofMRI), introduced in 2005 by Stanford scientists. We know the method as *optogenetics*, which introduces light-sensitive nanoparticulate matter into the molecules of specifically targeted neurons, multiple types of neurons, or tissue, and uses light on the scalp to activate or deactivate them.[5] This is a noninvasive, live process and, according to Dr. M. Stryker of UCSF, "has completely changed everything." The mere shining of light now pinpoints the neurons or network's role in a particular behavior/reaction.

Before optogenetics, the grossly invasive insert of electrodes into mindbrain tissue might stimulate or turn off thousands of neurons without the researcher knowing the precise involvement of specific cells.[6] "Over the past decade hundreds of research groups have used optogenetics to learn how various networks of neurons contribute to behavior, perception, and cognition," wrote Ed Boyden, a co-inventor of optogenetics, in an article in the November/December 2014 issue of *Scientific American Mind*.

The ability to locate the precise connection of axon tracts and the functionality of their source and destination to mindbrain areas, monitor the direction of neuronal signals, and turn a specific neuron on or off while following the resultant signal through its circuit opens an entirely new paradigm in mindbrain research. Scientists have taught mice a task, tracked the neurons that "learned" the task, and then erased the memory by eliminating those specific neurons.

Considering the progress made to date, there is good reason to believe these methods, in combination, will establish how various mindbrain activities elicit feelings, thoughts, and movements, as well as how they malfunction.

TO SEE, OR NOT TO SEE? THAT IS THE QUESTION

The curious have been looking for larger and larger images of smaller and smaller targets since peering through ye old optical (light) microscopes 400 EY ago. The laws of physics prevent the differentiation of one target from another if that target is less than half the wavelength of the visible light used in optical microscopes, which is about 200 nanometers divided by 2 nanometers, or 100 nanometers. In effect, it would be like trying to distinguish two separate targets as you are covering them. That has been a paradigm of physical law just as the speed of light is.

Consider that when the goal is to learn everything about living biological structures that are below the resolution limit—such as synapses, synaptic vesicles, and neuronal organelles of the mindbrain, to name just a few—most sophisticated microscopy does not work. When the incredibly exacting science of the brain requires live, time-sensitive, aberration-free color 3D imaging, and the recording and analysis of terabytes of data, ongoing technological innovation is mandatory. As science delves with ever more alacrity into these subcellular, molecular-size structures and processes that involve the triad's interconnected and interrelated streams of electrochemical life, necessity has fostered invention.

To work your way around a paradigm in any science, it takes a cumulative knowledge of the field, innovative expertise, and a determination that is stoic. By meeting that challenge in microscopy, three scientists, beginning with E. Betzig's work in 2006, received the Nobel prize in chemistry in 2014. The contribution was for a technique known as *super-resolution fluorescence light sheet microscopy*, which allows the resolution of a live target as tiny as twenty nanometers in scale, bringing microscopy into the living nano dimension.

By the time he received the award, Betzig had stated that he had made an even more important innovation to the original system. Colleagues and he had devised a system, beginning in 2010, that would emit less fluorescence, therefore being less toxic, and offer more clarity to a live target. He called it super-resolution fluorescence *lattice* light sheet microscopy, primarily used in biological studies using gentle thin beams of light that penetrate points on a target plane by plane.[7] There have been continuing improvements to the system by researchers such as multi-award-winning Ed Boyden (expansion microscopy, optogenetics) and others from the University of California at Berkeley, the Howard Hughes Medical Institute, and Harvard Medical School.

Two of the more significant improvements to super-resolution fluorescence lattice light sheet microscopy have been a method of stretching and expanding mindbrain tissue for imaging and the usage of conforming mirrors guided by a computer that *adapts* to and eliminates even minuscule wavefront distortions. Their cumulative effect is the ability to produce live, rapid 3D color pictures and videos at the nanoscopic level of any portion of the human mindbrain, sizable areas of the mouse mindbrain, and the entire zebrafish and fruit fly mindbrains. This now takes days, whereas it would have taken many EY[8] with the methods used as recently as 2016.

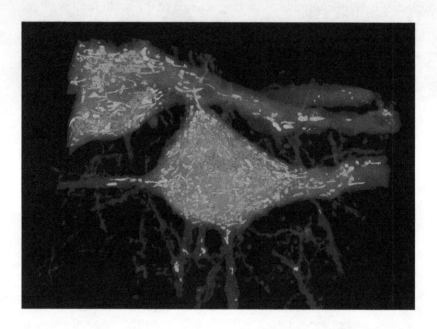

Scientists can identify organelles of various shapes and sizes (colored areas) inside mouse neurons imaged by a technique that merges expansion microscopy with lattice light-sheet microscopy. Credit: Gao.

THROUGH THE LOOKING GLASS

With the cumulative benefits of the work already done and the daunting amount of work yet to be accomplished, it will lure many bright young minds to the challenge. The goal of the coming research is to produce exacting live, real-time, color, aberration-free videos, of any sized biological/neurological processes which involve the human species. This will cause the consideration of the fourth dimension of time, along with the most resolution possible in space and time, anywhere within the organism itself, because it is only there that all the environmental factors that regulate its physiology are present.[10] With specific relevance to the theme of this book, Dr. Boyden envisions that enhancements to the current uses of super-resolution microscopy may lead to how mindbrain circuitry leads to memory, sensory input leads to a specific behavior, or how emotions interweave with decision-making.[11]

This segues very nicely into the continuing and advancing work being accomplished by researchers, discussed in the following section.

37

MINDBRAIN COMPUTER INTERFACE

"If you could read my mind, love, what a tale my thoughts could tell."
—Gordon Lightfoot

BRAIN-COMPUTER INTERFACE (BCI) technology is going to benefit humankind in a growing number of ways, some of which are unimaginable today. I will address BCI here only as it concerns the research into the mindbrain from the standpoint of enhancing our knowledge of how we think, that which we think, how we emote, and how we behave as we do.

(The medical area also uses BCI noninvasively, through EEG and EMG machines, to read mindbrain and muscle activity interpreted by various artificial intelligence computer applications.[12] This use of BCI enhances and enables a patient's mobility, cognition, and communication through their ability to control prosthetic devices and computers. For readers interested in furthering their knowledge of this aspect of BCI, see the references section.)

IDENTIFYING THOUGHT, EMOTION, AND INTENT

At Carnegie Mellon University, the functional MRI produces images of the scanned mindbrain of a subject while researchers ask them about a word or picture that is presented to them.

As a result, certain areas of their mindbrain show activity which is then immediately processed with specifically designed computer code; the specific words or pictures causing the mindbrain activity are unknown to the computer. Upon completion of the test, researchers make queries to the computer to associate each scan produced by the subject with a choice of one of two words/pictures, one of which caused that specific scan result. The accuracy of the computer's answers in correlating what word/picture caused the resulting mindbrain activity is perfect. Emotions such as hypocrisy, kindness, and love also show specific patterns in the mindbrain. Work to determine autism and suicidal tendencies is being successfully tested as well, with thought suggestive input and pictures, with high accuracy.

The same researchers could determine whether a person had been at a specific location at a prior time—by viewing their mindbrain patterns in reaction to visual presentations of different scenes.

Most significantly, the results of the testing done are consistent across the human spectrum, regardless of the subject's race, language, or ethnicity. Members of the species Homo sapiens exhibit similar mindbrain patterns, as deciphered by the fMRI computer, simply because we have the same equipment.

IDENTIFYING THE QUALITY AND EFFICIENCY OF THOUGHT

With the natural evolution of the human mindbrain, future innovations in BCI, MRI, quantum supercomputers, and AI, besides the ever-growing advances in microscopy, we may understand the differing qualities and efficiencies of human thought. Are there any molecular differences in a thought's quality or in their neurobiological source?

In describing qualities of thought, one category is dull, routine, habitual, or reflexive, and another group is insightful, reasoned, critical, imaginative, creative, or intuitive. Exactly what makes one mindbrain more efficient and more focused than another? Is it the glucose or oxygen available, the density of neurons or glial cells, neurotransmission and neurotransmitter factors, currently unknown genetic factors? What effect does the psyche (personality) of an individual have on the efficiency of their mindbrain?

These are the questions that we should attempt to answer so that we can understand the processes that define the content and operation of a human being's mindbrain. This will help inform us of why we have limited knowledge of self, the subtle effects of suppressed traumatic experiences, motivations that are not understood, and behaviors we cannot control. This should also give us a greater understanding of the nonhuman mindbrain, which will give us the awareness and understanding to treat them with greater humility. One might consider this understanding, if it may occur, another key step forward on the path away from devolution, toward realization.

PARTXII
MINDBRAIN THROUGH SPACETIME

"Life, that brief episodic spacetime experience betwixt the onset of your being, through to that of your non-being, is all you have and all you need to inform you to maximize your awareness and understanding of your experience in the Universe, and thereby reconcile you with your source, Nature."
—Symmetrias

"Future progress should be less the measure of that which we forge and optimize about us, and inarguably more the measure of that which we forge and optimize within us."
—Anonymous

WE KNOW, using the age of the universe and the Earth's fossil records, that primitive stimuli processing in certain species took 13.3 billion EY to first appear. That was approximately 500 million EY ago—because of Nature's ongoing propensity to weave energy into complex matter.

It began with a basic, direct, and overt antenna-like sensing of any stimuli of importance to a species' survival, such as the registering of light in the receptors of a primitive visual system or waves of sound through a nascent auditory mechanism. Those structures developed in complexity to enable the covert attention to stimuli, whereby a species did not have to attend directly to it but could know it through experience.

To select out and process ever greater amounts of information, to promote their survival and propagation, some species developed ever more complex structures, and with the evolution of reptiles around 350 to 300 million EY ago, a new structure emerged called the *hyperpallium*. Mammals inherited the hyperpallium from their reptilian ancestors about 200 million EY ago, now called the cerebral cortex, which has had an enormous evolution in growth since then.[1] These features developed into the mindbrain. Depending on the species, each is capable of awareness to varying degrees; many are the subjects of extensive and continuing research as described in parts 10 and 11. What is to become of the mindbrain as Earth precesses through spacetime?

DO SOMETHING; WE ARE LISTENING

In this vast unexplored universe, the conditions for mindbrained life may or may not be exceptional. As of now, science has no definitive answer. We are using radio telescopes to listen for electromagnetic transmissions from outer space and are assuming they originate from intelligent sources. We are still listening, but there are no signs as of this writing. It is possible that we are listening for the wrong signals, and there may be other forms of communication with which we are unfamiliar that extraterrestrials are transmitting through spacetime. Because of the sheer number of existing stars, solar systems, and galaxies, it is probable that there is extant life other than us.

Amongst the possibilities that exist, might we contact species that present forms of sentience we are unfamiliar with? Could it be that other species are familiar with dimensions we are not yet aware of and facets of the mindbrain or energies that might advance our scientific understanding? Are there other species who have already reached levels of mindbrain that have increased their AUQ and allowed their realization en masse?

These are intriguing questions, but unless we can locate and communicate with extraterrestrial life forms (or vice versa) that can help inform and awaken our species to raise our AUQ on Earth, they remain interesting and important unanswered questions that we may or may not have the luxury of spacetime to answer.

We must continue our exploration of the universe. It is most fortunate that we will, as curiosity is a natural attribute of a developed mindbrain.

PURPOSEFUL OR NOT?

Ever since Nature developed the ever-increasing complexity of mindbrain in many of its species, modern humans have had the native curiosity to enquire how all we know, and all that there is yet to know, could have developed.

One interpretation of evolution is that Nature may have intended there be an understanding of its skilled creativity by availing some of its species with highly conscious mindbrains. This would allow for awareness of environment, sensation, emotion, thought, memory, and self. Some species, such as cetacea, cephalopods, mammals, birds, and primates, possess these attributes. Our genus has also evolved the capability with which to exchange, record, execute ideas, and construct material forms.

Did Nature evolve our species with the complexities and qualities of mindbrain that would not only facilitate a continuing growth in the awareness and understanding of ourselves and all species—but of Nature itself?

There may be a *purposeful energy* at work in Nature that suffuses all it develops, given the precision of each of its prolific creations. Whatever energy Nature employs has grown from the divergent to the convergent and emerged as some extraordinarily complex entities. This could not be a mere coincidence, could it?

Or was it all by mere chance; could it be that Nature has no such purposeful energy at work at all? This universe, or multiverse, may very well be a phenomenon that is taking place within an infinite spacetime whereby anything and everything is possible, and all Earthly life is only one of the chance results—a huge *quantum* puzzle.

Whatever the case, our curiosity may someday yield an answer, the chance outcome of an infinite number of possibilities in an infinite spacetime, or the inevitable combination of both. I submit to you—the most relevant query to be answered presently is not if Nature is purposeful or not; it is whether we eventually realize it is up to each one of us to be aware and understand our place in the whole of Nature, which inevitably may lead to an enhanced AUQ and our realization.

AUQ VIS-à-VIS v. IQ

I have referred to AUQ in earlier sections as a measure of the level of *inter* plus *intra*. It represents a human being's in-depth awareness and understanding of all that exists other than the self.

The IQ is a measure, using standardized testing, of an individual's innate/inborn cognitive skills inclusive of problem-solving logic, and reasoning.[2] It does not automatically follow that a person with an above-average IQ may be more apt to have a higher AUQ as well, as that depends on where one directs their IQ. One could say the IQ is more a matter of how you think, whereas AUQ is more a matter of what you think. And, as the mindbrain develops and its effectiveness grows, we may augment intelligence in the future through genetics, pharmacology, mindbrain-computer linking,[3] and means yet to be developed.

The IQ may speed up the elevation of the AUQ with the following caveat: it will happen only at such spacetime as there is a confluence of IQ with an AUQ that has experienced several generations of an *inter/intra* educational curriculum, parental guidance, and proper leadership. part VIII, "Education," describes this.

The key to fostering a global AUQ will be the effectiveness of the efforts we make in introducing and increasing the AUQ through parenting, education, and leadership. However, the IQ, which is increasing through natural selection and may be augmented as described above, has led to a global IQ.

GLOBAL IQ

The evolutionary journey from the beginning of spacetime to the increase in the mindbrain's power of certain species, with the focus on Homo sapiens for this discussion, has brought us to a juncture whereby we can discuss the global reach of intelligence.

We include the following in the global IQ: the recorded cumulative amount of information available from recorded history to the present, the acceleration (frequency, speed) of that information, its ubiquitous distribution, and the ability of an individual to process that information. If one takes the preceding as the criteria for the intelligence of the human species, intelligence is already global. Human beings have inherited the accumulated knowledge that created our cultures, societies, sciences, and everything we have produced in recorded history. We live upon a readily accessible, continually innovating, technologically advancing, and increasingly mechanistic "smart" world.[4]

PAST FOUR THOUSAND YEARS:

Information-interactions within populations of humanity on Earth:[5]

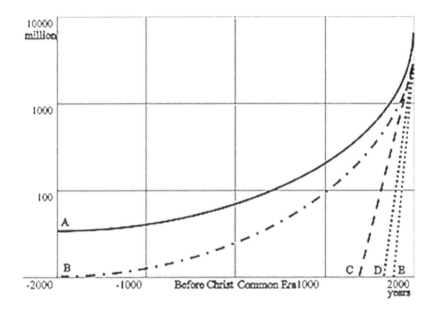

A—world human population: 7.8 billion;

B—number of literate persons: 6.8 billion,

C—number of reading books from the beginning of printing: 129.7 million,

D—number of radios/TVs: 2 billion+,

E—number of phones: 8.3 billion, computers 2 billion, internet users 3.9 billion.

Eryomin, A, "Noogenesis and Theory of Intellect," Krasnodar, 2019 updated.

With the neurological enhancements made biologically and genetically to eliminate disease, and to optimize the operation, energy, and power of the mindbrain, we may expect an acceleration in the rise of the future global IQ.

GLOBAL AUQ?

Nature has increased the power of our mindbrains by magnitudes sufficient to impress anyone, given to serious reflection. It enables or controls life and thought, and is the store of memory, ego, psyche, character, values, emotions, and varying degrees of acuity.

Further proof of the reach of our mindbrain is the fact that we are aware of our inner life, all life, and things about life, and a vast universe that we are not only curious about but can investigate and manipulate.

Each of us is an exclusive array of highly driven individualistic, societal, and symbiotic needs. To put it another way, our *self-interest*, and the interest of the *greater good*. Since we experienced our first dawn, it has heretofore caught human beings in turbulent webs of both progress toward and regress away from an equanimity of mindbrain and cooperation across the peoples on Earth. Most coherent, reasonable, and rational people understand that the elevation of a peaceful and thriving global population is the goal; the conundrum is that we do not know if we are any closer to that outcome nor whether we will ever attain it.

GREEN SHOOTS

Should we view our recent history for events and information, accumulated during our meandering quandary on Earth, which may serve to inform us of the possibility of achieving an elevated AUQ? An AUQ robust enough to precipitate global participation that can foster the realization of our species.

The common self-interest, of the leaders and populations of different nations, works in harmony when they deem it useful to do so, away from violence and discord, toward unity. They sign treaties, agreements, and accords, and have done so throughout the history of civilization. Add those to the cooperative organizations formed and projects undertaken, and they suggest the possibilities that they might be useful as blueprints for more significant enterprises as we grow our AUQ.

We have witnessed varying populations of differing political and economic structures agree to use nuclear energy peacefully, ban bacteriological and nuclear testing, and share access to space.[4] More recently, from the onset of the twenty-first century, there have been large worldwide ventures and cooperation to observe space and intensify nano level and brain study.[5] The possibility of networking and sharing research and information everywhere will help accrue to humankind the solution to the myriad problems concerning our health and welfare.

These efforts are a sign that, as communication on the Earth becomes more ubiquitous, people may become more cooperative as well. But it will require future generations of parents, educators, and leaders to inform the populations on Earth—how to elevate their mindbrains in word and deed, to ever-higher levels of AUQ to achieve that cooperation.

Steven Pinker, in his book, *Better Angels of Our Nature: Why Violence Has Declined*, gives us robust documented evidence showing that, for the past thirty EY, the number of wars and rates of death from wars are at an all-time low in our recorded history. The respect for the welfare of women and nonhumans is at the highest levels in the history of humanity. These are promising signs, but does this mean we are on an irreversible path to a time when there will be no more widespread violence or the denigration of women and nonhumans? He does not say that, and no one else could. What we can say is that it depends upon our determination to take the steps necessary, by elevating our AUQ, to maintain this near-term beneficial trend into the future.

AUQ ACCELERANTS

It is probable that, in due spacetime, newborns will have their genomes mapped, their genes corrected for defects, and their immune systems fortified, before release from their birthing facility. By calibrating and balancing their neurochemicals, we will ameliorate mental imbalances such as depression, bipolar disorder, panic disorder, ADHD, and more.

We will accomplish this by utilizing state-of-the-art quantum computing analysis and detection. These technologies will offer human beings a path to enhance their *inter* and *intra* toward realization, through the better health and balance of their mindbrain and an increased lifespan within which to achieve it. Our education, having a solid foundation in Nature/science explaining how our mindbrain is shaped and operates, will make us more aware of what promotes our ideation and behavior.

PART XIII
CONTINUING TO BECOME

"A human being is a part of a whole, called by us 'universe,' a part limited in time and space. One experiences oneself, one's thoughts and feelings as something separated from the rest . . . a kind of optical delusion of one's consciousness. This delusion is a kind of prison for us, restricting us to our desires and to affection for a few persons nearest to us. Our task must be to free ourselves from this prison by widening our circle of compassion to embrace all living creatures and the whole of nature in its beauty."
—Albert Einstein

IF YOU HAD the visual acuity to visualize with the naked eye the fields of energy and pressure created by matter, living or inert, you would see that they form, combine, and continually flow about us and within us. Nature crafts all forms of matter in the universe perfectly, or they could exist intact and in harmony. Continually converging and emerging throughout evolution, sometimes existing for nanoseconds and sometimes for billions of years, some of this energy has developed into living matter.

One of the more recent forms of energy to have developed into living matter is modern man, what one could call the *current* version of the genus Homo, known as Homo sapiens. Your energy comprises the same energy in all there is, differing only in its configuration, which affords you the capacity to think critically, influence, affect the environment, create, and search for your source.

Of the seven species of the genus Homo that have ever existed, approximately five were still extant on Earth about 100,000-200,000 EY ago, and we are still speculating how we alone remain. Since matter is a perfect form, did something go wrong with the genus Homo? No, but if one wishes to regard extinction as "something going wrong," consider that of all the perfectly formed species ever existing on Earth, though 99 percent are now extinct, many millions remain, and new ones constantly develop.[1] Many species become extinct because of climate and human intrusion, and rarely, if ever, is it self-destruction. Most likely we, the current version of the genus Homo, are so recently evolved that we have not yet had sufficient spacetime to go extinct.

What we can say is that—amongst all the known or to-date unknown Earthly species that have ever been—we can in fact survive and be the stewards of this planet. Given our highly altricial state, complex mindbrain, physical ability, and complex societal structure, the question is whether we can produce the paradigm changes in parenting, education, and leadership to elevate our AUQ, and realize the potential of our gift of Nature's perfectly formed energy.

Each one of us is the key to the next door opening, and we must walk through it so that the next generation may do the same, and so on. If any future generation cannot maintain the doors that have opened and push through the next doors that need to be opened, we will become the first failed form of any known species to make the decisions that cause its own extinction. This is our major challenge.

Fortunately, true to Nature, the more robust the mindbrain, the greater its curiosity to pursue the unknown and make it known. The robust mindbrain never believes the unknown to be unknowable, nor the undone to be undoable, and that is the power of its timeless energy and source—the decision by an individual to think and act in harmony and coherence with this energy and not in discord with it is realization.

One may say that with the mindbrain we already possess—and a continuance of its development—there is a reasonable expectation that our species or any of its successors may resolve the obstacles that have impeded our realization to date. On Earth, we are the only known interpreters of the universe. We are wasting spacetime waiting for the discovery of a "mysterious" something to make itself known and guide us—a force that rewards us with *eternity* for being *good* and *punishes* us for being *bad*, as if you are forever a child that has not experienced the maturity and wisdom one accrues going from childhood to adulthood. You need to be guided by the cumulative high AUQ knowledge of prior generations of parents, educators, and leaders, and to be individually responsible for elevating your AUQ.

This will entail total power and control over *your* being, with no interest in power and control over others. Until such a spacetime, as there is a *critical mass* of the combined AUQ of enough individuals on Earth to ignite the realization of our entire species, we risk existential ennui or imposed extinction.

Altricial Being hatched or born or having young that are hatched or born in a very immature and helpless condition to require care for a lengthy period.

Ardipithecus The earliest known, now extinct, genus of the zoological family Hominidae living an estimated 5.8 million years ago to 4.4 million years ago. The first group that includes humans and excludes great apes; the ancestor of Australopithecus (4.4 million years ago to 1.4 million years ago). A group closely related to and often considered ancestral to modern human beings.

AUQ "Awareness Understanding Quotient" A quotient measuring your in-depth awareness and understanding of all species of living beings other than yourself, and your in-depth awareness and understanding of oneself.

Cetacea The order of mammals that includes whales, dolphins, and porpoises.

Continental 8 An organization of a population of various countries on a given continent speaking a continental language as a second language.

Cosmic Calendar A calendar visualization of the evolving universe wherein 13.8 billion years are represented in a 365-day Earth-year calendar. An Earth Day in the cosmic calendar represents 37.8 million years of "cosmic" time, while a single Earth second is equivalent to 438 years of cosmic time. In this representation, the big bang occurs at midnight on January 1, with the universe expanding, cooling, and gravitating since. The present-day is shown at the very end of the cosmic calendar year, on December 31.

Cosmic time The equivalence of the 13.8 billion year time elapsed in the universe, relative to the time elapsed in one Earth year.

Cro Magnon Now known as early modern humans or anatomically modern humans were people who lived on Earth circa 40,000–10,000 EY ago.

Devolution Deterioration; decline; degeneration.

Diffusion Tensor Imaging Diffusion tensor imaging tractography, or DTI tractography, is an MRI (magnetic resonance imaging) technique that measures the rate of water diffusion between cells and is used primarily to visualize and quantify the orientation and direction of white matter fiber tracts in the brain.

Functional MRI (fMRI) Measures brain activity by detecting the changes in blood oxygenation and flow that occur in response to neural activity. When a brain area is more active it consumes more oxygen and demands increased blood flow to the active area. fMRI can be used to produce activation maps showing which parts of the brain are involved in any mental process.

Genus A taxonomic category ranking below a family and above a species, designating a group of species that are presumed to be closely related and usually exhibit similar characteristics. In a scientific name, the genus name is capitalized and italicized, for example, Ovis for sheep and related animals.

Homo The genus inclusive of the extant modern human species, Homo sapiens, and their close now-extinct relatives. The genus is estimated to be between 1.5 and 2.5 million years old.

Homo sapiens The species to which all modern human beings belong and the only member of the genus Homo that is extant. The earliest fossils of the species date to about 250,000 years ago.

Inter Describes your in-depth awareness/understanding/feeling for all of Nature's animate, and inanimate creations.

Intra Describes your in-depth awareness/understanding of yourself.

IQ A measurement derived by standardized testing, of human cognitive or intellectual abilities required to obtain knowledge and to best use that knowledge to solve problems that have well-described goals and structures. The average score is 100.

LUCA Stands for the "last universal common ancestor" of all living things on Earth. The originating entity of all prokaryote and eukaryote life dating back to 3.8 billion EY ago.

Market-oriented mixed economy A mixed economy is an economy organized with some free-market elements and some socialistic elements, which lies on a continuum somewhere between pure capitalism and pure socialism. Allegiance, however, is always demanded by the central government power, and their priorities for the economy, rule the day.

Mindbrain The reality that there is no longer a division between what had been viewed in the past as a mind, soul, or spirit as separate from the skull protected organ formerly known as "brain."

Mindbrain/Brain computer interface (BCI)' A technology that sends and receives signals between the brain and an external device. In doing so, it collects and interprets brain signals and transmits them to the connected device, which in turn outputs the correlated commands which initiated the brain signals received.

Nature Is derived from the Latin word natura, or "birth." *Natura* is a Latin translation of the Greek word physis (φύσις), which originally related to the intrinsic characteristics that plants, animals, and other features of the world develop of their own accord. The concept of Nature, the physical universe, is one of several expansions of the original notion.

Neanderthal A species of extinct hominins (Homo neanderthalensis) that lived throughout most of Europe and western and central Asia, circa 200,000 until 30,000 years ago.

Nidopallium Meaning nested pallium. The rear region of the avian brain is used mostly for some types of executive functions and other higher cognitive tasks. The avian equivalent of a primate prefrontal cortex coordinating cognition in the pallium layer of the brain.

NIH BRAIN Initiative Brain Research through Advancing Innovative Neurotechnologies® (BRAIN) Initiative is aimed at revolutionizing our understanding of the human brain. By accelerating the development and application of innovative technologies.

Non-Human Person Status The law divides the world between two entities: "things" and "persons." According to the Nonhuman Rights Project, personhood is best understood as a container for rights. Things have no rights, but when an entity is defined as a person, it can obtain some rights. A *nonhuman person* refers to an entity that is guaranteed some rights for limited legal purposes.

Optogenetic Functional MRI Technique that combines high-field fMRI readout with optogenetic stimulation (light and radio activated genes) allowing for cell type-specific mapping of functional neural circuits and their dynamics across the entire living brain.

OTH Acronym for "Other than human," and representing all living species other than human beings.

Personal primary psyche needs Inborn, grounded in our genome these needs cause mental predispositions from birth, and are a predominant influence on our behavior throughout our entire lives.

Precocial Active and able to move freely from birth or hatching and requiring little parental care; the opposite of altricial.

Psyche Used in this work as equivalent to personality.

Realization Becoming aware and understanding of your being and that of all other species, seamless and absolute, within the being of Nature's cosmos.

Species The final taxonomic category ranking just following the genus. Species is one of the most specific classifications that scientists use to describe animals. This system uses the genus as the first name, which is always capitalized, and the species name as the second name, always lowercase.

Speciesism The practice of treating members of one species as morally more important than members of other species.

Super-resolution fluorescence light sheet microscopy Super-resolution technologies are either based on tailored illumination or the precise localization of single molecules. Overall, these new approaches have created unprecedented new possibilities to investigate the structure and function of cells.

Taxonomy The branch of biology that classifies all living things. It has eight ranks from general to specific as follows: domain, kingdom, phylum, class, order, family.

MISCONCEPTION, PHILOSOPHY, IDEOLOGY

1. Smith, 1994.
2. Anderson, 2012.
3. Ibid.
4. Cherry, 2018.
5. Chrisomalis, 1996.
6. Stuart, 2013.
7. Rosser & Barkley, 2003.
8. Gregory & Stuart, 2013, p. 30.
9. Samuelson & Nordhaus, 2004.
10. American Govt.ushistory.org, Independence Hall Assoc., Phil., 2008-2013.
11. Cinpoes, 2010, p. 70.
12. Pauley & Payne, 2003, pp. 117-119.
13. Pew, 2019.
14. Roser, Our World in Data, blog, 2016.
15. Salk, In conversation with J. Krishnamurti, 1983.
16. Bagdy,1998, p. 357-363. Humble & Wistedt,1992, pp. 21- 40. Zimmerberg & Farley,1993, pp.1119- 1124.
17. Baylor, 1977, p. 27. Neusner,1999, p.523. Suchocki,1994, p.29, p.188. Dieter, Easterday & Gundry,1996.
18. Cavolina, Kelly, Allen & Stone, 1984, pp. 123-124.
19. Shahîd, 1984, p. 65-93; Pohlsander, 1980, pp. 463–73.
20. Gottheil, Strack & Jacobs, 1901–1906. Dundes,1991.
21. Turvey, 2008, p. 3. Chanes, 2004, pp. 34–45. Goldish, 2008, p.8.
22. Gottheil, Strack, & Jacobs, (1901-1906). Dundes,1991.
23. Chanes, 2004, pp. 34–45.

24. Greenfield, 2014.
25. Cannon, 2014.

HEREDITY AND COMPLEXITY

1. Timeline: Organisms that have had their genomes sequenced.
2. Kampourakis, 2014, pp. 127–129.
3. Doolittle, 2000.
4. Glansdorff, Ying & Labedan, 2008.
5. Schopf, Kudryavtsev, Czaja, & Tripathi, 2007.
6. Borenstein, 2017.
7. Bell, Boehnike, & Harrison, et al., 2015.
8. Wade,2016.
9. McKinney, 1997, p. 110.
10. Novacek, 2014.
11. Wynne, 2013.
12. Stringer, 1994.
13. Ghosh, 2014.
14. Ruse & Travis, 2015, p. 265.
15. Richter, Gnerre, 2006, pp. 1103–8.
16. Gibbons, 2012.
17. Blanchard, 1995.
18. Sagan, 1980.
19. Minkowski, 1908
20. Paul, 20121.
21.J. Krishnamurti, 1954.

INTER, INTRA AND THE AUQ

1. Janis, 1972.
2. Snyder, Lopez, Shane & Pedrotti, 2011.
3. Pijnenborg, Spikman, Jeronimus, & Aleman, 2012, Klein.
4. Hodges & Klein, 2001.
5. Begley, 2017.
6. Mount Sinai Medical Center, 2012 2013.
7. Gu, Gao, Wang, Liu, Knight, Hof, & Fan, 2012.
8. Wagner, 2012.
9. Schacter, Gilbe and Weger, 2009.
10. Gordon, 2012.
11. Nevid, 2015.

12. Camp, 2015.
13. Cacioppo, & Gardner, 1999.
14. Davidson, 2000.
15. Wolchover, 2013.
16. Bell, 2011.
17.Papez, 1937.

VIVE LA DIFFÉRENCE

1. Bell, 1997.
2. Trei, 2002.
3. Brizendine, 2006, p.127.
4. Kristof, 2010.
5. Smith, 2017.
6. Caprioli, & Boyer, 2001.
7. Nye, 2012.

VIOLENCE

1. Smith, 2012.
2. Pinker, 2012.
3. Smith, 2007, pp. 79-80.
4.Grant, apud Ryan, C., 2013.
5. Engelhaupt, apud Gomez, J.M., 2016, p.2.
6. Engelhaupt, apud Gomez, J.M., 2016, p.3.
7.Goodall, 1986, p.357.
8.Sussman, 2005.
9. Wrangham, 2019.
10. Bekoff, 2016.
11. Bekoff, 2015.
12. Bohannon, 1997, p.26.
13. Pinker, 2012.
14. Sell, Hone & Pound, 2012, pp. 30-44.
15. Bohannon, 1997. P. 26-32.
16. Abe, Kearns & Fukunaga, 2003, pp. 436-440.
17. Goetz, 2010, pp. 15-21.
18. Ellis, 2011, pp.707-722.
19. Wilson & Herrnstein, 1985.
20. Buss & Dedden, 1990, apud Fitzgerald & Whitaker, 2009, p. 469.
21. Cambell & Muncer, 1987.

22. Bjorkqvist, Lagerspatz & Kaukainen,1992.
23. Levine & Wolff, 1985.
24. Dorian, 2018.
25. Abe., Kearns &, Fukunaga, 2003, pp. 436-440.
26. Berkowitz,1993, p.475.

PARENTING
1. Ehrlich,1988.
2. Angier,1996, p.1.
3. Broad, Curley, & Keverne, 2006.
4. Axness, 2017.
5. Narvaez, 2011.
6., Hewlett & Lamb, 2005.
7. Stein & Newcomb,1994.
8. W. Wan, 2014.
9. Suttie, 2015.
10. Suttie, 2014.
11. Gauld, 2012.
12. ibid.
13. Narvaez, 2014.
14. Starkey, 2014.
15. Axness, 2015?
16. Rector, 2014.
17. Sheffield & Rector, 2014.

GOVERNMENT: TO ORGANIZE AND SERVE
1. Kramer, 1963.
2. Glyn, 2003.
3. Student, 2015.
4. Pareschi, Boschi & Favalli, 2006.
5. Soanes, 2006, p. 546.
6. Field, & Higley, 1980.
7. Winter, 2007, pg. 558.
8. Rothschild, 2015.
9. Prince, 1904.
10. Bartz & König, 2001.
11. Jarus, 2017.
12. Rothschild, 2015.

13. Hawking, 2016.
13.5 Nye, 2008.
14. Ruthven, 2002, p.7.
15. Moin, Khomeini, 1999, pp.249, 251.
16. Brumberg, 2001, p.123.
17.Smith, 2007, pg.11.
18.Caprioli, & Boyer, 2001.
19. Pew Research Center, 2017.
20. Sinan, 2016.
21. Hedges,2003.
22. Keen, 1991, pp.10-11, 30.
23. Leod, 1991.
24. Home Office: Country Information and Guidance Vietnam: Religious minority groups, December 2014, Hanoi, Viet Nam, 2014.
25. Elleman, 2001, p. 89.
26. Craughwell, 2009.
27. Correll, 2007.
28. Logevall,1999.
29. Correll, 2007.
30. Perlstein, 2008.
31. Lewy, 1978, pp. 442–453.
32. McNamara & VanDeMark, 1995.
33. Weiner, 2009.

EDUCATION

1. Bahar, 2014.
2. Clark, November 4, 2010.
3. Data Sources: National Vital Statistics Reports, Vol. 50, No.6., Life Expectancy at Birth, by Race and Sex, Selected Years 1929-98.; National Vital Statistics Reports, Vol. 49, No.12.Deaths, Preliminary Data for 2000.; U.S. Census Bureau. P23-190 Current Population Reports: Special Studies. 65+ in the United States.
4. Massachusetts School Laws and Massachusetts Education.
5. Gray, 2013.
6. Gray, 2008.
7. Principe, Jan. 2019.
8. Ellis, 2004.

9. Greenberg, 2016.
10. Ganly, 2012.
11. Krishnamurti,1954.
12. Lange, 2014,
13. Syms, 2016.

ARTISTIC EXPRESSION, INVENTIVENESS, AND SCIENTIFIC EXPLORATION

1. Wilkie,1995.
2. Wilford & Marsh, 1981, 1995.
3. Hays, 2009.
4. Netburn,2018.
5.White,2018.
6.Hirschler,2018.
7. Gardner,1970, pp. 450–45.
8. Michelangelo at Encyclopedia Britannica.
9. Reynolds, 1772.
10. Marsh, 1981.
11. Brian. & Cohen, 2007.
12. Browne, 2013, p. 319, p. 427.
13. National Human Genome Research Institute, 2015.
14. Dodd, Papineau, Dominic, Grenne, Tor, Slack, Rittner, Martin, Pirajno, Franco, O'Neil, Jonathan, Little, Crispin, 2017.

YOUR TREATMENT OF: NONHUMAN LIFE: A MAJOR SIGNPOST ON YOUR WAY

1. Kidd, 2013.
2. Smallwood, 2014.
3. Mueller, 2011.
4. Aptowicz, 2016.
5. Friedman, 1990.
6. Dadds, 2006.
7. Griffiths, 2016.
8. Coleman, 2018.
9. Becker, 2018.
10. Marler-Ball, 2018.
11. Conant, 2017.
12. Paterniti, 2017.

13. Ibid.
14. Sibeko, 2015.
15. Peek, 2017.
16. Pate, 2017.
17. Smith, & Molde, 2014.
18. Conservation Increasingly Funded by Non-Hunters, 2017.
19. Smith & Molde, 2014.
20. Thuermer, 2014.
21. Gibson, 2006.
22. Villavincencio, 2007.
23. Mann, 2007.
24. Villavincencio, 2007.
25. Mann, 2007.
26. Villavincencio, 2007.
27. Lynch, 2016.
28. Lawler, 2014.
29. Larson, 2015.
29.1 Ojibwa, 2018.
29.2 Capritito, 2019.
30. Pimm & Raven, 2000.
31. Fessenden, 2015.
32. Embury & Dennis, 2018.
33. Toliver & Zachary, 2019.
34. Clover,1999.
35. Fur Farming Legislation Around the World, Information.com.
36. Ibid.
37. Rousi & Vaittinen,et. al. 2015.
38. Eagle, 2000.
39. Scottish parliament, 2012.
39.1 Singer, 2009.
40. Ryder, 2009.
41. Smith, D., 2009.
42. Griffiths, 2016.
42.1 Roth, 2015.
43. Duncan, 2006, pp 11-19; Balcombe, 2009, pp. 208-216.
44. Bekoff, 2008.
44.1 Roth, 2015.
45. Relax, I'm an Entomologist; Do insects feel pain?, 2013.

46. Gibson, Gonzalez, & Fernandez et al., 2015.
47. Faerman, 2017, pp. 1-15.
48. Hance, Guardian, 22 Feb 2018.
49. Roth, 2015.
50. Webvet.com, 2012.
51. Smith & Strickland, 2015
51.1 Prior, Schwarz, & Gunturkun, 2008.
52. The ten smartest animals, how humans compare to other intelligent creatures, Science-NBC News, 2019.
53. Alt, 2016.
54. Ibid.
55. McCarthy, 2006.
56. Brakes, 2014.
57. Dale & Plotnik, 2017.
58. Prior, Schwarz, & Gunturkun, 2008.
59. Holland, 2014.
60. Elephant voices Charity, 2019.
61.Taylor, 2009, pp.8; 19-20.
62. Rowlands M., 2013.
63. Szűcs, Geers, Sossidou & Broom, 2012.
64. Morgan, 2010.
65. Messenger, 2011.
66. Elegans, 2012.
67. Bekoff, 2012.
68. Goodall & Bekoff, 2003.

MISSION: INNER SPACE

1.Moskowitz, 2011.
2. Eliceiri, Berthold, & Goldberg, et al., 2012.
3.Nasr, 2018.
4.Mehta, 2014.
5.Ghani, 2016.
6.Calderone, 2014.
7. Critchley, 2019.
8. Trafton, 2019.
9. Hell, Sahl, & Bates, et al., 2015.
10. Tsung-Li, Upadhyayula, & Milkie, et. al, 2018.

11. Trafton, 2019.
12. Song, 2017.

MINDBRAIN THROUGH SPACETIME

1.Graziano, 2016.
2. Pietrangelo, 2020.
3. Licklider, 1960.
4. Mamedova, 2015. p. 245.
5. Eryomin, 2005, p.356.

CONTINUING TO BECOME

1. Novacek, 2013.

Abe, T. & Kearns, C.F.& Fukunaga, T. Sex differences in whole body skeletal muscle mass measured by magnetic resonance imaging and its distribution in young japanese adults. British Journal of Sports Medicine, 37, 436-440. 2003.

Aptowicz, C. Could you stomach the horrors of 'halftime' in ancient rome?, Live Science, February 4, 2016.

Axness, M. (2012). Parenting for Peace: Raising the Next Generation of Peacemakers. Boulder, CO: Sentient Publications.

Axness, M. Mental health begins in the womb .https://marcyaxness. com/parenting-for-peace/mental-health-begins-in-the-womb/.

Axness, M. 7 Principles for peaceful parenting. excerpted from her book Parenting for peace: raising the next generation of peacemakers. Boulder, Co.: Sentient publications, 2012. https:// marcyaxness.com/parenting-for-peace/7-principles-peaceful-parenting/. 2019.

Bagdy, G. Serotonin, anxiety, and stress hormones: Focus on 5-HT receptor subtypes, species and gender differences. Annals of the New York Academy of Sciences, 851.1: 357-363.1998. Humble, M. & Wistedt, B. Serotonin, panic disorder and agoraphobia: short-term and long-term efficacy of citalopram in panic disorders. International clinical psychopharmacology, 6: 21-40, 1992. Zimmerberg, B. & Farley, M. Sex differences in anxiety behavior in rats: role of gonadal hormones. Physiology & behavior. 54.6: 1119-1124, 1993.

Bahar, G. Babies' amazing brain growth revealed in new map. Live Science, August 11, 2014.

Balcombe, J. Animal pleasure and its moral significance. Applied Animal Behavior Science, pp. 208-216, 2009

Bartz,G. & König,E., The louvre: arts and architecture. Rheinbreitbach, Rheinland-Pfalz, Germany: Ullmann, 2013.

Baylor, M. Action and person: conscience in late scholasticism and the young luther, studies in medieval and reformation thought, Volume XX. Leiden: E. J. Brill, 1977. Neusner, J. The theology of the oral torah: Revealing the justice of god. The failure to violate original sin in relational theology. Brill, 1999. Suchocki, M. Five views on sanctification. 1994. Dieter, M. & Gundry, S. The other is 'deliberate violation of God's known will. 1994

Becker, Kenya announces death penalty for poachers. Mercola, 2018.

Begley, S. Brain organoids get cancer, too, opening a new frontier in personalized medicine. STAT, 2017.

Bekoff, M. The emotional lives of animals: A leading scientist explores animal joy, sorrow, and empathy, and why they matter. Novato, Ca., New World Library, 2008.

Bekoff, M. Animals are conscious and should be treated as such. The New Scientist, 215 (2883):24–25, September 2012.

Bekoff, M. Violent humans are animals, but not behaving like animals-it's about time media and others get the behavior of nonhuman animals right. Psychology Today, June 24, 2015.

Bekoff, M. Murderous Humans Are Not "Acting Like Animals" "When it comes to murderous tendencies, 'humans really are exceptional.'" Psychology Today, September 28, 2016.

Bell, E, & Boehnike, P., et al. Potentially biogenic carbon preserved in a 4.1 billion-year-old zircon. Proc. Natl. Acad. Sci. U.S.A. Washington, D.C.: National Academy of Sciences, 112 (47): 14518–14521, November 24, 2015.

Bell, M. Ohio (musical composition). Marsan Music, 1997.

Bell, M. I think therefore I may become: Personal primary psyche need. KUS, 2011.

Berkowitz, L. Aggression: Its causes, consequences, and control. New York: McGraw-Hill,1993.

Bjorkqvist, K.,Lagerspatz K. & Kaukainen A. Do girls manipulate and boys fight? aggressive behavior. Google Scholar,18, pp.117–127,1992.

Blanchard, T. The Universe At Your Fingertips Activity: Cosmic Calendar. Astronomical Society of the Pacific,1995.

Bohannon, R. Reference values for extremity muscle strength obtained by hand-held dynamometry from adults aged 20 to 79 years. Archives of Physical Medicine and Rehabilitation, Vol. 78, pp. 26-32, 1997.

Borenstein, S. Hints of life on what was thought to be desolate early earth. NY: Mind Interactive Network Associated Press, October 19, 2015.

Brakes, P. Are orcas non-human persons? WDC (whale and dolphin conservation), October 30, 2014.

Brian, R. & Cohen, R. Hans Christian Oersted and the romantic legacy in science. Philosophy of Science, 241, 2007.

Brizendine, L. The female brain. Random House, Inc., Random House Audio, a division of Random House, Inc., 2007.

Broad, K., Curley J., & Keverne E. Mother–infant bonding and the evolution of mammalian social relationships. Philosophical Transactions of the Royal Society B-Biological Sciences, November 6, 2006.

Browne, M. Physics for engineering and science. Schaum, N.Y: McGraw Hill, second edition, 2013.

Brumberg, D. Reinventing Khomeini. Chicago: University of Chicago Press, 2001.

Buss, D. apud Fitzgerald, Whitaker, 2009, p. 469. Women use only language in competitive strategies. 1990.

Cacioppo, J. & Gardner, W. Emotion. Annual Review of Psychology, 50, 191–214,1

Calderone, J. 10 Big Ideas in 10 years of brain science. Scientific American, November 6, 2014.

Cambell, A. & Muncer, S. Models of anger and aggression in the social talk of women and men. Journal for the Theory of Social Behaviour, 17(4),1987.

Camp, J. Decisions are emotional, not logical: The neuroscience behind decision making. Big Think, June 11, 2012.

Cannon, M. 2 1/2 years of undergraduate/graduate chemistry. Sargent Degree level applied chemistry, Apr 14, 2016.

Caprioli, M. & Boyer, M. Gender, violence, and international crisis. Journal of Conflict Resolution, August 1, 2001.

Capritito, J. CNET, August 5, 2019.

Chanes, J. Antisemitism: A Reference Handbook. "Among the most serious of these [anti-Jewish] manifestations, which reverberate to the present day, were those of the libels: the leveling of charges against Jews, particularly the blood libel and the libel of desecrating the host." ABC-CLIO, 2004.

Cherry, K. Using 10 percent of your brain myth. verywell mind-web, October 31, 2018.

Chrisomalis, S. Weird words. Athenaeum anti libraries,

Cinpoes, R. Nationalism and Identity in Romania: A history of extreme politics from the birth of the state to accession. London: IB Tauris, 2010.

Clark, G. PowerPoint Presentation, November 4,2010.

Clover, C. Europe kicks up a stink over British move to ban mink. Telegraph.co.uk, May 13,1999.

Coleman, P. Young animal abusers can grow up to commit unspeakable violence. Miami Herald, April 04, 2018.

Conant, E. Gender revolution. National Geographic, January 2017.

Conservation Increasingly Funded by Non-Hunters. Center For Wildlife Ethics-web, April 28, 2017.

Correll, J. The Pentagon Papers. Air Force Magazine, February 2007.

Craughwell,T. The Vietnam war top 10 mistakes by U.S. presidents, Encyclopedia Britannica Blog, January 22, 2009.

Critchley, L. A guide to lattice light sheet microscopy. AZOM-web, Jan.28,2019.

Dadds, M. Associations among cruelty to animals, family conflict, and psychopathic traits in childhood. Journal of Interpersonal Violence, April 1, 2006.

Dale, R. & Plotnik,J. Elephants know when their bodies are obstacles to success in a novel transfer task. Scientific Reports,12 April 2017.

Data sources: Life expectancy at birth, by race and sex: Selected years 1929-98. National Vital Statistics Reports, Vol. 50, No.6.

Deaths, preliminary data for 2000. U.S. Census Bureau. P23-190, National Vital Statistics Reports, Vol. 49, No.12. 65+ in the United States. Current Population Reports: Special Studies.

Davidson, R. Cognitive neuroscience needs affective neuroscience and vice versa. Brain & Cognition,42:89–92,2000.

Deardoff, A. Glossary of international economics. Elddis.org., Jan. 2005.

Dodd, M. Papineau, D. et. al. Evidence for early life in earth's oldest hydrothermal vent precipitates. Nature, 543, 2 March 2017.

Doolittle, D. Uprooting the tree of life. Scientific American, February 2000.

Dorian, F. Homo Aggressivus: Male aggression: Why are men more violent? Psychology Today, September 22, 2018.

Duncan, I. The changing concept of animal sentience. Applied Animal Behaviour Science, pp.11–19, October 2006.

Dundes, A. The blood libel legend: A casebook in antisemitic folklore. Madison: University of Wisconsin Press, 1991.

Eagle, M. MP's vote to ban fur farms. BBC News, 22 November 2000.

Ehrlich, P. The Birther's Handbook. New York: Simon & Schuster, 1988.

Elegans, C. A Difference of Degree and Not Kind, Science and Dogs, May 23, 2012.

Elephant voices charity, 2019.

Eliceiri, K. Berthold,M. & Goldberg,I. et al. Biological imaging software tools. Nature Methods:9, 697–710, 2012.

Elleman, B. Modern Chinese warfare,1795–1989. Psychology Press (illustrated ed.), p. 89, 2001.

Ellis, A. Exemplars of curriculum theory. Larchmont, N.Y.: Eye On Education, Inc., 2004.

Ellis, L. Evolutionary neuroandrogenic theory and universal gender differences in cognition and behavior. Sex Roles 64(9):707-722, May 2011.

Embury-Dennis T. Norway raises limit on number of whales hunters can slaughter, Independent-web, 7 March 2018.

Engelhaupt, E. How human violence stacks up against other killer animals. National Geographic, September 28, 2016.

Eryomin, A. Noogenesis, and the theory of intellect. Soviet Kuban: Krasnodar, 2005.

Faerman,J. Don't kill that bug: New research shows insects do have feelings and emotions just like you, pp. 1-15, Dec., 2017.

Fessenden, M. A Hint That a Saturnian Moon Could Have Hydrothermal Vents—And Support Life. Smithsonian Magazine, March 12, 2015.

Field, L. & Higley, J. Elitism. United Kingdom: Routledge and Kegan Paul Ltd., 1980.

Friedman, I. The other victims: First person stories of non-jews persecuted by the Nazis. Boston: Houghton Mifflin, 1990.

Fur farming legislation around the world. Information.com.

Fur farmers backed into a corner. Finland.com/fashion, January 2, 2007.

Ganly, S. Educational Philosophies in the Classroom, Contributor Network, 2012.

Gardner, H. Art through the ages. Harcourt, Brace and World, 1970, pp. 450–456.

Gauld, M. Recognizing the parent's role in character education. Education Week, August 29, 2012.

Ghani, N. Neurotechnology: A look back at President Obama's BRAIN initiative. ECR Community: PLOS Blogs, September 7, 2016.

Ghosh, P. New dates rewrite neanderthal story. Science correspondent BBC News, August 20, 2014.

Gibbons, A. Plants & Animals. Evolution: Biology, Jun. 13, 2012.

Gibson, H. Detailed Discussion of Dog Fighting, Animal Legal & Historical Center: Michigan State University College of Law,2005.

Gibson, W., Gonzalez, C., Fernandez C, et al. Behavioral responses to a repetitive visual threat stimulus express a persistent state of defensive arousal in drosophila. Current Biology, 25 (11):140, 2015.

Glansdorff, N., Ying, Xu., & Labedan B. The last universal common ancestor: Emergence, constitution, and genetic legacy of an elusive forerunner. Biology Direct London: BioMed Central, 3: 29, 2008.

Glyn, D. The first civilizations: The archaeology of their origins. New York: Phoenix Press, 2003.

Goetz, A. The evolutionary psychology of violence. Psicothema, 22:1, February 2010.

Goldish, M. Jewish questions: Responsa on sephardic life in the early modern period. N.J.: Princeton University Press, 2008.

Goodall, J.& Bekoff, M. The ten trusts: what we must do to care for the animals we love. Harper San Francisco, Division of HarperCollins Publishers, 2003.

Goodall, J. Foreword. The emotional lives of animals: A leading scientist explores animal joy, sorrow, and empathy—and why they matter, by Marc Bekoff, New World Library, Novato, Ca., May 28, 2008.

Goodall, J. The chimpanzees of Gombe. Harvard University Press, 1986.

Gordon, S. L. Classification of emotions. inc.com, 30 April 2012.

Gottheil, R., & Strack, H. et. al. Blood Accusation. New York: Funk & Wagnalls, Jewish Encyclopedia, pp. 1901–1906.

Grant, S. Ten reasons humans are naturally evil. Listverse.com: Science, May 23, 2013.

Gray, P. School is a prison, and damaging our kids. Salon.com,2013.

Gray, P. Freedom to learn-a brief history of education. Psychology Today, August 20, 2008.

Graziano, M., A new theory explains how consciousness evolved: A neuroscientist on how we came to be aware of ourselves. The Atlantic, June 6, 2016.

Greenberg, D. A Place to Grow . Mass. :Sudbury Valley School Press, 2016.

Greenfield, D. Islam's religious war with everyone: Separating the real religious oppressors from the oppressed. Hindu Speaks-fineWordPress.com, 2014.

Gregory, P. & Stuart, R. The Global Economy and its Economic Systems. Ohio: South-Western College, 2014.

Griffiths, M. The psychology of animal torture. Psychology Today, Nov 23, 2016.

Gu, X. Gao, X. Wang, X., Liu, R., et. al. Anterior insular cortex is necessary for empathetic pain perception, Brain, 135 (9):2726.

Gu, X. Area of the brain that processes empathy is identified. ScienceDaily, 24 October 2012, 2013.

Hance, J. Birds are more like 'feathered apes' than 'bird brains.' The Guardian, Feb 22, 2018.

Hawking, S. This is the most dangerous time for our planet. The Guardian, Dec. 4, 2016.

Hays, J. Facts and Details.com, 2009.

Hays, P. Integrating evidence-based practice, cognitive–behavior therapy, and multicultural therapy:Ten steps for culturally competent practice. APA PsycNet, 2009.

Hedges, C. What every person should know about war. New York:Free Press, 2003.

Hell,S., Sahl, S., Bates, M., et al., The 2015 super-resolution microscopy roadmap. Journal of Physics D: Applied Physics-IOP Publishing Ltd, October 14, 2015.

Hewlett, M. & Lamb, B. Hunter-gatherer childhoods: Evolutionary, developmental, and cultural perspectives: Evolutionary foundations of human behavior. N.J.: Transaction Publishers, 2005.

Hirschler, B. Primitive art: Neanderthals were Europe's first painters, Science News, May 22, 2018.

Hodges, S. & Klein K. Regulating the costs of empathy: the price of being human. Journal of Socio-Economics, 2001.

Holland, J. Surprise: Elephants comfort upset friends. *National Geographic*, February 18, 2014.

Home office: Country information and guidance Vietnam: Religious minority groups. Hanoi, VietNam: Department of Justice, July 31, 2014.

Independence Hall Association, Phil. American government. ushistory.org, 2008-2013.

Janis, I. Victims of groupthink. Mass: Houghton Mifflin, 1972.

Jarus, O. Catherine the great: Biography, accomplishments & death. Live Science, May 23, 2017.

Jones, S. & Martin, R. Cambridge encyclopedia of human evolution. Cambridge, England: Cambridge University Press, 1992.

Kampourakis, K. Understanding evolution. Cambridge, U.K: Cambridge University Press, 2014.

Keen, S. Faces of the enemy. San Francisco: HarperCollins (2nd edition), 1991.

Kidd, E. Beast-hunts in Roman amphitheaters: The impact of the Venationes on animal populations in the ancient Roman world. historyoftheancientworld.com, 2genus, and species.

Klein, K.J. Regulating the costs of empathy: the price of being human. Journal of Socio-Economics, 2001.

Kramer, S. History begins at Sumer. Phil., Penn.: U. of Pennsylvania Press (3rd edition),1981.

Krishnamurti, J. 5th Talk to students, Rajghat School, Banaras, India, January 8, 1954.

Kristof, N. Religion and Women. New York Times, Jan. 9, 2010.

Lange, S. Strategies to Promote Critical Thinking in The Elementary Classroom. Partnership for 21st Century Learning: Volume 1, Issue 5, No.8, p.21, June 1, 2014.

Larson, P. Rodeos, inherent cruelty to animals. Humane Society Veterinary Medical Association, January 15, 2015.

Lawler, A. Birdmen: Co-partnership for 21st century learning cockfighters spread the chicken across the globe. Science: The State of The Universe, Dec. 2, 2014.

Leod, M. The Vietnamese Response to French Intervention, 1862-1874. Westport, Conn: Greenwood Publishing, 1991.

Levine, R. & Wolff, E. Social time: The heartbeat of culture, Psychology, p.77, 1985.

Lewis, E. American govt. Independence Hall Association, Phil.-ushistory.org., 2008-2013.

Lewy, G. America in Vietnam. New York: Oxford University Press, 1978.

Licklider, J. Man-computer symbiosis. IRE Transactions on Human Factors in Electronics, vol. HFE-1, p. 4-11. Mar 1960.

Logevall, F. Choosing war: The lost chance for peace and the escalation of war in Vietnam. Berkeley: University of California Press, 1999.

Lorenz, K. Behind the mirror: A search for a natural history of human knowledge. New York: Harcourt Brace Jovanovich, 1977.

Louann, B. The Female Brain. Newsweek, p. 127, 2006.

Lynch, C. Cockfighting is 'alive and well' in Ontario. Farmers Forum, August 12, 2016.

Mamedova M.D. The Concept of "Mind" in Chinese and Russian Linguistic World-images on the material of phraseological units, proverbs and sayings. Dushanbe: Russian-Tajik (Slavonic) University, 2015.

Mann, B. Illegal dog fighting rings thrive in U.S. cities, NPR, July 20, 2007.

Marler-Bal, T. Master Fitness Trainer & Nutritional Consultant, June 2, 2018.

Marsh, J. The universe and Dr. Sagan. Thriftbooks.com,1981.

Massachusetts School Laws and Massachusetts Education. Mass. gov.

McCarthy, M. Intelligent, emotional, ingenious: the amazing truth about whales and dolphins, independent.co.uk., 5 October 2006.

McKinney, M. The biology of rarity. Population & Community Biology Series, p. 110, 1997.

McNamara R. & VanDeMark, B. In retrospect: The tragedy and lessons of Vietnam. Norwalk, Conn: Easton Press,1995.

Meara, M. et. al. Growing up catholic. Dolphin Books, 1993.

Mehta, A. Brain scans: Technologies that peer inside your head. Brainfacts.com, Feb 26. 2014.

Messenger, S. Haunting footage reveals how chimps mourn death. nationalgeographic.com/video, January 31, 2011.

Michelangelo. Encyclopedia Britannica.1911.

Minkowski, H. Address to the 80th assembly of German natural scientists and physicians. scihi.org. September 21,1908.

Moin, B. Khomeini:Life of the ayatollah. London:I.B. Tauris, 1999.

Morgan, N. The hidden history of Greco-Roman vegetarianism. advocacy.britannica.com, August 10, 2010.

Moskowitz, C. What's 96 percent of the universe made of; astronomers don't know, Space.com, May 12, 2011.

Mueller, T. Unearthing the colosseum's secrets. Smithsonian Magazine, January 2011.

Music, G. "The good life: wellbeing and the new science of altruism, selfishness, and immorality. Routledge, 2014.

Narvaez, D. Moral landscapes: Dangers of "crying it out" damaging children and their relationships for the long term. Psychology Today, December 11, 2010.

Narvaez, D. Neurobiology and the development of human morality, evolution, culture, and wisdom. New York: W.W. Norton & Company, October 20, 2014.

Nasr, S. How Brain Mapping Works, Howstuffworks.com, 2018.

Netburn, D. Case closed Oldest Known Cave Art Proves Neanderthals As Sophisticated as Human Facts and Details, Science Now, Feb. 22, 2018.

Nevid, J. Feeling your thoughts; Are emotions and thoughts really as separate as people may think?. Psychology Today, Dec 23, 2015.

Nixon, R. How to eat smart. Livescience, 2009.

Novacek, M. Prehistory's brilliant future. New York: *The New York Times* Company, November 8, 2014.

Nye, J.S. Jr. When women lead. project-syndicate.org. February 8th, 2012

Nye, J.S. Jr. Bound to lead: the changing nature of American power. Oxford University Press, 2008.

Papez, J. A proposed mechanism of emotion. Journal of Neuropsychiatry Clinical Neuroscience, 7 (1): 103–12, 1937.

Pareschi, M. Boschi, E. & Favalli, M. Lost tsunami. Geophysical Research Letters, 33 (22): 2006.

Paterniti, M. Should we kill animals to save them? National Geographic Magazine, October 2017.

Paul, A. Why morning routines are creativity killers; Everything about the way we start our day runs counter to the best conditions for thinking creatively. Creativity Post, August 27, 2012.

Pauley, B. Hitler, Stalin, and Mussolini: Totalitarianism in the Twentieth Century. Wheeling, Il: Harlan Davidson, Inc.,1997.

Payne,S. A History of Fascism: 1914-1945, London: Routledge, 2001,

Peek, K. Vast majority of Americans oppose elephant and lion trophy hunting. Humane Society of the U.S. Dec. 5, 2017.

Perlstein,R. Nixonland: The rise of a president and the fracturing of America. New York: Simon and Schuster, 2008.

Pew Research Center, 2017.

Pietrangelo, A. What IQ measurements indicate-and what they don't. Healthline January 28, 2020.

Pijnenborg, G. Spikman, J., Jeronimus, B., & Aleman, A. Insight in schizophrenia: associations with empathy. European Archives of Psychiatry and Clinical Neuroscience, 263 (4): 299–307.

Pimm, S. & Raven, P. Biodiversity: Extinction by numbers. Nature, 403, pp. 843-845, 2000.

Pinker, S, Better angels of our nature: why violence has declined. London, England: Penguin Publishing Group. September 2012.

Prince, J. Dyneley review:The code of hammurabi. The American Journal of Theology,.University of Chicago Press, (3): 601–609, July 1904.

Principe, G. Free to Learn: Does The Hunter-Gatherer Style Of Education Work? Evolution Institute, Jan. 2019.

Prior, H., Schwarz, A., & Gunturkun O. Mirror-induced behavior in the magpie (pica-pica): Evidence of self-recognition. PLOS Journal-Biology, 6 (8) e202, August 19, 2008.

Raston, D.-Temple, Using AI in Malawi to save elephants. NPR-Illinois, September 17, 2019.

Rector, R. How Welfare Undermines Marriage and What to Do About It. Heritage Foundation, November 17, 2014.

Relax, I'm an entomologist; do insects feel pain? Tumblr, May 25, 2013.

Reynolds, J. Seven discourses on art, discourse 5, delivered to the students of the royal academy on the distribution of the prizes. Public Domain Books, December 10, 1772.

Richter, P., Gnerre, S., Lander, E., & Reich, D. Genetic evidence for complex speciation of humans and chimpanzees. Nature, 2006, 441 (7097): 1103–8.

Robinson, B, Ontario Consultants on Religious Tolerance. religioustolerance.org, July, 2016.

Roser, M. Our world in data. blog, 2016.

Rosser, M. & Barkley, J. Comparative economics in a transforming world economy. Cambridge, Mass: MIT Press, 2003.

Roth, G. Convergent evolution of complex brains and high intelligence. London: Royal Society Publishing, Dec. 19, 2015.

Rothschild, M. List rules: World leaders with progressive yet realistic approaches that bettered the lives of their people. n.p., 2015.

Rousi, H., Vaittinen, M._et. al. Demand an end to fur farming in Finland. thepetitionsite.com-Care2, May 21, 2015.

Rowlands, M. Animal rights: all that matters. New York: McGraw-Hill, August 6, 2013.

Ruse, M., & Travis, J. Evolution: The First Four Billion Years. Cambridge, Massachusetts: Belknap Press of Harvard U. Press, 2015.

Ruthven, M. A Fury For God: The islamist attack on america. London: Ranta, 2002.

Ryder, R. Speciesism, painism and happiness: A morality for the twenty-first century. Exeter, England: Imprint Academic, 2009.

Sagan, C. The shores of the cosmic ocean-cosmos: A personal voyage. Cosmos: Episode 1,1980.

Salk, J. In conversation with Krishnamurti Krishnamurti Foundation of America, Ojai, Ca.,1983.

Samuelson, P. & Nordhaus, W. Economics. New York:McGraw-Hill, 2004.

Schacter, D., Gilbert, D., Nock, M., & Weger, D. Acetylcholine receptors; Introduction to serotonin. University of Bristol, 2009.

Science-NBC News. The ten smartest animals: How humans compare to other intelligent creatures. Science-NBC News, May 15, 2008.

Sell , A., Hone, L. & Pound, N. The importance of physical strength to human males. Human Nature,Vol. 23(1), pp. 30-44, March 2012.

Shahbazi, A., et. al. Xenophon ,cyropaedia of xenophon,The life of cyrus the great, cyrus the great: The decree of return for the Jews, 539 BCE. Shiraz University Publication, No. 19, 1970.

Shahîd, I. Rome and the Arabs. Washington, D.C.: Dumbarton Oaks, 1984.

Sheffield, R. & Rector, R. War on poverty after 50 years. The Heritage Foundation, Sept. 15. 2014.

Sibeko, S. Photography. Reuters, Nov 22, 2015.

Sinan, K. The Myth of the 'Female' Foreign Policy. Atlantic Monthly Group, August 25, 2016.

Singer, P. Animal liberation: the definitive classic of the animal movement. N.Y.C.: Harper Collins, 2009.

Smallwood, C. 10 Cruel and unusual facts about the colosseum animal fights, Listverse, January 15, 2014.

Smith, D. Less than human: Why we demean, enslave, and exterminate others. N.Y.C.: St. Martin's Griffin, 2012.

Smith, D. The most dangerous animal: Human nature and the origins of war. N.Y.C.: St. Martin's Press -reprint edition, August 7, 2007.

Smith, H. The World's Religions. Erdman Handbook to the World's Religions, 2009.

Smith, M. & Molde, D. Wildlife conservation and management funding in the U.S. Nevadans For Responsible Wildlife Management.

Smith, K. Crows may be as intelligent as apes, scientists say. Sydney Morning Herald, 24 June 2015.

Snyder, C. R., Lopez, S. J., & Pedrotti, J. T., Positive Psychology: An international team led by researchers at Mount Sinai School of Medicine in New York has for the first time shown that one area of the brain, called the anterior insular cortex is the activity center of human empathy, whereas other areas of the brain are not. The Scientific and Practical Explorations of Human Strengths, Second ed. Los Angeles:SAGE, pp. 267–75, 2011.

Soanes, C. Compact Oxford english dictionary for university and college students. Oxford: Oxford University Press, 2006,

Song, E. Brain-computer interface based neuro-prosthetics. Duke SciPol, May 19, 2017.

Starkey, C. & Bryant, L. Getting Inside our Heads:What is character and how do we get it? Clemson University: The Newstand, September 2014.

Stein, J. & Newcomb, M. Children's internalizing and externalizing behaviors and maternal health problems. *Journal of Pediatric Psychology*, (5):571-93, Oct. 19, 1994.

Stringer, C. Evolution of early humans. Cambridge, England: Cambridge University Press,1994.

Stuart, D. The Global Economy and its Economic Systems. South-Western College Pub., 2013.

Student, A. A comparison between ancient Egyptian and Sumerian civilization history essay. *UK Essays*, March 23 ,2015.

Sussman R.& Garber, P. & Cheverud, J. Importance of cooperation and affiliation in the evolution of primate sociality. American Journal of Physical Anthropology, 2005 Sep;128(1):84-97.

Suttie, J. How parents influence early moral development. Greater Good Magazine, September 29, 2015.

Suttie, J. What is a good life? Greater Good Magazine, October 1, 2014.

Sweetlove, L. Number of species on earth tagged at 8.7 billion. Basingstoke,U.K.: *Springer Nature*, 2011.

Syms, C. 3 ways to upgrade your staff with team building. Museum Hack, July 20, 2016.

Szűcs, E. & Geers, R. et. al. Animal Welfare in Different Human Cultures, Traditions and Religious Faiths. *Asian-Australasian Journal of Animal Sciences*, November 2012 25(11):1499-506.

Taylor, A. Animals and ethics: An overview of the philosophical debate. Calgary, Canada: *Broadview Press*, 2009.

The economist intelligence unit. 25. Democracy Index 2016: Revenge of the "deplorables," *Red Bird Review*, January 2017.

Toliver, Z. Victory! Germany's last fur farmer gets out of the business. PETA, 2019.

Thuermer, A. Study: Non-hunters contribute most to wildlife. WyoFile, November 18, 2014

Timeline: Organisms that have had their genomes sequenced, Facts, Jan 19, 2015. .

Trafton, A. Mapping the brain at high resolution. *MIT News Office*, January 17, 2019.

Trei, L. Women remember disturbing, emotional images more than men, study shows. *Stanford Report*, July 24, 2002.

Tsung-Li, L., et. al, Observing the cell in its native state: Imaging subcellular dynamics in multicellular organisms. *Science*, April 20,2018.

Turvey, B. Criminal profiling: an introduction to behavioral evidence analysis. Academic Press, "Blood libel: An accusation of ritual murder made against one or more persons, typically of the Jewish faith," 2008.

Villavincencio, M. A History of dogfighting, *NPR*, July 19, 2001

Wade, N. Meet Luca, the ancestor of all living things. *New York Times*, July 25, 2016.

Wagner, A. M.I.T. discovers-the-location-of-memories in individual neurons. Extremetech. March 23, 2012.

Walden, J. Epigenetics: Using applied consciousness to wellness and wellbeing. Scribd.com, 2009.

Wan, W. Singapore kindness movement, moral education: Parents have a more vital role. *Straits Times Forum*, January 18, 2014. War on poverty after 50 years. Cato Institute, May, June 2015.

Webvet. Are parrots smarter than dogs? Webvet.com, August 9, 2012.

Wein, H. Human genome map yields insights into development, disease. National Human Genome Research Institute, March 13, 2015.

White, A. Neanderthals were artistic like modern humans. Southampton, England: University of Southampton, February 22, 2018.

Wilford, J. & Marsh, J. Noble neanderthals and modern humans coexisted longer than thought. The Universe and Dr. Sagan, Archives, May 1, 1981.

Wilkie, T. The quality of science and medical reporting. *The Science News*, June 12,1995.

Wilson, J. & Herrnstein, R. Crime, and human nature. New York: Simon and Schuster, 1985.

Winter, D. Things i've learned about personality from studying political leaders at a distance. *Journal of Personality*, May 7, 2005.

Wolchover, N. Have we been interpreting quantum mechanics wrong all this time? *Quanta Magazine, Science*, June 2013.

Wrangham, R. The goodness paradox. Pantheon; First Edition January 29, 2019.

Wynne, P. How much loner 18, 2013.

Zeitlin, S. The blood accusation. Vigiliae Christianae:50, No. 2, pp. 117–119,1996.

3/20/23

$19.95

46 637546